Local Government Tax and Land Use Policies in the United States

STUDIES IN FISCAL FEDERALISM AND STATE–LOCAL FINANCE

General Editor: Wallace E. Oates, Professor of Economics, University of Maryland

This important new series is designed to make a significant contribution to the development of the principles and practices of state–local finance. It will include both theoretical and empirical work. International in scope, it will address issues of current and future concern in both East and West and in developed and developing countries.

The main purpose of the series is to create a forum for the publication of high quality work and to show how economic analysis can make a contribution to understanding the role of local finance in fiscal federalism in the late 20th century.

Books already published in the series:

Financing Decentralized Expenditures
An International Comparison of Grants
Edited by Ehtisham Ahmad

The Fiscal Behavior of State and Local Governments
Selected Papers of Harvey S. Rosen
Harvey S. Rosen

Financing Federal Systems
The Selected Essays of Edward M. Gramlich
Edward M. Gramlich

Local Government Tax and Land Use Policies in the United States
Understanding the Links
Helen F. Ladd

Local Government Tax and Land Use Policies in the United States

Understanding the Links

Primary Author

Helen F. Ladd

Professor of Public Policy Studies and Economics,
Terry Sanford Institute of Public Policy, Duke University, US

STUDIES IN FISCAL FEDERALISM AND STATE–LOCAL FINANCE
IN ASSOCIATION WITH THE LINCOLN INSTITUTE OF LAND POLICY

Edward Elgar
Cheltenham, UK • Northampton, MA, USA

Published by
Edward Elgar Publishing Limited
8 Lansdown Place
Cheltenham
Glos GL50 2HU
UK

Edward Elgar Publishing, Inc.
6 Market Street
Northampton
Massachusetts 01060
USA

in association with
Lincoln Institute of Land Policy
113 Brattle Street
Cambridge
MA 02138-3400
USA

A catalogue record for this book
is available from the British Library

Library of Congress Cataloguing in Publication Data
Ladd, Helen F.
    Local government tax and land use policies in the United States :
understanding the links / primary author, Helen F. Ladd.
        — (Studies in fiscal federalism and state–local
finance)
    Published in association with the Lincoln Institute of Land
Policy.
    Includes bibliographical references.
    1. Land use–Effect of taxation on—United States.   I. Lincoln
Institute of Land Policy.   II. Title.   III. Series.
HD205.L3   1998
333.73'13'0973—dc21   97–27158
                                                                   CIP

ISBN 1 85898 657 5

Typeset by Manton Typesetters, 5–7 Eastfield Road, Louth, Lincolnshire LN11 7AJ, UK.

Printed and bound in Great Britain by MPG Books Ltd, Bodmin, Cornwall

Contents

Figures

Tables

List of Contributors

Jeffrey I. Chapman is Professor of Public Administration at the University of Southern California. His recent research focuses on how state and local governments respond to fiscal stress. He co-edited *California Policy Choices* volume 9 (1994).

William Fischel teaches economics at Dartmouth College and chairs the local zoning board. He is the author of *Regulatory Takings* (Harvard University Press, 1995) and *The Economics of Zoning Laws* (Johns Hopkins University Press, 1985).

William F. Fox is Professor of Economics and Director of the Center for Business and Economic Research at the university of Tennessee. Active in the National Tax Association, he does research on taxation, especially sales taxation, and economic development.

Robert P. Inman is Professor of Finance and Economics at the University of Pennsylvania, and a Research Associate of the National Bureau of Economic Research. He has also been a Visiting Professor of Economics at the University of California, Berkeley and at Stanford University and a Research Fellow at Harvard University, Australian National University and the Center for the Advanced Study in Behavioral Sciences, Stanford.

Helen F. Ladd is Professor of Public Policy Studies and Economics at Duke University where she also directs the graduate program in public policy. An expert on state and local public finance, she is the co-author (with John Yinger) of *America's Ailing Cities: Fiscal Health and the Design of Urban Policy* (Johns Hopkins University Press, 1991) and the editor of *Holding Schools Accountable: Performance Based Reform in Education* (Brookings Institution, 1996).

Thomas Luce is Assistant Professor of Public Affairs and Planning at the Hubert H. Humphrey Institute of Public Affairs, University of Minnesota. In addition to his work on tax-base sharing for this volume, his recent research examines Minnesota state budget policies, the potential impact of congestion pricing on employment sub-centers, welfare reform, and city fiscal management.

Peter Mieszkowski is Cline Professor of Economics at Rice University. A specialist in public finance, he has a long standing interest in the work of Henry George and related issues in local finance and public goods theory. His current research interests include the relationships between international trade and income-distribution and the normative foundations of federal grants.

Adele C. Morris is a senior economist with the Council of Economic Advisers. She was previously at the Office of Management and Budget, where she was responsible for regulatory oversight of the Department of Agriculture.

Matthew N. Murray is Associate Professor of Economics and Associate Director of the Center for Business and Economic Research at The University of Tennessee, Knoxville. His general area of expertise is state and local public finance, with a current focus on the sales tax.

Dick Netzer is Professor of Economics and Public Administration at the Robert F. Wagner Graduate School of Public Service, New York University. For more than forty years, he has done research on and written about the property tax.

William H. Oakland is Professor of Economics at Tulane University. His research interests are in public finance and regional economic development.

Wallace E. Oates is Professor of Economics at the University of Maryland and University Fellow with Resources for the Future in Washington, D.C. His principle research interests are in public finance (with particular attention to fiscal federalism and state-local finance) and environmental economics.

Robert M. Schwab, a Professor of Economics at the University of Maryland, works primarily on public economics issues with an emphasis on state and local government. His recent research focuses on urban land taxation, the link between infrastructure investment and regional economic growth, education finance reform, the distribution of education resources, and the relative efficiency of public and Catholic schools.

William A. Testa directs the regional programs in the research department of the Federal Reserve Bank of Chicago. He has recently completed an economic assessment of the Midwest economy's past performance and long-term outlook.

Michelle J. White is Professor of Economics at the University of Michigan. She has written many articles on urban land use when employment is decentralized and on urban commuting patterns. She is a member of the editorial board of the *Journal of Urban Economics*.

John Yinger is Professor of Economics and Public Administration at the Maxwell School, Syracuse University, and Associate Director for the Metropolitan Studies Program at the Maxwell School's Center for Policy Research. A specialist in state and local public finance, racial and ethnic discrimination in housing, and urban economics, he recently published *Closed Doors, Opportunities Lost: The Continuing Costs of Housing Discrimination* (Russell Sage Foundation, 1995).

Acknowledgements

This book summarizes the current thinking of urban and public finance economists on the interactions between tax policy and land use policy as pursued by local governments in the United States.

The views in this book were aired and debated at the Fall 1995 Annual Conference of Taxation, Resources and Economic Development (TRED), a group that has been managed and financed by the Lincoln Institute of Land Policy in Cambridge, Massachusetts for over 20 years.

The Lincoln Institute initially commissioned Helen Ladd to prepare a monograph on the interactions between local tax and land use policies. This monograph provided the structure for the TRED conference and this volume.

The conference was organized by Helen Ladd with the assistance of Dick Netzer and Ben Chinitz. They invited members of TRED and other academic experts in the field to contribute short papers to augment Helen Ladd's work and to critique and expand various sections of her monograph. In his capacity of Faculty Associate (and former research director) of the Institute, Ben Chinitz provides the link with the Lincoln Institute. Dick Netzer served as the primary editor of the commentaries that appear in this volume.

The editors are extremely grateful to the Lincoln Institute for financial and logistical support throughout this project. In addition, Helen Ladd would like to thank Gretchen Eisenach of Duke University for research support during the final stages of the project.

Lincoln Institute of Land Policy

The Lincoln Institute of Land Policy is a non-profit and tax-exempt educational institution established in 1974. Its mission as a school is to study and research land policy, including land economics and land taxation. The Institute is supported by the Lincoln Foundation, established in 1947 by John C. Lincoln, a Cleveland industrialist. Mr Lincoln drew inspiration from the ideas of Henry George, the 19th-century American political economist and social philosopher.

Integrating the theory and practice of land policy and understanding the forces that influence it are the major goals of the Lincoln Institute. The Institute explores both the public and private decisions that shape land use and regulation; the taxation of land and buildings; and land values, ownership and property rights.

1. Introduction

Helen F. Ladd

The two most important functions of local governments in the United States stem from their power to tax and their power to regulate local land use. The power to tax permits local governments to raise revenue to provide services such as public safety, health, transportation, education and social services. The power to regulate land use permits local governments to segregate land uses, to restrict various types of land use and to slow the pace of local development. The goal of land use regulation is presumably to achieve a 'better' pattern of land use (at least from the perspective of local voters) than would result from the operation of an unfettered land market.

Regulatory tools are used primarily to achieve land use goals and local tax instruments are used primarily to raise revenue. Nonetheless, land use policy and tax policy interact in complicated ways. These interactions, some of which are intended and some of which are not, are the subject of this book. Neither a review of the extensive literature on land policy alone, nor a review of local tax policy, this book focuses on the nexus between the two.

INTRODUCTORY OVERVIEW: WHY EXAMINE THESE INTERACTIONS?

The 19th-century social reformer, Henry George, found it quite natural to look at land and tax policy together. According to George, a tax on land rents would provide the correct incentives for landowners to use their land most productively and would eliminate the need for all other taxes. In particular, it would allow jurisdictions to reduce reliance on other taxes that distort economic behaviour, including the property tax which applies to improvements as well as land. Thus good tax policy would be synonymous with good land policy.

Henry George's ideas, plus the extensive use of the property tax in the United States, have generated a wealth of theoretical research on land and property taxes. Was the self-made economist Henry George correct that a single tax on land is desirable? Is it true that the property tax distorts housing

and investment decisions and that the tax is regressive? Would a shift away
from the property tax towards a tax on land value generate more development? Using the mathematical tools of modern economics, contemporary
economists have a lot to say about these issues. Hence the first goal of this
book is to examine Henry George's ideas from the perspective of contemporary economics. The theoretical literature on these issues is summarized in
Chapter 2.

A second reason to look at land and tax policy jointly is that land use
regulation, as implemented through zoning, subdivision controls and other
mechanisms, is often used explicitly to promote fiscal goals. Representing
the interests of established resident voters who wish to keep their tax rates
down, local officials may encourage the development of fiscally 'profitable'
land uses, such as business activity or high-income housing, and may discourage fiscally 'unprofitable' uses, such as multi-family housing. The use of
local land use controls for fiscal purposes reflects in part the fact that local
governments are part of a spatially fragmented governmental system and that
they rely heavily on property taxes. Potential residents with low income
might well want to live in inexpensive housing in wealthy communities
where they would receive the same public services as other residents but
would pay relatively low property taxes on their low valued houses. Consequently, such households are often viewed as fiscally undesirable by established residents, who support zoning restrictions to keep them out of the
community. Because low income households are denied access to communities with high quality public services, this fiscally motivated use of zoning
raises serious concerns about fairness. At the same time, economists have
praised such zoning for creating communities in which residents have similar
preferences for public services, and thereby increasing the efficiency with
which local public services are provided. Chapter 3 is devoted to examining
the equity and efficiency implications of using land policy as a fiscal tool and
also to examining changes in the conventional wisdom about the fiscal effects
of new development and various patterns of land use.

An additional reason for scrutinizing the interactions between land and tax
policies is that taxes used by subnational governments in the United States
might have large effects on land use. Almost all taxes are presumed to affect
economic decisions by firms and consumers and thereby to affect the amount
of economic activity. However, taxes used by state or local governments
potentially affect not only the amount of such activity but also its spatial
location. For example, a high tax on the use of business capital in one
community relative to another may not only induce a firm to invest less
overall but may also induce it to move some of its investment to the jurisdiction with the lower tax rate. Listening to business executives, one would
conclude that these spatial effects are huge; such executives continually claim

that high taxes may force them to move their firm to another jurisdiction or that local taxes are too high for them to consider that location as a site for a new plant. Starting with John Due's (1961) review of the literature, the conventional wisdom among economists has been that the adverse location effects of taxes were grossly exaggerated and that taxes in fact have little or no effect on the location decisions of firms. Only recently have economists re-evaluated the conventional wisdom. The research that has produced this reconsideration is reviewed in Chapter 4.

The final reason for examining the interactions between tax and land policy is that tax policy is often used as an explicit tool of land policy. Thus instead of simply serving as a source of revenue, tax policy is often designed to promote various land use goals. For example, tax policy is frequently used to promote development. As discussed in Chapter 5, the main tool for this purpose is local tax abatement, or, in its geographically targeted form, enterprise zones. Other tools for this purpose include tax increment financing and shifting away from the property tax to a tax on land value, both of which are discussed in Part II. Alternatively, tax policy might be used to slow down economic development, as with the use of preferential tax treatment of agricultural land as a means of preserving farmland and open space in urbanizing areas. Sometimes the land use goal of financing instruments is unclear. The recent use of fees and exactions to finance the infrastructure associated with new development fits into this category. From one perspective, fees and exactions may appear to limit growth. From another perspective they may appear to facilitate local growth. Parts II and III of this book provide new research by public finance experts on some of these interactions.

Thus the interactions between land and tax policy are interesting from both a theoretical and a policy perspective. However, the subject has yet to be treated in a comprehensive and accessible manner. This book is designed to fill this gap by summarizing the best current thinking on these issues by US urban and public finance economists in a way that will be accessible to non-specialists. Helen Ladd was initially commissioned by the Lincoln Institute of Land Policy to write Part I of the book as part of the Institute's larger investigation of land use policy. Given the centrality of the interactions between land use and tax policy to the mission of the Lincoln Institute, the Institute sponsored a conference in September 1995 to discuss that material and to provide a forum for additional work on those interactions. This book is the outcome of that process. Part I includes four overview chapters by Helen F. Ladd, supplemented with commentary by five conference participants. Parts II and III represent research by various authors on specific tax policies that affect land use. The final section of this chapter briefly summarizes the current status of various challenges to the conventional wisdom on many of these issues.

BACKGROUND AND TRENDS

The literature reviewed in subsequent chapters presumes some knowledge of the taxing and regulatory powers and practices of local governments. As background, this section provides an introductory overview, first of local tax policy and second of land use regulation. It ends with a discussion of exactions on developers, which can be interpreted as a hybrid of tax policy and land use regulation.

To be sure, various taxes used by the federal government also exert major impacts on land use. A case in point is the federal personal income tax. Through its favourable treatment of owner-occupied housing and its provisions relating to rental property and other investments, the federal tax code can have large effects on housing and other types of investment. Similarly, federal estate and gift laws may have large effects on when land is put up for development. The land-related impacts of the federal income and wealth taxes notwithstanding, this study focuses on state and local taxes and activities. This focus reflects the observation that explicit land use policies tend to be the responsibility of local – and increasingly state – policy-makers. Therefore, a focus on state and local taxes rather than federal tax policies, highlights the interactions between land and tax policy-making.

Local Tax Policy

The power of local governments to tax local residents and activities derives from state, in contrast to federal, constitutions and statutes. Consequently, these powers vary from one state to another. For example, some states empower their local governments to use no broad-based tax other than the property tax. Other states empower specified categories of local governments to supplement local property taxes with local sales or earnings taxes, or both. Moreover, even within states, localities with similar spending powers may differ in the types of taxes they use. This within-state variation occurs because state legislation often enables, but does not require, local governments to enact a supplemental tax, because state legislation may differentiate among governments by size, or because states confer home-rule powers on some cities that give them more freedom than other local governments to choose their local taxes. Regardless of what other broad-based taxes they authorize, however, all states empower their general-purpose local governments to raise revenue from a tax on property. Moreover, property taxes have historically been the dominant tax source for local governments.

The role of the property tax

The property tax originated as a local tax in the United States and has continued as the main tax used by local government. During the 18th and 19th centuries, the tax was collected from a broadly defined base that included intangible property. However, by the end of the 19th century, the property tax had evolved into a more selective tax on real estate (both residential and business) and business personalty (equipment and inventories).

Figure 1.1 documents the trends since 1927 in the role of the property tax as a revenue source for local governments. (See also Appendix, Table 1A.1.) The top line depicts local property taxes as a percentage of local government taxes and the bottom line as a percentage of all local revenue, which includes intergovernmental aid and revenue from charges and fees as well as from taxes. The pattern is one of general decline in the role of the property tax to 1980, with the most rapid declines occurring during the 1930s and 1940s and during the 1970s and early 1980s. Since the mid 1980s, the pattern has been reversed, and reliance on the property tax has been rising somewhat.

In 1927, the property tax accounted for 97 per cent of total local taxes, and over 69 per cent of total local government revenue. The collapse of income and property values in the 1930s, combined with ongoing needs for local government revenues, forced many states to respond to the crisis brought on by the Depression by increasing state aid to local governments. This state action significantly reduced the dependence of local governments on the property tax during the 1930s and the 1940s. Another significant decline in local reliance on the property tax occurred in the 1970s as the federal government provided assistance directly to local governments, states increased their assistance to local governments (especially to finance education) and authorized additional local taxes, and local governments turned to non-tax sources such as user charges.

Local governments come in many different sizes and shapes. In 1992, more than 53 000 general-purpose local governments were distributed by type as follows:

Counties	3 043
Municipalities	19 279
School districts	14 442
Townships and towns	16 656

Source: US Census Bureau, 1992 Census of Governments, Governmental Organization, Table A12.

An additional 31 555 special districts provided specific public services such as fire protection, transit, parks or water.

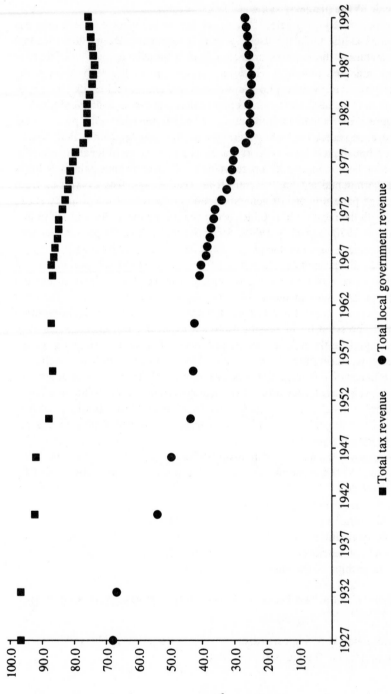

■ Total tax revenue   ● Total local government revenue

Figure 1.1   Property taxes as a percentage of total tax revenue and total local government revenue

Table 1.1 documents that the property tax remains the major tax source for each type of local government, but that it is more important for some types of local government than for others. The first column shows that, as of 1992, property taxes accounted for more than half of the local taxes for each type of government and over 97 per cent for local school districts. Significantly, property taxes accounted for only 52.6 per cent of municipal tax revenues, a drop from 73.2 per cent in 1962. The second column puts the property tax into the broader context of all local government revenues. Because of inter-governmental aid, other taxes and user charges (especially for special districts), property taxes accounted for only about 30 per cent of the total amount of revenue received by local governments. Thus while the property tax remains the dominant local tax, its role as a source of general revenue for local governments has diminished quite dramatically over time.

Table 1.1   Property taxes by level of government, 1991–92

	As a percentage of taxes	As a percentage of general revenue
All Local Governments		
Counties	74.3	27.9
Municipalities	52.6	23.1
Townships	93.0	56.9
School Districts	97.4	37.5
Special Districts	67.6	11.0
States	2.0	1.1

Source: US Department of Commerce, Bureau of the Census, *Government Finances: 1991–92*, Table 2, 'Summary of Government Finances by Level and Type of Government'.

Limitations on the property tax base and revenues

A variety of interrelated trends have narrowed the property tax base over time (Netzer, 1993). Over time, states have increasingly exempted personal property from the tax base, where personal property is defined as property other than land and buildings, such as the motor vehicles owned by individuals and inventories and equipment owned by firms. State actions, many of which have been taken to improve a state's competitive position, have reduced the share of the property tax base that is personal from 17 per cent in 1956 (Netzer, 1993, p. 59) to less than 9 per cent in 1991. States have also narrowed the base by allowing homestead exemptions for some or all of the owners of residential property, by assessing agricultural property at its value in current use rather than its market value, by classifying property into categories with differing effective tax rates, and by allowing local governments to provide property tax abatements to promote economic development.

Many of the homestead exemptions, and some of the classification programmes were introduced during the 1930s as a way of reducing the burden of the tax on homeowners. Preferential tax treatment of farmland began in Maryland in 1957 and has since spread to all 50 states in an attempt to preserve farmland or to provide fiscal relief for farmers, or both. Local tax abatements reflect the continuing efforts of large cities, especially the older cities of the North and the Midwest, to use the tax system to offset overwhelming economic pressures for firms to move to the suburbs where land prices are lower, or to the South where wages are lower. Many of these tax policies are explicitly undertaken to affect land use and, consequently, are discussed in detail in subsequent chapters.

The combination of market forces and policy actions has produced the distribution of assessed property values shown in Table 1.2. (Unfortunately, the detailed breakdown is not available for a year more recent than 1986.) As a rough approximation, residential property accounts for about 50 per cent of

Table 1.2   Gross assessed property values by type

Type of Property	1991 Amount (In billions of dollars)	1991 Percentage of Assessed Value	1986 Percentage of Assessed Value
Total assessed value	6 924.2	100.0	100.0
State assessed	285.9	4.1	5.0
Locally assessed	6 638.3	95.9	95.0
Real Property	6 043.6	87.3	85.2
Residential (non-farm)	n.a.	n.a.	52.1
Single-family houses	n.a.	n.a.	45.3
Commercial	n.a.	n.a.	14.7
Industrial	n.a.	n.a.	6.0
Farm acreage	n.a.	n.a.	6.4
Vacant platted lots	n.a.	n.a.	3.9
Other	n.a.	n.a.	2.0
Personal property	594.7	8.6	9.8

n.a.   signifies not available.

Sources: US Department of Commerce, *1987 Census of Governments: Vol. 2: Taxable Property Values, 1989, No. 1: Assessed Valuations for Local General Property Taxation*. Table 1: Gross and Net Assessed Value of Property Subject to Local General Property Taxation: 1986. US Department of Commerce, *1992 Census of Governments: Vol. 2: Taxable Property Values 1991, No. 1: Assessed Valuations for Local General Property Taxation*. Table 1: Gross and Net Assessed Value of Property Subject to Local General Property Taxation: 1991.

the gross assessed tax base, and commercial and industrial property accounts for about 35 percent. The latter percentage is the sum of locally assessed commercial and industrial real estate, personal property (most of which is business property), and state-assessed property (the bulk of which is utility property). This 1986 pattern reflects a significant redistribution of the tax away from business property towards residential property. In 1956, for example, residential property accounted for only about 40 per cent (Netzer, 1966, Table 2.1) of assessed valuation, well below its 52 per cent share in 1986.

In addition to policies that narrow the tax base, many states have now imposed binding restrictions on the level of the local tax rate or on the growth rate of local property taxes. Although constitutional limitations on property taxes have existed for more than a century, the new limitations differ in that they bind. The most stringent limitation measures are California's Proposition 13, which in 1978 rolled back all local tax rates to 1 per cent of market value and limited the growth of assessed values, and Massachusetts' Proposition 2½, which rolled back tax rates in that state to 2.5 per cent of market value and restricted the rate of growth of levies to 2.5 per cent, well below the rate of inflation. In these two cases, the limitation was imposed by a statewide referendum with no clear promise that state aid would be forthcoming to offset the tax cuts. In other states, such as Minnesota in 1971, limitations were imposed as part of a package that included additional state aid for local governments and where the role of the limitation measure was to ensure that the increased aid was not offset by increased spending. These limitations reduce reliance on the local property tax and limit the flexibility of local governments to make choices about spending and taxes.

Current pressures on local taxes
Two interrelated trends with potential impacts on local tax policy are worth noting: the deterioration in the fiscal condition in many large US cities, and the outlook for significant devolution of responsibilities from the federal government to state and local governments. The outflow from cities of middle and upper income households in search of better schools, lower taxes and lower crime in the suburbs, has led to an increasingly poor and dependent population in many large cities, and has thereby increased the need for public spending in the cities. These spending pressures have been exacerbated in recent years by nation-wide trends such as homelessness, drug addiction and teen pregnancy, problems that are disproportionately represented in large cities and that add to the pressure on city spending. At the same time, the decreasing demand for housing and the decline of manufacturing activity have reduced the ability of cities to raise revenue, particularly from the property tax. This rising pressure on spending, combined with a declining capacity to raise revenue, has made it increasingly difficult for cities to meet

the service needs of their residents at reasonable tax burdens (Ladd and Yinger, 1991).

The structural problems of many large US cities are caused in part by the structure of many metropolitan areas, and in particular the ease with which many metropolitan residents can avoid the fiscal burdens associated with big cities. In the South and Southwest, cities have often been able to share in the wealth of the metropolitan area as a result of their power to annexe surrounding areas as the urban area expands. In the older cities of the Northeast and Midwest, annexation is not an option and central cities have become increasingly impoverished at the same time as suburban areas have flourished. The fiscal problems of central cities reflect as well a variety of federal policies, including the federal tax subsidy to home ownership and federal financial assistance for new roads and sewer systems, that favour the suburbs over the central city, and the fact that public housing has concentrated many poor households in central cities. In addition, however, the suburbs themselves are culpable. As discussed in Chapter 3, they have used their zoning powers in many cases to exclude low income households from the suburbs, thereby exacerbating the problems of the cities.

A strong case can be made that the solution to the fiscal problems of large cities must be found outside the city itself in the form of additional assistance, broadly defined, from higher levels of government (Ladd and Yinger, 1991). However, because the property tax is a significant revenue source for big cities, policy-makers in large cities naturally turn to the property tax as a policy tool for solving their fiscal problems. One approach, used by many cities, is to provide tax abatements for business property in an attempt to retain existing firms and to induce new firms to locate in the city. Unfortunately, tax abatements are typically not very successful at countering the larger economic forces that induce firms to move out of the city or that lead them to locate elsewhere. In addition, tax abatements have the counterproductive effect of raising tax burdens for other residents and firms. A second policy option is the sharing of new property tax revenues among all local governments within the metropolitan area. As described more fully in Chapter 12, the Minneapolis–St Paul experience provides a good example of metropolitan-wide tax base sharing, but one that has not proven politically feasible in other metropolitan areas.

The other current issue is the potential for significant devolution of responsibilities to state and local governments, as proposed in 1995 by the Republican majority in Congress. Central to the devolution is the shift away from the current federal approach to funding Medicaid and Aid to Families with Dependent Children in favour of block grants, the removal of the federal entitlement to welfare and medical care for the poor, and a reduction in the amount, and growth, of federal aid to state and local governments. Such a devolution is likely to lead to increased pressure, either directly or indirectly, on state and local government taxes. If the states respond by offsetting the cuts in federal aid, they will have to raise state taxes or find other programmes to cut, one of which may well be state aid to cities and other local governments. If the states do not respond, the people who bear the burden will be the service recipients, who disproportionately live in cities. Consequently, their demand for services will increase and their ability to pay taxes will decrease, which will lead to a further deterioration in the fiscal position of the cities in which they reside. Finally, the devolution is likely to lead to increased competition among local jurisdictions for economic activity, thereby exacerbating the pressure for cities to use tax abatements to attract economic activity and for the suburbs to continue to zone out low income households. Thus the possible devolution of responsibilities is likely to exacerbate many of the pressures and patterns of economic behaviour discussed in this book.

Local Land Use Policy[1]

Land use regulation is allowed under the police powers of local governments. Under these powers, local communities are empowered to zone land for specific purposes, to regulate and restrict the height and size of buildings and the percentage of the lot that may be occupied, and to impose subdivision regulations to further the health, safety and general welfare of the local community. Such controls were traditionally justified as a way to minimize the negative externalities, such as noise, pollution and congestion, that can arise when factories are located near residential property. As the powers of local government to impose land use controls have evolved over time, the purposes of those controls have expanded to include the preservation of community character, the maintenance and enhancement of property values, the minimization of adverse fiscal impacts, and the pursuit of orderly growth and development. To many observers, these other rationales for zoning appear to be rationalizations for what in many cases amounts to zoning for exclusionary purposes such as excluding low income households (see, for example, Mills (1979) and Ellickson and Tarlock (1981)).

Zoning for exclusionary purposes increases the value of property for some people but may decrease it for others. When zoning is used to limit development, the most notable losers are the owners or developers of undeveloped land who are thereby prohibited from developing their land in the most profitable way. In that sense, zoning reduces the value of their property and might be viewed by some as a regulatory 'taking' similar to the taking of private property by eminent domain. However, because zoning is justified under the police powers of the local government, no compensation need be paid to the losing parties. The case for no compensation is clear when zoning is used to minimize negative externalities. However, to the extent that zoning is used for exclusionary purposes, the absence of compensation has significant implications for the behaviour of local voters. Because the use of zoning or other land use controls forces no explicit balancing of the social benefits to existing residents against the costs to potential residents or to surrounding communities, established residents have an incentive to zone more aggressively than they would if they bore the costs as well as the burdens of the exclusionary zoning or if potential residents could vote. This issue is discussed more fully in Chapter 3.

Legal history of zoning
The legal history and evolution of zoning and other land use controls reflects a struggle between the interests of three different groups: landowners or developers, present residents of the community as represented by the municipal government, and potential residents. Landowner interests dominated for the first quarter of the 20th century and then, for next 40 years or so, the interests of established residents dominated. Not until the early 1970s did the courts pay much attention to the third group, potential residents.

During the first quarter of the 20th century, landowner interests dominated as the courts were reluctant to support governmental intervention into the land market in a country committed to a *laissez-faire* economic and social philosophy. As a result, the drafters of local zoning ordinances were correspondingly cautious and restricted their regulations to those that separated housing, commerce and industry (Babcock and Bosselman, 1973, p. 25). Not until the US Supreme Court decided the *Euclid v. Ambler* case in 1926, did the pendulum swing towards the interests of the current residents and the municipal government. In that celebrated case, the Ambler Realty Company lost its argument that the zoning ordinance of the village of Euclid extended beyond the police powers of the community and represented a 'taking' of property. That case, for the first time, firmly established the constitutional validity of zoning for the promotion of the general health, safety and welfare of local residents.

Like most powers of local governments, the power to zone and impose other land use regulations must be explicitly granted through state constitutions or statutes. The promulgation of a model state zoning enabling act by the US Department of Commerce in 1926 dramatically increased the number of states with such enabling statutes and the local governments with comprehensive zoning ordinances.[2] Subsequently, local zoning expanded rapidly, with the specific powers of local governments evolving over time in response to decisions by the courts. By the late 1930s, most large cities and many suburbs and small towns had zoning ordinances, with increasingly fine classifications of types of residential, commercial and industrial property (Mills, 1979, p. 517).

During the 40 years between the mid 1920s and the mid 1960s, communities used their zoning powers in part to segregate the various types of land uses in ways that arguably could be defended as promoting the health and safety of the residents. For example, restricting industrial property to industrial zones, retail property to commercial zones and residential property to residential zones could be justified as a means of minimizing the adverse spillovers from one activity to another. In addition, however, local governments used their zoning powers to impose minimum lot sizes, to rule out multi-family housing and to impose other restrictions on the size and type of buildings, restrictions that both limited access to the community by potential residents and that had potential spillover effects on other communities. For example, minimum lot sizes and limitations on multi-family housing served to keep out low income families with children who were deemed undesirable in part because they were likely to receive more in local public services than they would pay in local property taxes. Those families in turn then had to find housing in other communities, which affected housing prices and tax and service levels in those other communities. That many of the local zoning ordinances were exclusionary either by design or effect during this period received little judicial attention.

The 1968 urban riots changed the situation as civil rights groups began to attack exclusionary zoning on the grounds that it violated the equal protection clause of the US constitution. However, this legal theory was undermined as housing was deemed not to be a fundamental right, that wealth need not be a suspect category, and that racial discrimination required a discriminatory intent that was often hard to prove. Hence while the federal courts ruled out zoning that discriminated on the basis of race, they were reluctant to rule out zoning that discriminated on the basis of income.

The opponents of exclusionary zoning were only slightly more successful in the state courts. Only in a few notable cases have state courts declared that exclusionary zoning is illegal and tried to combat it. The most famous of these are the Mt Laurel cases in New Jersey. The first Mt Laurel case in 1975 required the community, which is a suburb of Philadelphia, and other 'developing' communities like it to rezone to accommodate low income housing. Frustrated by the recalcitrance of the communities to comply and the hostility of the legislature, the New Jersey court went even further in the second Mt Laurel decision in 1983, and imposed an affirmative obligation to build low income housing in every New Jersey community. A final case, popularly known as Mt Laurel III, approved the New Jersey Fair Housing Act of 1985 (Fischel, 1995, pp. 336–8). In the end, communities were allowed to buy their way out of part of their obligation by contracting with other, less affluent, communities to provide the low cost housing units. Hence the final result was significantly less than that for which reformers had hoped.

A 1975 California case focused attention on another type of land use control, those designed not simply to limit housing for low income households, but rather to limit all forms of development. Responding initially to the problem of a sewer treatment plant that was over-loaded by unexpectedly rapid growth, the City of Petaluma ultimately imposed stringent growth controls that excluded people of all types, not just low income people, by severely limiting building permits and rationing them with a point system that gave added weight to costly design features. Although subsequent studies have shown that controls of this type significantly raise the price of housing and thereby make it less available, especially for low income households, the US Court of Appeals upheld the Petaluma Plan and praised it for providing some incentives for moderate income housing. This decision facilitated the introduction of such growth controls in many other California cities (cited in Fischel, 1995, pp. 222–3).

In summary, local governments have significant authority to limit the uses of land within their jurisdiction. Moreover, because the courts have interpreted quite broadly the requirement that zoning be used to further the health, safety and general welfare of the community, most rationales for zoning continue to be legitimate uses of the police powers of local governments in most states. Although zoning for the explicit purpose of exclusion is not likely to pass judicial muster, communities can usually find other, more acceptable, rationales to achieve the same ends.

Exactions as a Policy Tool

Communities subject to population pressures have increasingly turned to exactions and fees on developers to finance additional public services associated with development. Although they resemble taxes in that they generate revenue, exactions are similar to zoning regulation in that they are based not on the taxing power but rather on the police power of local governments. While exactions on developers are not new – large developers have traditionally been required to provide on-site infrastructure for their projects – jurisdictions are now asking developers to provide funds for off-site infrastructure such as parks and schools. The intent is to force the new development to pay for the fiscal burden it imposes on established residents. In some areas, these fees are very high. One study showed that in California, where fees are used most frequently, the mean fee on a 2000 square foot home was $6496, with 10 per cent of the cities imposing fees of over $10 000 (cited in Gyourko, 1991, p. 244).

One common interpretation of these fees is that they are simply another form of land use control comparable to zoning. According to this interpretation, impact fees slow down development by raising its costs. Moreover, they particularly harm low income households which cannot afford the higher priced housing.

Recent work has emphasized a different interpretation of fees and exactions. This new interpretation views impact fees as a means of facilitating growth, given the incentives for fiscal zoning that arise in their absence. The starting point in these analyses is that, in the absence of impact fees, public services would be financed by a property tax that applies at the same rate to existing and new property. To the extent that development does not pay its way, it imposes fiscal burdens on established residents and thereby provides a reason for them to limit development. Fees on new development reduce the burden on established residents and may make new development more politically acceptable.

This argument that fees may facilitate new development has been made by both economists and political scientists. Economists have developed an economic model in which the fees transfer some of the consumer surplus that low income households gain from living in the community to established residents. Compared with the situation without fees, both groups are made better off and more low income housing is provided (Gyourko, 1991). The political argument is that the flexibility of fees allows politically skilful officials to use fees and exactions to transform contention over development from a zero-sum game between pro- and anti-development forces into a distributive game in which differences can be reconciled as the balance of forces dictates (Altshuler and Gómez-Ibáñez, 1993, Chapter 9).

STATUS OF THE CONVENTIONAL WISDOM

Local government land use and tax policies are closely intertwined in the United States largely because of our highly decentralized fiscal system. Many of the land use effects of taxes occur because firms and households can move from one taxing jurisdiction to another. The smaller and more spatially fragmented are the local jurisdictions and the greater are the spending responsibilities they bear, the larger is the impact on land use of local fiscal decisions. Similarly, the effects of land policies on land prices and taxes vary with the size of the jurisdiction and the mobility of people and households across jurisdictions.

The interactions between land and tax policy also reflect the institutional fact that local governments in the United States have extensive powers to determine how local land will be used. Because local governments have used this power not only to offset the traditional form of negative externalities that arise from having smoke-producing firms near residential neighbourhoods, but also for other purposes such as preserving the character of the community, minimizing adverse fiscal impacts and limiting growth, land use regulation has exacerbated fiscal inequities among jurisdictions.

The interactions between local land use and tax policies are complex and have received a lot of attention in both the theoretical and empirical literature. Over time a number of common views have developed and have been used both in research and to guide policy. At the same time, many of these views have been challenged by the research of others. The review of the existing research in Part I of this book, combined with the new research in Parts II and III, sheds new light on many components of the conventional wisdom and evaluates the challenges to that common wisdom.

Conventional Wisdom: A Tax on Land does not Distort Land Use Decisions

According to the 19th-century US social reformer, Henry George, a tax on land is superior to all other forms of taxation because it does not distort behaviour. A tax on land *rents* (that is, the return to land) does not distort the behaviour of landlords who, provided they singlemindedly seek to maximize profits, have no incentive to change the intensity of land use after a tax is imposed.

This conventional wisdom handed down from Henry George that a tax on land *rents* has no effect on the intensity of land use remains intact. However, the research reviewed in Chapter 2 shows that a tax on the capitalized value of expected future returns may affect the timing of development. By increasing the carrying costs of holding land, a tax on land value, where value is defined in this way, may induce landowners to develop the land sooner than they otherwise would. A tax on true site value, in contrast, would not distort landowners' economic behaviour. Thus whether a tax on land value is likely to distort landowner decisions depends largely on how land value is determined for purposes of taxation.

Conventional Wisdom: In Contrast to a Tax on Land Alone, a Tax on Property (Including Improvements) Distorts Land Use Decisions

The standard conclusion that property taxes – that is, taxes on improvements as well as on land – distort investment and location decisions has been challenged on the grounds that under certain conditions the property tax acts like a benefit tax (see Chapter 2 and commentary by William Fischel). Central to this challenge to the conventional wisdom is the existence of many local governments within a metropolitan area, all with the power to set local property tax rates to pay for locally provided public services. With the additional assumption that each community will zone its land in such a way as to ensure that all housing is of similar value, the property tax paid by residents in each community acts like a user charge for locally provided services, and hence does not distort economic decisions. Controversy remains about the extent to which zoning achieves this goal in practice. At best, zoning may approximate this outcome in suburban areas that have multiple small jurisdictions. However, even here some distortions are likely to remain. Given that the property tax is a major revenue source for many types of jurisdiction other than small, homogeneous suburban communities, it is reasonable to conclude that, in general, the tax distorts investment and housing decisions (but see commentary by William Fischel for the alternative view).

Conventional Wisdom: The Property Tax is Regressive

The conventional wisdom is that the property tax imposes a larger burden on households with low income than on households with high income. Implicit in the conventional wisdom is that the property tax is not a benefit tax, that is, one for which the burden of the tax across households would be perfectly offset by the benefits they receive from local public spending. The conclusion that the tax is regressive appears to be valid, but only from the perspective of policy-makers in relatively small-taxing jurisdictions such as cities or counties, that is, jurisdictions from which investment can easily be withdrawn in favour of a lower taxing jurisdiction. For example, when the mayor of a large city is contemplating raising the local property tax rate, she can expect the burden to fall disproportionately on the lower income residents in the city. For the country as a whole, the property tax is more appropriately viewed as a tax on capital, the burden of which is distributed among households in a progressive manner. As a result, any attempt through federal policy to reduce reliance on the property tax is likely to benefit high income citizens more than low income citizens. This conclusion holds despite variations among communities that lead to additional burdens on consumers of housing and other taxed goods in communities with high tax rates and lower burdens on consumers in communities with low tax rates. Differentials around the average may offset the overall progressive pattern somewhat, but only to the extent that low income households disproportionately reside in jurisdictions with above-average tax rates.

Conventional Wisdom: New Development Generates Fiscal Profits (an Excess of Revenues over Additional Public Spending)

Many US studies of the fiscal impacts of development have typically indicated that, with the exception of inexpensive housing, new development pays its fiscal way and that business property yields a clear fiscal surplus. As discussed in Chapter 3, this conclusion is currently being challenged in the United States. Both changing economic circumstances and more sophisticated analysis suggest that new development may impose greater fiscal burdens than was once believed. In particular, new development may require more additional local public spending, especially on public infrastructure, than was previously believed, so that the additional costs of development may exceed the additional revenues associated with the new development. Recent studies by economists of the fiscal impacts of population growth generally support the revisionist view that development may not pay its fiscal way. However, a recent study of the Chicago area (see Chapter 10) provides new, but limited, statistical support for the conventional view that new business development, as distinct from residential development, yields fiscal benefits to established residents.

Conventional Wisdom: High Density Development Puts Less of a Burden on Spending and Taxes than Spread-Out Development

Modern urban planning starts from the premise that compact development decreases the costs of public facilities and services relative to urban sprawl. Hence according to this conventional wisdom of planners, compact development should be encouraged as a way of reducing spending and taxes. As spelled out in Chapter 3, this conventional wisdom is currently under attack from economists who find that public sector costs may bear a U-shaped relationship with population density: that is, both sparsely populated and densely populated areas generate higher public sector costs than moderately dense areas.

Conventional Wisdom among Economists. In Practice, Variations in State and Local Tax Rates have Little Effect on the Location and Investment Decisions of Firms

Economic theory predicts that variations in tax rates across jurisdictions will affect the location and investment decisions of firms. However, early empirical studies found little impact. Hence until recently, applied economists typically held the view that tax rate differentials were not an important determinant of firm location. This empirically based conventional wisdom has changed quite dramatically in recent years as statistical models have become more sophisticated and the number of careful empirical studies has increased (see Chapter 4). Recent studies confirm the theoretical prediction that taxes significantly affect the location decisions of firms both among states and among communities within metropolitan areas.

Conventional Wisdom. Tax Policy Alone is not a very Effective Tool for Achieving Land Use and Related Social Goals

Tax policies are frequently used as tools of land policy. Sometimes, as with tax abatements and geographically targeted programmes in the form of enterprise zones, they are used to promote more intensive use of the land, and sometimes, as with preferential treatment of agricultural land, they are used to limit development and to preserve open space. Recent experience with tax abatements, especially in their geographically targeted form of enterprise zones, raises serious questions about their ability to achieve the broader social goals, such as jobs for disadvantaged households, that motivated the programmes to attract new business to distressed areas in the first place (see Chapter 5). For the programmes for which costs can be measured, the cost of attracting new jobs for disadvantaged households through enterprise zones is very high: the annual cost per new job for a disadvantaged resident appears to be $40 000 to $60 000. Thus the conventional wisdom among economists, although not always of policy-makers, that tax policy alone is not a very effective tool for helping disadvantaged residents in economically distressed areas, seems to be confirmed by the evidence reported here.

The effectiveness of tax policies designed to retain land in farming has not, until now, been carefully investigated. While most economists have been highly critical of the goals of such programmes, they had little empirical evidence on which to base conclusions about whether programmes that provided preferential tax treatment of farmland served to retain more land in farming than would otherwise have been the case. New evidence reported in Chapter 7 shows that such programmes may have increased the share of a typical county's land in farmland by about 10 percentage points over a 20-year period. However, this finding should not be interpreted as support for such programmes, given that the land that is retained may not be the land that provides the positive externalities that justify the programme.

Conventional Wisdom: A Shift Away from the Property Tax in Favour of Heavier Reliance on the Land Tax could Reinvigorate Declining Cities

The conventional wisdom is that a shift away from a tax on improvements in favour of a tax on land alone could have some positive economic effects on a city. However, most economists are careful to point out that the positive effects come not from the increase in the land tax, but rather from the reduction in the tax on improvements. Moreover, theoretical work shows that the tax restructuring is most likely to increase aggregate land values if the jurisdiction making the change is small relative to the economic region of which it is a part.

Unfortunately, empirical evidence to confirm this conventional wisdom is hard to obtain, since so few cities in the United States have experimented with this form of restructuring. A careful study of Pittsburgh's experience with tax restructuring provides evidence consistent with the conventional wisdom, but the evidence is not sufficient to rule out other explanations for Pittsburgh's recent growth and vitality (see Chapter 6).

Conventional Wisdom: Development Fees or Exactions are an Effective Way to Shift the Burden of Paying for New Public Infrastructure on to the New Residents who Require It

Many fast-growing communities impose exactions or fees on developers with the goal of shifting the burden of the new development on to the new residents. However, it turns out that not all the burden will end up on the new residents. In general, more than half of the burden of the fees is likely to fall on the owners of undeveloped land. Nonetheless, the popularity of development fees is not surprising: in general they confer a capital gain on existing homeowners and do not place any burden on developers (Chapter 11).

In general, special assessments appear to be a much fairer financing mechanism in that the burden falls entirely on the people who benefit from the new public infrastructure, namely the people who buy new housing, and established residents receive no capital gains.

CONCLUDING OBSERVATIONS

Throughout this book, we view the interactions between local government tax and land use policy through the lens of the economist, with its focus on economic efficiency, behavioural incentives and equity. Lurking close to the surface, but not directly addressed here, are significant issues of politics and values. Local governments are the arena in which the inherent conflict between national ideas of social justice and equality on the one hand, and individual mobility and market-driven choices on the other, is played out. Local land use controls, development strategies and the level of property taxes are the tools through which local governments seek to tailor local communities and the provision of public services to the needs of a relatively homogeneous set of local residents who have other choices. An important question for the next century is how the resulting local tax and land use decisions support or undermine the values of social justice and equality.

NOTES

1. The following discussion draws heavily on Mills (1979), Fischel (1985, 1995), Babcock and Bosselman (1973), Ellickson and Tarlock (1981).
2. Section 1 of this model enabling act spells out the basic purpose of zoning as follows:

> (Grant of Power.) For the purpose of promoting health, safety, morals, or the general welfare of the community, the legislative body of cities and incorporated villages is hereby empowered to regulate and restrict the height, number of stories, and size of buildings and other structures, the percentage of the lot that may be occupied, the size of yards, courts, and other open spaces, the density of population, and the location and use of buildings, structures, and land for trade, industry, residence, or other purposes (quoted in Sullivan, 1990, p. 282).

REFERENCES

Altshuler, Alan A. and José A. Gómez-Ibáñez (1993), *Regulation for Revenue: The Political Economy of Land Use Exactions*, Washington, DC: Brookings Institute and Lincoln Institute of Land Policy.

Babcock, Richard F. and Fred P. Bosselman (1973), *Exclusionary Zoning: Land Use Regulation and Housing in the 1970s*, New York: Praeger Publishers.

Due, John F. (1961), 'Studies of State-Local Tax Influences in Location of Industry', *National Tax Journal*, **14**, 163–73.

Ellickson, Robert C. and A. Dan Tarlock (1981), *Land Use Controls: Cases and Materials*, Casebook Materials Series, Boston, MA: Little Brown.

Fischel, William A. (1985), *The Economics of Zoning Laws: A Property Rights Approach to American Land Use Controls*, Baltimore: Johns Hopkins University Press.

Fischel, William A. (1995), *Regulatory Takings: Law, Economics, and Politics*, Cambridge, MA: Harvard University Press.

Gyourko, Joseph (1991), 'Impact fees, exclusionary zoning, and the density of new development', *Journal of Urban Economics*, **30**, 242–56.

Ladd, Helen F. and John Yinger (1991), *America's Ailing Cities: Fiscal Health and the Design of Urban Policy*, updated edition, Baltimore: Johns Hopkins University Press.

Mills, Edwin S. (1979), 'Economic Analysis of Urban Land-Use Controls', in P. Mieszkowski and M. Straszheim (eds), *Current Issues in Urban Economics*, Baltimore: Johns Hopkins University Press, pp. 511–41.

Netzer, Dick (1966), *Economics of the Property Tax*, Brookings Institute.

Netzer, Dick (1993), 'Property taxes: their past, present, and future place in government finance', Thomas R. Swartz and Frank J. Bowello (eds), *Urban Finance Under Siege*, Armonk, New York: M.E. Sharpe, pp. 51–78.

Sullivan, Arthur M. (1990), *Urban Economics*, Boston, MA: Irwin Publishers.

Table 1A.1   Local reliance on the property tax

| Year | Property taxes as a percentage of | |
	Total tax revenue	Total local government revenue
1927	97.3	68.8
1932	97.3	67.2
1940	92.7	54.0
1946	91.9	49.5
1950	88.2	43.7
1955	86.9	42.7
1960	87.4	42.3
1965	86.9	40.8
1966	87.4	40.2
1967	86.6	39.0
1968	86.1	38.2
1969	85.4	37.5
1970	84.9	37.0
1971	84.6	36.4
1972	83.7	36.2
1973	82.9	34.0
1974	82.2	32.4
1975	81.6	31.3
1976	81.2	30.8
1977	80.5	30.7
1978	79.9	29.9
1979	77.5	26.6
1980	75.9	25.4
1981	76.0	25.0
1982	76.1	25.0
1983	76.0	25.4
1984	75.0	25.3
1985	74.2	24.8
1986	74.0	24.7
1987	73.6	24.7
1988	74.1	25.7
1989	74.3	25.8
1990	74.5	25.8
1991	75.3	26.4
1992	75.6	26.5

Source: For 1927–89: Urban Finance Under Siege, Table 3.1 (US Census Bureau, Government Finance diskettes, 1989) for 1990–92: *Government Finances 1989–1990, 1990–1991, 1991–1992*, Table 2: Summary of Government Finances by Level and Type of Government. US Department of Commerce, Economic and Statistical Administration, Bureau of the Census.

PART I

Interactions between Tax and Land Policies

2. Theoretical controversies: land and property taxation

Helen F. Ladd

Historically, a tax on land has appealed to many people, both because it is neutral with respect to resource use – that is, it does not distort economic behaviour – and because it seems fair in that it applies to land rents that are caused not by the actions of the landowner but rather by population growth and public investments. In contrast, the primary land-based tax used in the United States, namely the property tax, has been frequently criticized for distorting housing and investment decisions and for imposing a heavier burden on households with low income than on those with high income. However, neither the virtues of land taxation nor the liabilities of property taxation are free from controversy. This chapter elucidates the nature of the theoretical controversies that surround both types of tax.

TAXES ON LAND: RESOURCE USE AND EFFICIENCY

According to the 19th-century social reformer, Henry George, a tax that appropriated all land rents would provide the correct incentives for landowners to use their land in the most productive manner and would eliminate the need for all other taxes. Thus in the ideal Georgian world, the only relevant tax would be a tax on land value. George's belief that land taxes do not distort land use and are the most efficient way to finance public services continues to appeal to many economists and his modern followers. It is worth asking, however, whether Henry George was right. That is, do his claims of neutrality stand up to the rigorous analysis of modern economists?

Are Taxes on Land Neutral?

A neutral or efficient tax is one that provides no opportunity for taxpayers to reduce their tax burdens by changing their behaviour. Provided the population in each jurisdiction is fixed, a head tax is neutral in that no taxpayer can avoid or reduce the tax by changing his or her behaviour.[1] In contrast, a tax on income, output or constructed real estate will distort economic decisions. Taxpayers can reduce their income tax burden by earning less, can reduce their sales tax burden by consuming less or can reduce their property tax burden by building less. Because they provide incentives for altering behaviour, each of these other taxes is non-neutral or inefficient.

Land differs from other factors of production, such as labour or machines, in that the supply of land is fixed. Consequently, the standard view is that a tax on land rent – or, equivalently, the profit from land – is neutral with respect to resource use. The tax does not distort resource use because, provided landlords are profit maximizers, they have no incentive to use their land any differently after the imposition of a tax than before. The assumption that landlords always seek to maximize profits plays an important role in this assertion. The argument is that for any tax rate, t, the return to the landowner $((1-t)$ times land rent) will be maximized by the same behaviour that maximized land rents in the absence of the tax. But might not landowners try to reduce their tax burden by selling their land? The answer is no, because the tax will be fully capitalized into the price of land. That is, with the introduction of the tax, potential purchasers will reduce the amount they are willing to pay for the land by the amount of the present value of the stream of future tax payments to which they will be subject. Thus full capitalization implies that the current owner of the land cannot avoid the burden of the tax by selling his land. If he sells the land, he in effect pays the tax in the form of a lower sales price for the land.

Although economists agree that a tax on annual land rents is neutral, they disagree about the effects of a tax on land value. Several authors have argued that a tax on land value distorts the timing of development decisions by inducing landowners to develop the land sooner than they otherwise would. For example, Bentick (1982), Mills (1981) and, more recently, Duck-Ho Lim (1992) show that if the tax depends on the current market value of the land and developers have to choose among mutually exclusive development projects with different time streams, the tax raises the carrying cost of the land and increases the attractiveness of current relative to future development.

This challenge to the Georgian orthodoxy is valid but rests on the important assumptions that development is not reversible and that the tax applies to the current value of the land, which in turn depends on future development options that are affected by current decisions. Irreversibility means that if development is undertaken today, the option of developing that same parcel in a subsequent year at some other density is foreclosed. The underlying model posits that profit-maximizing landowners make decisions about when to develop their land by comparing the present value of the streams of returns associated with different times of development. In the absence of taxes,

developers will hold on to the land until the return from the land is just equal
to the opportunity cost of carrying the land in its vacant state, as measured by
the interest rate. The imposition of a tax on the value of land increases the
annual cost of carrying the land by the amount of the tax, and thereby induces
earlier development to compensate the developer for the higher costs of
holding land vacant.[2]

If, in contrast, the value of the land for tax purposes were based not on its
chosen use but rather on its 'highest and best' use, the land value tax would
not distort the timing of investment decisions (Vickrey, 1980; Wildasin, 1986).
The tax would be neutral because it would impose the same burden whether
the land were developed or not. Thus the controversy about the neutrality of
the tax is largely one of semantics. True believers in the neutrality of the
land-value tax argue that a tax that affects the timing of the development
decision should not be called a land-value tax, but rather should be referred to
as a tax on the present value of planned net income.[3] In practice, the neutrality (or lack thereof) of any specific tax on land values will depend on how the
tax assessors determine the value for tax purposes (see the discussion of the
Pittsburgh tax in Chapter 6).

In a provocative 1977 article, Martin Feldstein challenged the conventional
orthodoxy about who bears the burden of a tax on pure rent. However, his
conclusions in no way alter the conclusion that the tax is neutral. He develops
his argument in the context of a life-cycle model in which taxpayers try to
accumulate a certain amount of wealth during their lifetime. Because the
imposition of a land-value tax reduces the value of taxpayers' wealth, they
are induced to accumulate more wealth in the form of produced capital. The
increased capital reduces the net yield on capital, increases wage rate, and
generates a smaller reduction in the price of land than is predicted by the
standard model. Through this mechanism, some of the burden of the tax is
shifted away from landowners. However, this change in behaviour is in
response to an effective change in initial endowments and not to the presence
of a wedge between the return to savers and the productivity of capital.
Hence the standard conclusion that a tax on land is neutral is not affected.

In sum, the basic conclusion that true land taxes do not distort resource use
remains valid. Only when the tax applies to the present value of planned net
income does the tax distort the timing of the investment decision. Thus a
land-value tax can be viewed as a lump-sum tax in which the amount of the
tax paid by each person varies with the amount of land they own.[4]

Are Confiscatory Taxes on Land the most Efficient way to Finance Public Goods?[5]

In addition to the relatively straightforward assertion that taxes on land are neutral because people cannot avoid them by changing their economic behaviour, stronger assertions have been made about the efficiency of land taxes and their role in financing public services. The strongest form of the assertion is that in the context of a regional model in which the geographic area of each region is fixed, the economically efficient number of people in the jurisdiction will be achieved if the jurisdiction finances public services exclusively with a tax on land rents. This assertion is referred to as the 'Henry George theorem' because of its consistency with George's basic argument that all public services should be financed by a single tax on land value.

The basic model is based on the following assumptions. First, the region has a fixed amount of land and anyone who lives in the region also works in the region and receives no income from outside the region. The fixed quantity of land implies that the marginal productivity of labour falls as more people move to the region and that land rents increase. Second, land and labour in the region are used to produce output that can be used either for private or for public consumption. Third, the public goods are characterized by non-rivalry in consumption with no congestion (which means that the benefits received by one person do not adversely affect the benefits received by another person). This non-rivalry implies that the average resource cost of providing the public good falls as the number of people increases, and that the marginal cost of supplying public goods to an additional resident is zero. Consequently, when someone moves to the region, there are two effects on established residents: they are hurt by the decline in the productivity of labour but they benefit from the decline in the average costs of providing public services.

The omniscient planner (the one who knows and sees all and the one is who is evoked by the economist developing an abstract model) wishing to maximize the welfare of the typical resident, should admit new residents up to the point where the marginal productivity of labour is just equal to the per capita consumption of the private good. When this condition holds, the *net social* marginal product of the new worker (that is, the amount the worker contributes to total output net of what he takes out in the form of private consumption) is zero and exactly equal to the social cost he imposes for his share of the pure public good. Interestingly, the way to achieve this efficient outcome is not by using head taxes but rather by a 100 per cent tax on land rents. Head taxes in this context typically lead to inefficient outcomes.

Only in the uninteresting and unrealistic case in which all regions are identical would head taxes, used alone, lead to an efficient outcome. With differences across regions, say in land endowments, head taxes are inefficient because they can be avoided by moving to a different region. The inefficiency emerges because when people move out of a region to avoid a high head tax, they do not consider the effects of their relocation on remaining residents.

In this context, efficiency requires the use of 100 per cent taxes on land rents. This conclusion follows from the welfare-maximizing logic just presented. Assuming that workers are paid the value of their marginal product, welfare maximization requires that all wage income be used for consumption of the private good. The remaining portion of the regional income, namely the land rents, should be used to finance the public goods.[6] In this model, the land rents reflect the benefits from collective consumption of the public good that accrue from having a concentrated population. To ensure efficiency with respect to population movement, none of the land rents should go to private consumption. Instead they should all be used to finance the public good that generated them. Stated differently, the rents from the activity with decreasing returns (private production on the land) should be balanced against the costs of providing the activity with increasing returns (the provision of the public good).

Although the basic analytical model is quite simple and was developed initially in the context of a regional model, its essential logic applies to other situations as well (Mieszkowski and Zodrow (1989, p. 1136) and Wildasin (1986, p.26). For example, the model can also be applied to an urban area in which land rents are generated by a transportation system with large fixed costs. Under certain circumstances, the land rents generated by the presence of the transportation system will just equal the subsidy needed to cover the fixed costs and are appropriately taxed for that purpose. In this case the source of the population concentration is economies of scale in the production of transportation. Consequently, the land rents generated by the resulting concentration of population are appropriately used to finance the fixed costs of the system.

The Henry George theorem that land taxes alone should be used to finance public services needs to be modified when the public good is congested. With a congested public good, a new resident adversely affects the benefits from the public service available to established residents. To ensure efficient migration in this case, Wildasin and others have shown that a combination of land rents and head taxes is needed where the head taxes serve as congestion charges. Without the head taxes, migrants would not take into account the effects of their migration decisions on the quality of public goods. If the publicly provided goods are, in fact, comparable with private goods (in the sense of being fully rival) and are produced with constant returns to scale, public goods no longer provide an incentive for the concentration of population. In particular, they generate no land rents. As a consequence, they should be financed by head taxes rather than by taxes on land rents. (See additional discussion of head taxes below in the context of the Tiebout model and property taxes.)

This discussion puts into perspective Henry George's view that land taxes alone are the appropriate tax on efficiency grounds for financing local public services. As modern writers have clarified, the key point is that George's efficiency argument depends crucially on the assumption that publicly provided goods exhibit economies of scale with respect to population. These economies of scale may be generated by the publicness of the good itself, as in the case of uncongested pure public goods, or from increasing returns to scale in production. If average costs of providing the public good decline with population size, people have an incentive to concentrate, which produces land rents that are appropriately used to finance the public service. However, the conclusion differs quite dramatically in the absence of economies with respect to population size. In the case of fully congested or private goods, for example, no land rents are generated by the provision of public services, and efficiency considerations dictate lump-sum head taxes rather than taxes on land values as a cost of entry into the community. Given that local public goods are undoubtedly congested and not purely public, sole reliance on local land taxes is not likely to achieve an efficient outcome. [7]

A final point worth emphasizing is the regional nature of this model and the assumption of only one local public good. When there are many local public goods, with differing, but overlapping, spatial benefit regions, economists typically call for a decentralized system of overlapping local governments in which the boundary of each government corresponds to the spatial benefit area of each good (see Oates, 1971). However, this prescription is appropriate only when the public good is appropriately financed fully by user charges. When efficiency calls for financing by land rents – as if does when distance from the public facility affects the benefits enjoyed – there is no mechanism whereby the aggregate land rents can be allocated with the right incentives to all the separate local governments. Hence efficiency in this case requires a regional, or metropolitan-wide, government that includes all the overlapping jurisdictions (Hochman *et al.* 1995). In sum, a Georgist focus on land taxation has implications not only for the type of financing, but also more generally for the structure and organization of local governments. Moreover, as discussed in the next section, the efficiency claims for metropolitan or regional government that emerge from the Georgist view contrast sharply with the efficiency claims for a much more decentralized system of local government that emerge from the Tiebout approach.

THE PROPERTY TAX

The property tax has long been criticized, by both experts and the general public, for distorting investment and housing decisions and for placing a disproportionate burden on low income households. However, economists have recently challenged both of these criticisms. This section describes the nature of the challenges and the status of the current debate.

Does the Property Tax Distort Investment and Housing Decisions?

A property tax (as used in the United States) differs from a land-value tax in that it applies to improvements as well as to land.[8] Conventional wisdom holds that this tax on improvements distorts investment and consumption decisions. Provided the owners of the taxed property have alternatives that are not subject to the same tax, they are able to avoid the tax by changing their behaviour. The standard view is that, as used in the United States, the property tax is a tax on capital that reduces investment in general, shifts investment from highly taxed to less taxed sectors, and shifts investments from high to low tax jurisdictions. Thus investment in housing and other property is expected to be lower when revenue is raised from a property tax than when the same amount of revenue is raised from a land value tax. (See Brueckner (1986) for a modern statement of this view.)

This standard view has been challenged by Bruce Hamilton (1975, 1976), who argues that, under certain conditions, the property tax can be viewed as a non-distorting benefit tax. Because the US property tax is primarily a local tax, he argues that one should look at it in the context of a model of the type initially specified by Tiebout (1956) in which voters choose among local jurisdictions in a metropolitan area the jurisdiction that provides their preferred spending and tax package. Tiebout's original assumption that all jurisdictions used non-distorting head taxes led to his conclusion that decentralized provision of public services would be efficient. In effect, the head tax is similar to a user charge for living in the community which entitles the user to the available public services.

In practice, of course, local communities do not use head taxes. Instead they rely heavily on local property taxes which, as described above, are generally viewed as distorting. In the context of a Tiebout-like model with no non-residential property and in which public goods are like private goods, Hamilton (1975) shows that the property tax can be made equivalent to the non-distorting head tax envisioned by Tiebout by the addition of a binding zoning constraint. Perfect zoning in this context means that each community strictly enforces the constraint that every resident must have a certain minimum amount of housing. This constraint ensures that all residents of a jurisdiction will end up in similarly valued houses. Residents who wish to live in housing valued at less than the minimum – and thereby to pay below-average taxes for the public good – are precluded by the zoning ordinance. Residents who wish to live in more expensive houses will move to another community to avoid paying an above-average share of the cost of the public good. With all residents of a particular jurisdiction having housing of similar value, they all pay the same property tax, which is then identical to Tiebout's head tax.

In a subsequent paper, Hamilton (1976) generalizes his argument to a model in which some communities have heterogeneous housing. Assuming the heterogeneous communities are fully developed, full (relative) capitalization of taxes into housing values ensures once again that the property tax is a non-distorting benefit tax. Extensions by White (1975) and Fischel (1975) show that the taxation of commercial and industrial property can also be converted to non-distorting taxes by appropriate zoning ordinances. Zoning plus perfect mobility of firms can result in an efficient outcome in which the taxes paid by firms just equal the cost of providing public services to them plus the environmental costs they impose on the community.

The central components of the Hamilton approach are: (1) the fact that households are mobile and each will choose to reside in the community that provides its preferred tax and expenditure bundle; and (2) perfect zoning. Mieszkowski and Zodrow (1989) show that it is the binding zoning constraint, and not the mobility assumption, that converts the property tax from a distortionary tax to a non-distortionary tax. The intuition for the importance of zoning is clear. In the absence of the zoning constraint, households would respond to the property tax by altering their consumption of housing, even if they are mobile, in response to fiscal differentials among jurisdictions. However, if zoning regulations precisely determine the amount of housing, no leeway remains for the property tax to distort decisions about how much housing households will purchase, and the property tax becomes a lump-sum tax that can be viewed as the cost of entry to the community.

Whether the property tax should be viewed as a non-distorting benefit tax has emerged as a controversial issue in the field of local taxation. Its staunchest supporter is William Fischel (see commentary on this chapter), whose vast research on zoning and first-hand experience with a local zoning board have convinced him both that local communities have the tools to zone for fiscal purposes and that they use them effectively (Fischel, 1992, 1995). To support his position, Fischel cites various empirical studies that document the importance of fiscal motives as a determinant of zoning decisions, such as studies of New Jersey municipalities and Boston suburbs (Fischel, 1995, pp. 262–4). In addition he notes that local communities have a range of substitutable zoning tools that allow them to fine-tune their decisions. For example, by imposing expensive building standards for four-bedroom houses and more lenient standards for housing for the elderly, local officials can match the value of the housing to the costs of providing services to that housing. In response to critics who use the observation that developers often exceed regulations about minimum lot size to argue that zoning is not binding, Fischel emphasizes the substitutability among tools. By using other tools, such as minimum floor area and frontage requirements on a public road, local officials are able to control the value of housing on the larger lots (Fischel, 1992, p. 173; 1995, pp. 264–5). In addition, he emphasizes that in practice – in contrast to the simplified world of theory – efficiency need not require that all households in a community end up with housing of exactly the same value. The fact that housing for the elderly puts a smaller burden on local public spending than does housing for families with children means that different housing values for the two groups can be consistent with efficiency.

Fischel continues his case by pointing out that local voters have a strong economic interest in ensuring that development pays its fiscal way; if new homeowners impose greater fiscal costs than they pay in taxes, the value of the homes of established residents will decline. Consequently they have a strong incentive to zone out development that does not pay its fiscal way, and will do so provided they have the political power to do so. This type of reasoning leads Fischel to distinguish between suburban communities, where evidence suggests that political outcomes reflect the view of local voters, and large cities, where political outcomes reflect competition among interest groups and in which developers are able to play a more significant role (Fischel, 1992, p. 174).[9]

Finally, Fischel points to the evidence on capitalization which shows that suburban zoning lowers the value of undeveloped land and raises existing home values. Although he recognizes that this evidence need not imply that suburban communities engage in effective *fiscal* zoning, he argues that it is strongly suggestive (Fischel, 1992, p.175). The weight of Fischel's evidence has convinced others, such as Wallace Oates, to take the benefits view seriously. In a recent review of the literature on fiscal federalism, Oates concludes that it is, 'impossible to reject ... the benefits view' (Oates, 1994).

On the other side of the debate are Peter Mieszkowski and George Zodrow (1989) and Stephen Ross and John Yinger (forthcoming). Both sets of authors view the assumptions of the Hamilton model, especially the assumption about perfect zoning, as extreme, and not consistent with the evidence. Neither set of authors disputes Fischel's argument that suburban communities engage in zoning for fiscal purposes. However, neither accepts the conclusion that zoning is perfectly constraining. The fact that suburban communities engage in fiscal zoning need not mean that they engage in the perfect zoning required for the Hamilton model. As Ross and Yinger emphasize, zoning for fiscal purposes is also consistent with other models of local sorting among communities. Moreover, despite their multiplicity, the tools of zoning are still too blunt to control housing precisely. And finally, they show that voters would have to be exceptionally foresightful to set zoning barriers at exactly the right level of housing (Ross and Yinger, forthcoming).

Ross and Yinger also highlight the phenomenon of capitalization. In the basic Hamilton model, fiscal packages of taxes and services have no impact on housing values, presumably because all residents pay property taxes that serve as prices for public services. However, Ross and Yinger point out that the conclusion of zero net capitalization is built into the model by an unrealistic assumption. In particular, Hamilton assumes that housing is infinitely available at a given price for any package of services and property taxes. For housing to be infinitely available, either existing jurisdictions would have to have flexible boundaries so that additional housing could be built with no rise in house prices, or developers would have to be able costlessly to form new communities to replicate existing ones. Neither assumption is consistent with the data. Without these assumptions, the process of bidding for housing is likely to lead to the capitalization of packages of public services and taxes into house values. Hence the capitalization that Fischel cites in favour of the efficiency of the Hamilton model in fact provides evidence against the model.[10]

In reality, the answer is somewhere in between. Fischel himself notes that fiscal zoning, even in suburban communities, is not perfect zoning in the Hamiltonian sense (Fischel, 1995, section 7.8). For some purposes the benefit approach is most useful and for others the standard view that the property tax distorts housing and investment decisions is preferred. As with all abstract models, the challenge is to determine when the model sufficiently approximates reality that it becomes useful for making predictions and drawing conclusions.

This pragmatic approach leads to the following conclusions. The benefit view of the property tax is best suited to those suburban areas where zoning is sufficiently powerful to produce taxes that closely replicate user charges. Even in this situation, the model does not perfectly describe reality (Fischel, 1995, section 7.8). For example, no one would disagree that the property tax would distort decisions about minor expansions and repair that are beyond the purview of the zoning authority but not the tax assessor. Nonetheless, the benefit view captures something important about the situation and is useful, especially for inferences about the efficiency with which public services are provided.

However, in many other situations the benefit view clearly does not ring true. Even Fischel would agree that it does not apply to large and heterogeneous cities, to exurban areas and to rural areas. Thus for these areas, which comprise a significant proportion of the US population, the property tax is not appropriately viewed as a benefit tax and therefore distorts land use and investment decisions. These distortions emerge in three main forms. First is the distortion associated with the reduction in the average after tax rate of return to capital throughout the country; second is the distortion that arises from differential property taxation of business and housing; and third is the distortion that arises from interjurisdictional differences in tax rates.[11]

The magnitude of the first distortion is hard to measure given disagreement among economists about the responsiveness of saving and investment to the net rate of return. Given the difficulties of estimating such elasticities, the likelihood of estimating this distortion with any precision is low. Of more relevance for the land use question is the extent to which the property tax on housing distorts housing decisions or simply offsets the generous tax treatment of housing under the federal income tax.[12] Note that even with full capitalization of tax differentials into land values within a metropolitan area, the housing decision can still be distorted.

Within a metropolitan area, various theoretical studies suggest that the distortion associated with using the property tax (rather than a land tax) is low when people are relatively immobile, but much larger when residents are perfectly mobile between metropolitan areas. This finding suggests that the distortion has more to do with the structure, powers and responsibilities of local governments than of the property tax *per se,* a theme to which I shall return.

Is the Property Tax Regressive?
Most studies of the distributional effects of the property tax treat the tax as if it is not a benefits tax. From this perspective, the traditional view of the property tax is that it is regressive, that is, that the burden of the tax as a percentage of income is higher for households with low income than for those with high income. This view is based on the assumption that the property tax on both residential and business structures is fully shifted forward to the consumers of housing and other goods and services. Because spending on housing and on other goods and services represents a higher share of income for low- than for high-income households, the tax burden declines with income.

In contrast, the 'new view' of the incidence of the property tax starts from the idea that because the property tax is essentially a tax on capital, its primary effect is to reduce the net rate of return on capital. Provided that most forms of physical capital are taxed in all jurisdictions, the owners of capital have no easy way to avoid the tax and, consequently, suffer from a reduced rate of return. This view implies that the property tax burden is progressive because income from capital is concentrated among high income households. This conclusion holds despite variations among communities that lead to additional burdens on consumers of housing and other taxed goods in communities with high tax rates and lower burdens on consumers in communities with low tax rates. Differentials in tax rates around the average may offset the overall progressive pattern of the burden somewhat, but only to the extent that low income households disproportionately reside in jurisdictions with above-average tax rates.

Importantly, the traditional view is neither inconsistent with the new view nor wrong. The traditional view remains useful for understanding the distributional impact of an increase in the property tax rate in a single jurisdiction. For a single jurisdiction, the assumption of full forward shifting is relatively plausible, despite the fact that for all jurisdictions taken together the owners of capital cannot avoid the tax. As the property tax is raised in one jurisdiction, the owners of capital – that is, investors in housing and business activity – may respond by investing more heavily in other jurisdictions that have not raised their rates. Consequently, from the perspective of the mayor of an individual city, the property tax is reasonably viewed as regressive. However, from the perspective of national policy-makers, the new view implies that the property tax is more appropriately viewed as proportional or even progressive (see Aaron (1975) and McLure (1977)). As a result, any attempt through federal policy to reduce reliance on the local property tax is likely to benefit high income citizens more than low income citizens.

EFFECTS OF SHIFTING FROM A PROPERTY TAX TO A LAND-VALUE TAX

Because the property tax distorts land use decisions more than does a tax on land, many people have advocated that local communities, especially distressed urban areas that are trying to promote economic development, reduce their reliance on the property tax in favour of heavier reliance on a land-value tax. In fact, however, Pittsburgh is the only major US city to have moved its tax policy in that direction. An empirical analysis of the impacts of that shift are discussed in Chapter 6. Here, the focus is on what theory predicts about the effects on land use of shifting away from taxes on improvements to a tax on land.

Almost all analysts agree that restructuring the property tax towards land will affect land use primarily by reducing the distortionary tax on structures rather than by increasing the tax rate on land value. Because a tax on structures reduces the incentive for landlords to invest in property, a reduction in the tax is predicted to increase investment in structures. In this way, tax restructuring increases the long-run capital intensity of land use in the city. Importantly, however, how much additional investment is induced will depend in part on whether the tax on improvements is reduced in a single city or whether it is reduced in all cities. If the tax on improvements is reduced in only one city, new investment in that city could be extensive as firms choose to invest in that city rather than elsewhere. The predicted effect on investment in any particular city will be much less if other cities also reduce their tax on improvements.

The only theoretical controversy relates to the effects of raising the tax on land. Here, however, the controversy is identical to that discussed earlier about whether the tax on land affects land use decisions. To the extent that land taxes are truly not affected by the planned use of the land, and if there are no other market failures, then increasing the tax on land value should have no land use effects. In the absence of other market failures, only if the tax on land value is applied in such a way that it affects the cost of carrying land, will it speed up development and thereby induce landowners to develop property earlier than they otherwise would.

Less well understood is the effect of the shift in the direction of land-value taxation on the value of land and on the distribution of windfall gains and losses among landowners. Does the value of land rise or fall as a result of the tax restructuring? And which types of landowner are likely to benefit most from the change? To examine these distributional issues, Jan Brueckner (1986) has provided a model of the long-run equilibrium effects of the tax change. Brueckner's contribution is to use modern economic methods to analyse a revenue-preserving shift to a graded tax, that is, one that taxes land more heavily than improvements. In addition to demonstrating the standard result that the reduction of the tax on improvements will increase the intensity of land use,[13] he uses the model to determine the effects of the tax shift on the total value of land. If the tax change applies to a small part of the market (sufficiently small so that the price of improvements, such as housing, is not affected), somewhat surprisingly the tax restructuring raises the value of land. The reduction in land values caused by the capitalization of the higher land tax is more than offset by the positive impact on land value from the increased intensity of land use. However, if the tax applies to a whole metropolitan area, the tax restructuring depresses the price of improvements (housing) and most likely reduces the value of land. According to Brueckner: 'These results suggest that while a small city in a large metropolitan area will generate capital gains for landowners by grading its tax system, metropolitan-area-wide gradation will leave landowners with capital losses while benefitting the ultimate consumers of housing' (1986, p.56).

With respect to the short-run windfall gains and losses, Brueckner challenges conventional wisdom by showing that the owners of the most intensively developed parcels suffer windfall losses in the form of higher taxes, while the least intensively developed parcels benefit from windfall gains.

This result may seem counterintuitive, since the parcels with high improvements gain the most from the lower tax rate on improvements. However, these same properties lose even more from the higher land tax because of their high land value. Applying this basic intuition to mixed land uses suggests that with a shift to a graded tax, many commercial and industrial properties would face higher taxes, while single-family homes would generally benefit from lower tax bills.

In sum, the distributional effects of a shift away from property taxation in favour of land-value taxation are more complex than first appears. Moreover – and this point is the important one – the distributional and land use effects of such a shift depend heavily on whether the tax restructuring is done in a single city or in all cities. The positive effects on economic development touted by proponents of land-value taxation emerge more strongly when the restructuring applies to a small part of the metropolitan area rather than the whole area, and reflect the reduction in the property tax not the increase in the tax on land value.

NOTES

1. The asumption of a fixed number of people rules out the possibility that the tax affects the number of children that people choose to have or the likelihood that people will commit suicide. In an intertemporal model even a head tax might not be neutral, as households change their tax burdens by changing the number of household members.
2. See Oates and Schwab, Chapter 6 in this volume, and Oates and Schwab (1997) for a fuller explanation of this argument.
3. Based on personal communication from Nicolaus Tideman, 23 June 1995.
4. Arnott and Lewis (1979) and Arnott (1996) extend the investigation of neutrality by looking at systems of property taxes. In the earlier paper, they showed that a property tax on land value prior to development causes development to occur earlier and at a lower density, while a tax on total property value after development delays development but does not alter its density. In his 1996 article, Arnott extends the analysis to demonstrate the possibility of constructing a system of property taxes that would be neutral with respect both to the intensity and timing of development of a specific parcel. Under the assumption that redevelopment rent is zero, a neutral property tax system would require a zero tax rate on pre-development land value, a positive tax rate on post-development site value, and a subsidy on the post-development structure value.
5. This discussion draws heavily on Wildasin (1986) and Mieszkowski and Zodrow (1989).
6. Implicit in this logic is the requirement that, given marginal cost pricing, the value of output just equals the value of the inputs, which according to Euler's theorem requires that production be characterized by constant returns to scale. This condition is met, but only at the optimal level of population. The planner's task is to select a population that will minimize the average costs of providing a given level of utility to the population. Given a U-shaped average cost curve, the minimum point will be characterized by constant returns to scale and hence the requirement is met. (I thank Richard Arnott for this point of clarification.) For additional clarification and intuition, see Mieszkowski and Zodrow (1989, p. 1135). Note in addition that the Henry George conclusion about the efficiency of land taxes is a first best result and applies only if there are no other distortions in the economy.

7. See the thoughtful discussion and evidence in Inman (1979). As he notes, empirical studies that are based on a structural model of the demand for service quality and the technology are likely to generate more meaningful estimates of the degree of congestion than are reduced form studies. The problem with the reduced form approach is that the so-called 'congestion parameter' is really the product of a congestion effect and a scale effect.

8. The focus here is on real estate taxes rather than taxes on personal property. Real estate includes land and structures. In the tax applies to both business property and to residential property. Residential property, both single family homes and rental property, accounts for slightly more than one-half of all assessed valuation.

9. Developers are also able to play a significant role in rural areas, where many voters are farmers or otherwise connected with the owners of vacant land and where concern about jobs and economic growth may offset concerns about fiscal subsidies to new residents (Fischel, 1992, p. 174).

10. Hamilton relaxed this assumption about the infinite elasticity of supply in a subsequent paper (Hamilton, 1976) but replaced it with another strong assumption, namely that the benefits from public services can be measured by local public spending. Ross and Yinger point out that this assumption requires unrealistically that both the income and price elasticities of demand for public services are equal to zero.

11. A fourth potential distortion relates to the provision of local public services. In simple models, the use of a tax on mobile capital leads to underprovision of the public good. In more complicated models in which housing and public goods are complementary, the outcome could be either under- or over-provision (see Mieszkowski and Zodrow, 1989, p. 1121).

12. In her 1973 study of the property tax, Ladd concluded that the differential burden on owner-occupied housing associated with the property tax was on average more than offset by the preferential treatment of owner-occupied housing under the federal income tax at that time.

13. In fact, Brueckner shows that this result holds only for the standard situation in which the increase in the tax on land permits a reduction in the tax on improvements. It is not impossible for the perverse result to obtain, namely that the rise in the tax rate on land requires an increase in the tax on improvements in order to maintain revenue.

REFERENCES

Aaron, Henry J. (1975), *Who Pays the Property Tax?: A New View*, Washington, DC: Brookings Institute.

Arnott, Richard (1996), 'Neutral property taxation', processed, Boston College, Department of Economics.

Arnott, R. and F. Lewis (1979), 'The transition of land to urban use', *Journal of Political Economy*, **87**, 161–70.

Bentick, Brian L. (1982), 'A tax on land value may not be neutral', *National Tax Journal*, **35** (1), 113.

Brueckner, Jan K. (1986), 'A modern analysis of the effects of site value taxation', *National Tax Journal*, **39** (1), 49–58.

Feldstein, Martin (1977), 'The surprising incidence of a tax on pure rent: a new answer to an old question', *Journal of Political Economy*, **85** (2), 349–60.

Fischel, William A. (1975), 'An evaluation of proposals for metropolitan sharing of commercial and industrial property tax base'. *Journal of Urban Economics*, **3**, 253–63.

Fischel, William A. (1992), 'Communication: property taxation and the Tiebout model: evidence for the benefit view from zoning and voting', *Journal of Economic Literature*, **30**, 171–7.

Fischel, William A. (1995), *Regulatory Takings: Law, Economics, and Politics*, Cambridge, MA: Harvard University Press.

Hamilton, Bruce (1975), 'Zoning and property taxation in a system of local governments', *Urban Studies*, **12** (2), 105–11.

Hamilton, Bruce (1976a), 'The effects of property taxes and local public spending on property values: a theoretical comment', *Journal of Political Economy*, **84** (3), 647–50.

Hamilton, Bruce (1976b), 'Capitalization of Intrajurisdictional Differences in Local Tax Prices', *American Economic Review*, **22** (December), 743–53.

Hochman, Oded, David Pines and Jacques-François Thisse (1995), 'On the optimal structure of local governments', *American Economic Review*, **85** (5), 1224–40.

Inman, Robert P. (1979), 'The fiscal performance of local governments: an interpretative review', in Peter Mieszkowski and Mahlong Straszheim (eds), *Current Issues in Urban Economics*, Baltimore: Johns Hopkins University Press.

Kim, Duck Ho (1992), ' The nonneutrality of the land value tax: impacts on urban structure', *Journal of Urban Economics*, **32**, 186–94.

Ladd, Helen F. (1973), 'The role of the property tax: a reassessment', in R.A. Musgrave (ed.), *Broad Based Taxes: New Options and Sources*, a supplementary paper of the Committee for Economic Development, Johns Hopkins University Press.

McLure, Charles E. Jr (1977), 'The "new view" of the property tax: a caveat', *National Tax Journal*, **30** (1), 69–75.

Mieszkowski, Peter and Zodrow, George R. (1989), 'Taxation and the Tiebout model: the differential effects of head taxes, taxes on land rents, and property taxes', *Journal of Economic Literature*, **27**, 1098–1146.

Mills, David E. (1981), 'The non-neutrality of land value taxation', *National Tax Journal*, **34** (1), 125–9.

Oates, Wallace (1971), *Fiscal Federalism*, New York: Harcourt, Brace, Jovanich.

Oates, Wallace (1994), 'Federalism and government finance', in John M. Quigley and Eugene Smolensky (eds), *Modern Public Finance*, Cambridge MA: Harvard University Press, pp. 126–51.

Oates, Wallace E. and Robert W. Schwab (1997), 'The impact of urban land taxation: the Pittsburgh experience', *National Tax Journal*, **50** (March), 1–21.

Ross, Stephen and John Yinger (forthcoming), 'Sorting and voting: a review of the literature on urban public finance', *Handbook of Regional and Urban Economics*, North Holland, Vol. 3, Elsevier.

Sinn, Hans-Werner (1985), 'Vacant land and the role of government intervention', *Regional Science and Urban Economics*, **16**, 353–85.

Tiebout, Charles (1956), 'A pure theory of local public expenditures', *Journal of Political Economy*, **64** (1), 416–24.

Vickrey, William S. (1980), 'Defining land value for taxation purposes', in Daniel Holland (ed.), *The Assessment of Land Value*, Madison, Wisconsin: University of Wisconsin, pp. 25–36.

White, Michelle J. (1975), 'Fiscal zoning in fragmented metropolitan areas', in Edwin S. Mills and Wallace E. Oates (eds), *Fiscal Zoning and Land Use Controls: The Economic Issues*, Lexington, MA: Lexington Books, pp. 31–100.

Wildasin, David E. (1986), *Urban Public Finance*, Amsterdam: Harwood Academic Publishers.

COMMENT

William Fischel

Economists have disputed for some years just what kind of tax the property tax is, and have searched for empirical verification of their own characterizations. There is another view of some importance in the real world: how voters see the tax and what this implies for both policy decisions and the way we economists can contribute to those decisions.

I believe that there is substantial evidence, especially in the exceedingly negative voter response to efforts in a number of states to 'recapture' some of the 'excess' school taxes levied in rich districts for use in poorer districts in the same state, that people feel differently about local government than about state government (Campbell and Fischel, 1996). A dollar in taxes paid to the state government is not equal to a dollar paid in taxes to one's local government.

At the local level, the property tax persists – despite caps and rollbacks – because it buys local public goods that enhance the value of property in that jurisdiction. In essence, voters have a proprietary interest in their local governments, in a way that is inapplicable to the state and federal governments.

In this commentary, I deal with these two points: first, that the local property tax really is a benefit tax; and second, that the tax is an appropriate one for municipal corporations seeking to maximize the value of the individual resident's property.

In Defence of the Benefit Tax Formulation

Ladd's chapter reviews much of the argument in the literature about whether the property tax is a distorting, but possibly progressive, tax – the Mieszkowski model – or a benefit tax – the Tiebout–Hamilton model. In recent work, I have defended the empirical realism of the Tiebout–Hamilton model, focusing on zoning (Fischel, 1992; 1995, Chapter 7). While zoning cannot actually dictate the minimum property values that the Tiebout–Hamilton model calls for, it is elastic and pervasive enough to accomplish the same thing by means of regulation of the physical attributes and the use of real property.

The criticisms of the Tiebout–Hamilton model fall into two general categories. One is the perfectionist criticism, which holds that the model's assumptions about zoning are unrealistic. The other is the empirical evidence suggesting that the Tiebout–Hamilton model is a special, rather than a general, theory of local government.

The perfectionist criticism points out that the Tiebout–Hamilton model requires 'perfect' zoning (Mieszkowski and Zodrow, 1989, p. 1108). The local government has to be able to discriminate perfectly among potential land users and enact binding zoning laws that will ensure that the $152 901 house will be occupied by no more than 0.72 children who will attend the public school and will generate 9.2 automobile trips per day. Otherwise, the property taxes generated by the house will not in fact cover the public costs of the house, and the tax will entail some deadweight losses. A related criticism is that the Tiebout–Hamilton model causes deadweight loss in the housing market by tying residence with local public services, especially schools (Ross and Yinger, forthcoming). The distortions arise because households have to find a community that matches both their housing demand and their school demand.

One response to the requirement of 'perfect' zoning is that none of the economic institutions that we normally invoke as embodying our theories operates in the perfect ways that those theories require. Moreover, like most of those institutions, zoning and related land use controls get an amazing amount of attention from market participants. Yet many economists claim that zoning is either a veil easily pierced by developers or a shadow that follows what the market would generate anyway. Public choice theory surely would suggest that apparently rational people, acting in their economic capacities, do not devote enormous amounts of time to processes that are irrelevant to economic outcomes.

To insist that zoning is a serious and rational (to the local voters) constraint on land use that cuts down on the deadweight loss of the property tax is not to deny that zoning often moves in the same direction as the otherwise unconstrained land and housing market (McDonald and McMillen, 1991; Wheaton, 1993). Most successful legal institutions attempt to get more people to do what most people would want to do without the legal constraints.

The quibble about imperfect zoning is echoed in the charge that the Tiebout–Hamilton model distorts the housing market because of a lack of enough communities to satisfy all demands for housing and public services. In concept, an unlimited supply of potential jurisdictions might be better, but a more elastic supply of communities is typically not the alternative policy being recommended by the critics. Their ideal policy is one in which a central authority sums the public's marginal rates of substitution and efficiently imposes taxes for the public good. This is perfectionism writ large. It is an unrealistic and unreasonable view of what large governmental entities can do, as well as being at odds with decades of public choice theory.

The criticism of the Tiebout–Hamilton model that is more persuasive comes from empirical work which suggests that the Tiebout model does not apply well to large cities. A fine study by Robert Wassmer (1993), using a sample of large central cities, concludes that the Tiebout model does not apply there, at least as far as the property tax is concerned. Hamilton from the outset conceded that his theory did not fit central cities (Hamilton, 1975). Although the majority of American urban populations now live in the suburbs, the number who still live in central cities is sizeable, and their problems are, too.

One response to this criticism is simple bifurcation. The Tiebout–Hamilton model works pretty well in the suburbs and in the small towns and cities, while the Mieszkowski view prevails downtown and in Hawaii, which has no local government to speak of. (The same bifurcation seems to apply to the median voter model, which is a necessary political supplement to the Tiebout–Hamilton model: it works in the suburbs and small towns, not in the big cities and the state legislature (Romer *et al*, 1992).) However, economists abhor such arbitrary distinctions. In this commentary, I propose a more general version of the Tiebout–Hamilton model.

Capitalization and the Nature of Local Government

The empirical evidence that is invariably invoked in favour of the Tiebout–Hamilton model is that fiscal differences are capitalized in home values. This shows that potential residents are at least aware of differences among communities, although there remains much debate about how much more is shown.

It is essential that there is some method by which interlopers are excluded from local government jurisdictions in order for differences in local government services to be capitalized. If there were no such method, developers would look around for communities with low tax rates and good schools, and they would build houses there to take advantage of the differential. A nice, double-wide house-trailer would accommodate families with a taste for good schools but less-than-average means to pay for them. Obviously, that would be costly to existing residents, whose taxes would have to go up or whose school spending would have to go down, with the result that their houses would not command any premium over those of any other community. Since we regularly do see such a premium, it follows that there must be some way to preserve the benefits of local government policies. Robert Nelson and I have argued at some length that zoning is the means by which such public property rights are established (Nelson, 1977; Fischel, 1985).

Capitalization is the linchpin of local government, not merely something that falls out of tests of the Tiebout model. Maximizing the present value of owner-occupied housing ought to be modelled as the objective of most local governments. Characterizing capitalization as something other than an objective causes researchers to miss the essentially economic nature of the local government process. By missing the essential objective, we economists have tried to fit local governments into Procrustean beds that make them look like little national or state governments.

A better way to characterize local governments is by their 19th–century legal designation, 'municipal corporations'. Modern economic analysis would profit by adopting this generic view of local government and applying the modern literature on corporate control.[1]

Why Does the Municipal Corporation Use Property Taxes?

A model of modern municipal corporations should include the following elements:

1. It must allow that all residents can vote and that non-residents cannot. The voting franchise cannot be limited to residents who are homeowners or property owners. Newcomer-residents and renters cannot be disenfranchised, and owners with especially valuable property cannot be granted more than one vote. In these respects, municipal corporations have no parallel with private corporations, which typically arrange voting by share ownership.
2. It must build on the empirical reality that homeowners are the most numerous voters in most American jurisdictions. This is usually true even when renters form a slim majority of the population, since homeowners are, according to the political science literature, more likely to vote and otherwise participate in public life.
3. A theory of municipal corporations must accept that state governments and constitutions set the boundaries of municipal corporate power. This allows that there is at least one non-market means to constrain municipal corporations. Such constraints may, however, be endogenous to the model.
4. It should explain why local governments rely as much as they do on the property tax, and why this reliance has declined in recent years.

This last criterion is a special challenge, both because the property tax is the subject of this volume and because it has been addressed by one of urban economics' most creative theorists, Vernon Henderson. Henderson (1995) constructs a formal model that incorporates the salient features of local government in the United States, and he then asks whether rational homeowners in that model would choose the property tax. One of Henderson's major accomplishments is to incorporate in it homeowner-voters who simultaneously see their houses as a major financial asset and as the repository of two major consumption goods: housing services and local public goods.

Henderson's primary and most consistent finding is that in none of his models does a rational homeowner-voter ever prefer the property tax (that is, the tax on the value of land and housing) to some feasible alternative, such as user fees, head taxes or land taxes. The homeowner-voters are interested in efficiency, and the property tax always has some deadweight loss. While Henderson recognizes that the property tax and zoning can reduce deadweight loss by preventing congestion of local quasi-public services, the property tax is never the best method of achieving this.

Henderson uses his findings to explain why the property tax declined between 1950 and 1988. (Henderson's figures understate the continued reliance on property taxes in the suburbs, where homeownership is most dominant but nonetheless reliance on it has diminished.) This decline can be partly accounted for by some other factors, notably the more-or-less exogenous school-finance decisions by many state courts, but Henderson has a point (Bahl *et al.*, 1990). However, as Thomas Nechyba remarked at the 1995 public choice meetings, it seems ironic that voters who are so interested in maximizing property values should subject it to so much taxation. Maybe the voters have figured this out.

One way to probe Henderson's theory is to analyse a real example of where it works almost perfectly. Private community associations, such as those which govern condominiums, are the closest private analogue to local governments (Ellickson, 1982). They need to raise revenues for various collective goods (typically common-property maintenance), and they do not use an *ad valorem* property tax. Community association dues are usually fixed per unit, regardless of their value. Sometimes a differential is established among types of unit, but the differential is seldom increased in proportion to changes in market value over time. The feature that gives rise to deadweight loss in property taxes – the knowledge that value increments affect one's tax liability – is absent in most private community associations.

The *ad valorem* Property Tax Helps Deter Expropriation

Henderson's theory may explain the absence of property taxes in private governments. The question here is why the property tax remains an important source of local government revenue.

My explanation: because asset-owners governed by municipal corporations cannot forswear one-person, one-vote rules, they will try to adopt (typically in state constitutions) rules to reduce opportunistic transfers from one set of owners to others. *Ad valorem* property taxes are one means of constraining opportunistic transfers while still maintaining a tax base that is roughly proportional to the benefits received. The inefficiencies inherent in the *ad valorem* property tax are accepted because the property tax offers fewer incentives for collective expropriation of their property by other voters. As an example of the property tax's protective incentives, consider a proposal to site a profitable toxic waste dump in a community. The dump's profit will be shared with the community by means of land use exactions, money paid by the developer in exchange for a re-zoning that permits the dump. The dump, however, will devalue nearby homes. If the devaluation of the homes is taken into account, the dump should not be built, even though a majority of the community would benefit.

The *ad valorem* property tax provides an automatic signal to all voters that the dump may not be the best use of the land. The reduction in the value of the homes will shift more of the burden of the property tax to other residents of the community. Because they anticipate this, the majority will be more cautious about allowing land uses that reduce the aggregate value of property in the community. Such a signal would not be present (except under the artificial conditions of the Coase theorem) if taxes were assessed on the otherwise more efficient basis of heads or land area.

An example of this principle at work is rent control. The puzzle about rent control is why it is not more common, given that tenants outnumber land-lords. One reason it is rare is because of the property tax. In places where homeowners are dominant, rent control is resisted because it devalues the tax base, shifting more of the burden of paying taxes from apartment-owners to homeowners.[2]

Evidence for this comes from the rapid rise of rent control in California following Proposition 13 in 1978. Proposition 13 was said to have encour-aged rent control because landlords did not reduce rents in response to the deep property-tax cuts. But this assumes that such moralisms were a con-straint on tenants' political behaviour prior to Proposition 13. A more rational explanation is that Proposition 13 insulated homeowners from the direct costs of rent control by freezing their assessments well below market levels and capping the tax rate at 1 per cent of that value. The tax bills of individual homeowners were now divorced from the taxes paid by apartment house-owners. Homeowners thus had less interest in forestalling rent control and tenant activists became more persuasive in local politics. There remained an opportunity cost to rent controls, in so far as devalued apartment buildings paid less to the public treasury, but this loss was tempered by the fact that school expenditures were essentially assumed by the state, as induced by *Serrano v. Priest*, and by the fact that Proposition 13's maximum allowable rate was low. The rise in rent controls in California after 1978 is consistent with the view that the property tax in other places ordinarily constrains opportunistic transfers within communities.

Conclusion: Not Quite Georgism

I have suggested an approach to a more general economic theory of local government. A model with some of the elements outlined here is needed to understand location-based economic activity. My major point for economists' evaluation of the property tax is that they should look up from the tax itself and examine more closely its institutional matrix. The unlovely property tax is a product of political choice, and the reasons people have for making that choice should inform our understandings of the tax. My arguments in favour of viewing local governments as constrained property-value maximizers warrant re-examination of a point in Ladd's chapter. The modern Henry George theorem shows that land-value taxation can be the most efficient form of financing local public services. My approach suggests, however, that we might more profitably re-examine the ideas of the original Henry George. George advocated public ownership of land, and the single tax was a means of accomplishing this without the administrative evils of outright public ownership. Nicolaus Tideman, George's most sophisticated contemporary advocate among economists, has shown that a version of George's plan provides the correct incentives for local governments to zone their land (Tideman, 1990). The reason is that the governments perceive both the costs and benefits of development if they reap through land taxes the incremental values from re-zoning.

Most local government officials actually try to behave in the way Tideman says they would under a Georgist regime. They seek to maximize the value of property owned by their residents.[3] On my analysis, Henry George may have come in the back door. Single-taxers have overlooked this possibility for the same reason that most economists have. Single-taxers, too, see the economic issue as one of taxes rather than one of organization of economic activity at contiguous locations.

My invocation of Georgism in support of the corporate analytical approach should not mislead the reader into believing that I think that confiscatory local land taxes are a good idea. Indeed I have argued at length that constitutional protections of property ought to be specially invoked against majoritarian rent-seeking at the local level (Fischel, 1995). However, I also have argued (in the same book) that such protections should be applied gingerly in order to provide an incentive for local governments to capitalize on value-enhancing public services. As Robert Ellickson has demonstrated in a wide-ranging article, a mixture of public and private control over land is observed in almost all successful (that is, durable) societies (Ellickson, 1993). The necessary mixture of private and public entitlements will always create a tension between such interests. Trying to resolve those tensions by moving to a libertarian position of wholly private ownership or a collectivist position of wholly public ownership will not succeed.

Notes

1. For a discussion of parallels between municipal and private corporations by a law professor steeped in the modern literature on public finance, see Vicki Been (1991).
2. Anthony Downs (1983, p. 141). Owner-occupied housing units comprise more than 50 per cent of all housing units in the overwhelming majority of municipal corporations that levy property taxes. A prominent exception is New York City. More than 70 per cent of its households are renters, and this super-majority may account for its long-standing rent controls. Other well-known exceptions are many college and university towns, some of which have had rent controls for more than 25 years.
3. Both Tideman and I stretch history somewhat, because George advocated the single tax for all governments, not just local units. However, in the United States of the late 19th century, local governments were the only ones that spent serious money, and therefore had to collect substantial revenue, and their tax was the property tax.

References

Bahl, Roy, David Sjoquist and W. Loren Williams (1990), 'School finance reform and impact on property taxes', *Proceedings of the Eighty-Third Annual Conference on Taxation*, Columbus, Ohio: National Tax Association–Tax Institute of America.

Been, Vicki (1991), '"Exit" as a constraint on land use exactions: rethinking the unconstitutional conditions doctrine', *Columbia Law Review*, **91** (April), 473–545.

Campbell, Colin D. and William A. Fischel (1996), 'Preferences for school finance systems: voters versus judges', *National Tax Journal*, **49** (March), 1–15.

Downs, Anthony (1983), *Rental Housing in the 1980s*, Washington: Brookings Institute.

Ellickson, Robert C. (1982), 'Cities and homeowners' associations', *University of Pennsylvania Law Review*, **130** (June), 1519–80.

Ellickson, Robert C. (1991), *Order without Law*, Cambridge, MA: Harvard University Press.

Ellickson, Robert C. (1993), 'Property in Land', *Yale Law Journal*, **102** (April), 1315–1400.

Fischel, William A. (1985), *The Economics of Zoning Laws: A Property Rights Approach to American Land Use Controls*, Baltimore, MD: Johns Hopkins University Press.

Fischel, William A. (1992), 'Property taxation and the Tiebout model: evidence for the benefit view from zoning and voting', *Journal of Economic Literature*, **30** (March), 171–7.

Fischel, William A. (1995), *Regulatory Takings: Law, Economics, and Politics*, Cambridge, MA: Harvard University Press.

Hamilton, Bruce W. (1975), 'Property taxes and the Tiebout hypothesis: some empirical evidence', in Edwin S. Mills and Wallace E. Oates (eds), *Fiscal Zoning and Land Use Controls,* Lexington, MA: Heath-Lexington Books.

Henderson, J. Vernon (1995), 'Will homeowners impose property taxes?', *Regional Science and Urban Economics*, **25** (April), 153–82.

McMillen, Daniel P. and John F. McDonald (1991), 'A Markov chain model of zoning change', *Journal of Urban Economics*, **30** (September), 257–70.

Mieszkowski, Peter and George R. Zodrow (1989), 'Taxation and the Tiebout model: the differential effects of head taxes, taxes on land rents, and property taxes', *Journal of Economic Literature*, **27** (September), 1098–1146.

Nelson, Robert H. (1977), *Zoning and Property Rights*, Cambridge, MA: MIT Press.

Romer, Thomas, Howard Rosenthal and Vincent G. Munley (1992), 'Economic incentives and political institutions: spending and voting in school budget referenda', *Journal of Public Economics*, **49** (October), 1–33.

Ross, Stephen, and John Yinger (forthcoming), 'Sorting and voting: a review of the literature on urban public finance', in Paul Cheshire and Edwin Mills (eds), *Handbook of Regional and Urban Economics*, Vol. 3, North-Holland: Elsevier.

Tideman, T. Nicolaus (1990), 'Integrating land-value taxation with the internalization of spatial externalities', *Land Economics*, **66** (August), 341–55.

Wassmer, Robert W. (1993), 'Property taxation, property base, and property value: an empirical test of the "New View"', *National Tax Journal*, **46** (June), 135–60.

Wheaton, William C. (1993), 'Land capitalization, Tiebout mobility, and the role of zoning regulations', *Journal of Urban Economics*, **34** (September), 102–17.

COMMENT

Peter Mieszkowski

Ladd begins her treatment of the theoretical controversies by examining Henry George's claims that land-value taxation is neutral. She concludes that taxes on land rents do not distort resource use, but that taxes on land values could generate some distortions in the timing of investment. She goes on to consider the George–Hotelling–Vickrey theorem that land taxes should be used to finance the fixed cost of decreasing cost industries or, more specifically, local communities should use confiscatory land taxes to finance non-rival public goods when they can control its population size so as to maximize per capita utility. The discussion following Wildasin (1989) and others indicates that this result holds only for non-congested public goods and in general a combination of head and land taxes should be used. This conclusion I classify as soft Georgist doctrine, namely that under certain conditions a single tax will do, though it is confiscatory.

Is a Land Value Tax more Efficient than a Property Tax?

Notwithstanding the claims of William Fischel that zoning is sufficiently precise to make the local property tax, effectively, a benefit tax (Fischel, 1992), Ladd treats the property tax as a distortionary levy. However, her principal conclusion is that a property tax, inclusive of improvements, is more distortionary than a land-value tax. But this conclusion seems to apply to a single jurisdiction. Ladd continues that, if a single jurisdiction shifts to a land-value tax, the additional investment may be substantial. But if all cities switch over to land-value taxation, changes in investment may be small; thus, 'the distortions from having all US local governments use a property tax rather than a land-value tax may be overstated'. This last conclusion may understate the case for moderate Georgist doctrine, which is the claim that land-value taxation dominates the property tax on efficiency grounds. This claim does not depend on the induced level of investment at the level of a jurisdiction or the nation as a whole. Wildasin, following up on the work of Zodrow and Mieszkowski, argues that the underprovision of local public goods, induced by fiscal competition or the concern that the taxation of mobile capital will decrease local output, is quite large quantitatively (Zodrow and Mieszolski, 1986; Wildasin, 1989). This conclusion is for a world where land (or labour) is in fixed supply in each jurisdiction, so that a land tax is neutral, and under the assumption that land is used only for the production of export goods. For this somewhat restrictive case, the moderate Georgist doctrine is already established.

However, it would be much more compelling to establish the case for land-value taxation when the demand and supply of land is not fixed. While the supply of raw land at the national level is fixed in supply, a very large portion of this land has little, if any, economic value. In contrast, the amount of *urban* land or the amount of economically viable land is not fixed. It is endogenous and depends on commuting costs and the demand for residential land. In the standard urban model, residents who commute to a central work place trade off commuting costs for space or residential housing services. Housing is produced with land and capital and, if land is taxed, it will become more expensive as the supply of residential land from agriculture is perfectly elastic. Housing production will be distorted by a land tax. Of course, even if the supply of capital is fixed at the national level, the taxation of capital used in export goods production and in housing will distort the demand for public goods and will induce local public officials to produce too few public goods.

If the public good is congestible, the neutral tax will be a head tax on labour, and the open question is whether the provision of public goods is distorted more by the property tax than by land-value taxes. If it can be shown that land should be taxed at a higher rate than capital, the case for Georgist doctrine will be established, even when the amount of urban residential land is endogenous. It probably is possible to establish that land should be taxed at a higher rate than capital. The proposition that land-value taxes should be the exclusive source of revenue is more questionable. The advantage of taxes on land is that the surplus on close-in land will be taxed, but as land values are small relative to the value of structures, the relatively high tax rate on land will distort land use.

Equity Considerations

If land-value taxation is substituted for property taxation, owners of centrally located property would lose while suburban landowners would gain. This substitution raises conventional equity considerations about the capital gains and losses associated with changes in tax regime. Differential impacts on property owners at different locations will be especially large for this tax 'reform'. To tax homeowners on the basis of whether they chose to live close to the centre and avoid commuting, or live further out on cheap land, seems arbitrary and inconsistent with benefit taxation. Equals are not treated equally.

Ladd, like many other writers, concentrates on issues of economic efficiency. It is of interest to re-read Henry George's *Progress and Poverty* and to rediscover the strong Ricardian flavour of his analysis. George's concern was with long-run trends in the distribution of income between land rents and wages and returns to capital. His key argument was that the fruits of economic progress, the returns to every improvement or invention, accrued to landlords. Every labour-saving invention has a tendency to increase rent: 'Wealth in all its forms being the product of labor applied to land or the products of land, any increase in the power of labor, the demand for wealth being unsatisfied, will be utilized in procuring more wealth, and thus increase the demand for land' (George, 1958, p. 249).

According to George, labour-augmenting technical change increases the size of the effective labour force. The productivity of individual workers will result in technological unemployment in the short run, increase competition between workers and extend the margin of cultivation, thus increasing land rents, absolutely and relatively, while the returns to labour and capital remain unchanged. During the second part of the 19th century, real wages appeared to fluctuate, though imperfect price deflators may mask wage increases. We now know that George's pessimistic conclusions about labour and capital not sharing in the fruits of technological progress depend on the assumption of quite low elasticities of substitution between labour and land. When this substitution parameter is relatively high, as for a Cobb–Douglas technology, labour will share in the technologically induced increase in output in proportion to its share in national output.

George, writing when he did, could not anticipate the decline of the relative importance of land in modern industrial societies, that new transportation technology and investment in railroads would increase the effective supply of agricultural land by decreasing shipping costs to major export nodes such as Chicago and St Louis. William Cronon's recent masterful history of Chicago describes the opening up of Midwest agriculture and the development of Chicago around the processing and shipment of wheat, meat and lumber (Cronon, 1991). His book describes in illuminating detail the economies of scale in processing and transportation and financial services. Most of these production processes are urban activities, requiring small inputs of land.

In a metropolitan setting, transportation innovations – streetcars, rail and finally the automobile and truck – increased effective commuting distance and allowed cities to grow at constant or declining real land values. *The supply of urban land is not fixed.* It represents less than 2 per cent of the total land area of the United States.

An understanding of the economic basis of Georgist doctrine should emphasize his dynamic theory of income distribution, as discussed above. After putting forth his proposal for a single tax, George examines the consequences of his policy in book 9 of *Progress and Poverty*. Chapter 1 is devoted to efficiency considerations. Here George discusses 'the elimination of other taxes that hamper every wheel of exchange and press up every form of industry' (p. 434). Savings and investment will be encouraged by the elimination of taxes other than the land tax. Also, the tax on land will increase the supply of land; the price of land will fall and land will not be held unless it is used – land speculation will decrease: 'Labor and capital would not merely gain what is now taken from them in taxation, but would gain by the positive decline in rent caused by the decrease in speculative land values. A new equilibrium would be established, at which the common rate of wages and interest would be much higher than now' (p. 442). Chapter 2 in book 9 makes it clear that George's primary policy objective is to equalize the distribution of income and to transfer land rents, which are growing as a share of national income, to the state so as to benefit the whole community. The cutting edge of George's paradigm is the predicted growing inequality in the distribution of income and growing land rents. If the theory underlying the proposition that land is the primary beneficiary of technical progress and economies of scale is faulty, the case for land-value tax, based on distributive considerations, the strong form of Georgist doctrine, is vitiated.

George's argument that labour and capital do not share in the fruits of technological improvements is inconsistent with facts that he did not have. But the historical statistics of the United States provide some basis for George's pessimism regarding the growth of real wages as the disruptions of the Civil War, and related inflation, decreased real wages by 20 per cent between 1860 and 1870 (US Bureau of the Census, 1975, Tables D.735–8). Real wages did not return to their pre-Civil War period until the early 1880s, a time just after the publication of *Progress and Poverty*. Real wages then increased by about 25 per cent to 1900, despite the very heavy inflow of immigrants between 1875 and 1900.

Modern Georgists, such as Mason Gaffney and Fred Harrison (1994), defend George against various neoclassical critics such as J. B. Clark and R. T. Ely. However, Henry George's grand dynamics are not discussed by these writers, and his dire predictions regarding the stagnation of real wages and growth of land rents are not mentioned, despite the slow growth of real compensation in the United States since 1973. The only reference to Robert Solow in the Gaffney–Harrison book, is to his pro-Georgist letter to Mikhail Gorbachev.

If George were alive today, he might be inclined also to tax the rents earned by Bill Gates, Steven Spielberg and Oprah Winfrey, instead of singling out the hard-working owners of the Irvine and King Ranches.

References

Bruecker, Jan (1986), 'A modern analysis of the effects of site value taxation', *National Tax Journal*, **39**, 49–57.

Cronon, William (1991), *Nature's Metropolis: Chicago and the Great West*, New York: W.W. Norton.

Fischel, William (1992), 'Communication', *Journal of Economic Literature*, **30**, 171–7.

Gaffney, Mason and Fred Harrison (1994), *The Corruption of Economics*, London: Shepheard-Walwyn.

George, Henry (1958), *Progress and Poverty*, New York: Robert Schbalkenbach Foundation.

US Bureau of the Census (1975), *Historical Statistics of the United States, Colonial Times to 1970: Part I*, Washington, DC: Government Printing Office.

Wildasin, David E. (1986), *Urban Public Finance*, Amsterdam: Harwood Academic Publishers.

Wildasin, David E. (1989), 'Interjurisdictional capital mobility: fiscal externalities and a corrective subsidy', *Journal of Urban Economics,* **25**, 192–212.

Zodrow, George R. and Peter Mieszkowski (1986), 'Pigou, Tiebout, property taxation, and the underprovision of local public goods', *Journal of Urban Economics*, **19**, 356–70.

3. Land use regulation as a fiscal tool

Helen F. Ladd

Local land use regulations were historically rationalized in terms of externalities. By separating different types of land use, a community could avoid undesirable spillover effects (in the form of factory smoke, for example) of one type of land use on another. However, land use regulations are also used – and perhaps increasingly so – for fiscal purposes, that is, to minimize the impacts of new development on the community's tax rate. Such use is particularly common in suburban communities in metropolitan areas.[1] By zoning out the types of development that would require more in public spending than they would generate in revenue and encouraging development that yields a fiscal 'profit', established residents try to keep their own tax burdens down.

The incentive for fiscal zoning emerges most clearly with the use of property taxes in a spatially fragmented governmental system. Local governments rely heavily on local property taxes to finance public services that are made available on an equal basis to all local residents and, for some services, to all business firms. The primary local service, education, provides direct benefits to households with children and no direct benefits to firms. According to the conventional wisdom, many types of business property generate a fiscal surplus because their property is sufficiently valuable that the property taxes they pay exceed the costs of the services they use. Among residents, households in high valued housing with few children tend to produce a surplus, while those in less expensive housing with many children produce a net fiscal deficit. To maximize their own welfare, established residents try to attract certain types of business firm and to zone out residential uses that produce a deficit. They typically achieve the latter goal by imposing minimum lot sizes or by excluding multi-family housing.

While planners tend to distinguish between land use regulations that limit specific types of land use, such as multi-family housing, and those that limit the overall growth of the community, economists tend to view the latter regulations simply as more stringent forms of traditional land use control. Like zoning, strategies to limit growth are based on the police power of the community and are typically justified as promoting the health, safety and general welfare of local residents by controlling the timing and sequencing of growth (see Fischel, 1985; Mills, 1990). Consequently, the discussion in this chapter applies both to traditional land use zoning and to the growth controls that emerged in many parts of the country during the 1970s and 1980s.

Another way in which land policy may be used to achieve fiscal ends relates to the density of development. Urban planners tend to take as a premise the view that urban sprawl increases the average costs of providing public facilities and services. Given this premise, planners often try to promote compact, high density development as a way of keeping down costs and taxes.

This chapter reviews various aspects of the use of land policy as a fiscal tool. The first three sections focus on fiscally motivated zoning and land use controls. Section 1 reviews the literature that evaluates such controls. Section 2 looks critically at fiscal impact analysis, the main analytical tool used to guide their use. Section 3 summarizes a recent regression-based national study of the effects of population growth on spending and taxes. Section 4 focuses on the relationship between density of development and public sector costs, and section 5 concludes with a summary of areas in which more research would be desirable.

EVALUATION OF FISCALLY MOTIVATED ZONING AND GROWTH CONTROLS

Because of the multiple motives for zoning, isolating the precise contribution of the fiscal motive is impossible. Nonetheless, the extensive use by planners of *fiscal impact analysis* – a tool to determine the additional spending requirements and additional revenues associated with development – testifies to the importance of this motive. Other evidence consistent with extensive use of fiscally motivated residential zoning includes the observation that many communities impose increasingly stringent land use controls as they develop, that many communities are quite homogeneous with respect to the income of residents, and that growth controls are disproportionately represented in high income communities (Mills, 1990, pp. 35–6; Fischel, 1992).

Economists have often pointed out that the scramble for fiscally productive tax bases can lead to undesirable and bizarre patterns of land use. Many communities try to attract industry and shopping centres but try to avoid housing their employees, especially those with low incomes and large families. As a result, we find both an absence of affordable housing for low wage employees adjacent to work places and peculiar patterns of development near community borders. As noted by one prominent economist in 1962: 'One consequence, not surprisingly, is that community A's industrial district ... is adjacent to community B's high school, hospital or quarter-acre residential area, with bizarre aesthetic and circulation effects' (Netzer, quoted in Cason, 1981, p. 340).

Despite these unaesthetic and distorted patterns of land use, some authors use a model based on the economic theory of clubs to justify fiscally motivated land use policy. Other authors use the rational choice theory of fiscally motivated zoning to show that, while land use controls may or may not be inefficient, they are clearly inequitable. Studies that make normative arguments about land use controls are the subject of the following subsections.

Models Based on the Theory of Clubs

Several authors (see references in Chapman, 1988) use the theory of clubs to argue that fiscally motivated government interventions into the land market are desirable. In standard club models, as developed initially by Buchanan (1965), the challenge is to determine both the size of the club (for example, the membership of the private swimming club) and the level of service to be provided (for example, the size of the pool). For any given size of pool, more members mean lower costs per member but, because of crowding, the pool yields lower benefits per member. For any membership level, a bigger pool means higher costs, but also greater benefits. The optimal combination occurs when the optimal size for the given membership level is consistent with the optimal membership level for the given size.

Chapman (1988) uses the club model most explicitly to justify fiscally motivated zoning. Chapman views each community as a club composed of homogeneous residents who decide both on the optimal level of public services and the level of development. In the absence of active government intervention into the land market, local governments are unlikely to reach the equilibrium between development and service levels that would emerge from unconstrained club behaviour; institutional constraints on their authority to raise revenue and the requirement that local government budgets be balanced produce a balanced-budget equilibrium (a combination of development and public services) that is likely to differ from the club equilibrium. Chapman concludes from this analysis that local government officials ought to intervene in the land market, with decisions guided by the fiscal impacts of new development.

However, Chapman's model is too narrowly fiscal (see Windsor, 1990). The demand for development presumably is not based on fiscal considerations alone. It also depends on more general quality-of-life considerations. Consequently, the appropriate analytical tool for land use interventions should be more encompassing than the narrow tool of fiscal impact analysis (see the section on fiscal impact analysis for a further discussion of this point). Moreover, the club model is a partial equilibrium model that ignores the consequences of being excluded from the club. While these consequences may not be a problem in the context of the private swimming pool example, they loom much larger in the context of local communities.

In sum, the club model apparatus has only limited usefulness for evaluating fiscally motivated zoning. At best it provides a positive model of how local communities behave. It is less useful for drawing normative conclusions about efficient and equitable outcomes.

Rational Choice Model of Fiscal Zoning

An alternative approach, the rational choice model of fiscal zoning (see Mills, 1990 for a summary discussion and Fischel, 1985, 1995), assumes that the zoning decision reflects the interests of local voters. In particular, voters will support zoning limitations that maximize the value of existing residential real estate. Empirical studies of the effects of zoning on the prices of existing housing generally support this theory by confirming that zoning increases the prices of existing houses.[2]

However, not everyone will benefit from the controls. In particular, owners of undeveloped land may be harmed by zoning restrictions that limit development. Hence the overall efficiency or welfare implications of zoning are unclear. As discussed in the next subsection, the efficiency issues may be elucidated by empirical studies of zoning. Equity considerations must be addressed separately.

Measuring the welfare effects of zoning.

The extensive theoretical literature on the welfare effects of zoning is inconclusive. One problem is that most of the theoretical models are incomplete in that they fail to incorporate all the effects of zoning (see Pogodzinski and Sass, 1990). Hence the predicted welfare effects vary with the initial assumptions of the model.

The best way to determine empirically whether zoning enhances welfare is to examine its effect on aggregate land values (Fischel, 1985, 1995; Brueckner, 1990). The change in land values reflects both the benefits to existing residents and the potential costs to the owners of undeveloped land. Using the Hicks–Kaldor test of potential compensation, an increase in aggregate land values indicates that the benefits to existing owners of developed land are sufficiently large to allow them, in principle, to compensate the owners of vacant land.

Unfortunately, most of the empirical studies of zoning are partial in that they focus on the prices of existing homes rather than on all potential development. Only one study, George Peterson's unpublished 1974 study of zoning in Boston suburbs, exemplifies the appropriate approach of balancing the benefits to some against the losses to others. Peterson found that the losses to landowners whose development options were reduced by the controls exceeded the increased amenity values and fiscal gains to others and, consequently, that the suburban land use controls in the Boston area were inefficiently restrictive (cited in Fischel, 1985, p. 233).

Equity considerations

While fiscally motivated zoning of residential property may be in the economic interests of established residents, and may or may not be in the interests of the local community, it is clearly subject to criticism on equity grounds. Mills (1979), Mills (1990) and White (1978) make this argument most forcefully. Because the generators of fiscal deficits are likely to be poor households, many suburban areas pursue zoning policies that specify minimum lot sizes and restrictions on multi-family housing which work to exclude poor households. As a result, such households are unfairly denied access to the high quality services provided by wealthy suburban jurisdictions, the most important of which is education (Mills, 1990, p. 29).[3]

In addition, Mills questions whether local governments have the *right* to use their zoning authority to benefit high income residents at the expense of low and moderate income citizens. However, as was pointed out in Chapter 1, only one supreme court – New Jersey in the Mt Laurel cases – has ruled that the state government must use or 'delegate its police powers so as to serve the interests of all citizens and not permit them to be used against the interests of constitutionally sensitive minorities' (Mills, 1990, p. 29).

No- or slow-growth zoning differs from exclusionary zoning in that it does not distinguish among types of household; it simply excludes or limits the growth of all types of housing. Although motivated in part by concerns for the environment, this type of zoning may also be driven largely by fiscal considerations (see White (1978) for a strong endorsement of this position). Rapid growth may impose fiscal burdens on established residents by requiring additional infrastructure that must be financed at high interest rates and by increasing the demands on the public sector. White argues that: 'The no-growth movement should be seen for what it is – a new and modernized form of exclusionary zoning that plays on the environmental consciousness of the 1970s'.

Mills (1979, 1990) lays the blame for exclusionary zoning squarely on the property tax.[4] Because a resident's property tax contribution is determined by the value of the family's housing, suburban jurisdictions have incentives to zone out low valued housing. Starting from the premise that most local zoning is exclusionary and that income redistribution cannot be accomplished at the local level, Mills (1979) goes so far as to propose that local property taxes be replaced with local head taxes, that local land use controls be completely eliminated, and that communities be encouraged to buy land for open space at the fair market price if they wish to preserve the environment. In fact, the empirical findings of Ladd (see below) that population growth increases per capita spending and tax burdens suggest that a shift to head taxes would not completely eliminate the fiscal incentive to keep new residents out. Moreover, England's recent experience with the poll tax testifies to the political unpopularity of head taxes. Nonetheless, Mill's analysis usefully highlights the close interaction between locally raised taxes and zoning.[5]

FISCAL IMPACT ANALYSIS

To use land use policy as a fiscal tool, local planners need to understand how land use affects local taxes and spending. Since the 1940s, the tool most commonly used for this purpose has been fiscal impact analysis (also called cost–revenue analysis). The goal of fiscal impact analysis is to estimate the additional revenues that the new development is expected to generate and the additional spending needed to provide public services. If expected revenues exceed expected expenditures, the new development is deemed to be fiscally profitable; if the reverse is true, the development does not pay its way and would raise the tax burden on established residents.

In practice, fiscal impact analysis is straightforward and quite crude. Spending requirements are typically calculated by multiplying average spending per unit – for example, per vehicle, per student or per person – by the number of additional units generated by the development. Differences between marginal and average impacts are often ignored. Revenues are typically calculated by multiplying the local tax rate by the projected assessed value of property and adding in other revenues that can be attributed to the development (such as sales tax, fee revenue and intergovernmental aid, if applicable). The analysis can be performed for a specific development project or for general categories of land use. (The mechanics are discussed in great detail in Burchell and Listokin (1978); a short recent summary appears in Burchell and Listoken (1992).)

The conventional wisdom that emerges from fiscal impact analysis has two parts. First, business property is more profitable than residential property; and second, low income housing is fiscally undesirable. With the exception of low income housing, the conventional wisdom suggests that development is fiscally advantageous for the community. However, recent research questions whether business property pays its way. Also, recent considerations suggest that the relative fiscal disadvantage of low income households may have declined over time and that possibly no type of residential property pays its way. This more recent research may help explain the increasing willingness of many communities to shift from land use regulations that limit certain types of property to more stringent regulations that limit all types of development.

The new wisdom partially reflects the changing circumstances of the 1980s. Cutbacks in federal aid for capital spending mean that local governments now have to pay for a larger share of local capital projects. In addition, the nation-wide revolt against property taxes during the late 1970s and early 1980s reduced effective property tax rates and consequently the amount of revenue generated from new projects (see Altshuler and Gómez-Ibáñez, 1993). Rapid inflation and high interest rates during the late 1970s and early 1980s also increased the fiscal burden of all types of new development. Established residents paid for their cheaper (in current dollars) infrastructure with fixed rate bonds at relatively low interest rates; inflation raises the annual debt service costs of replicating that infrastructure for new residents and, with property tax financing of debt service, imposes burdens on established residents (Fischel, 1985, pp. 324–5). Finally, court-ordered reforms that forced states to provide more aid to equalize education spending may have reduced some of the relative disadvantage of admitting poor households in some states. More education aid from the state reduces the adverse fiscal consequences of admitting households which have low or moderate income and children (Fischel, 1985, pp. 326–7). Because this also reduces the fiscal benefits of other types of development, it may also provide incentives for limiting all development.

Increased attention by analysts to capital spending and to the distinction between marginal and average costs may also help to explain the new attitude towards the fiscal impact of development. For a number of reasons, analysts in the past typically understated the capital costs of new development. For example, the typical practice of using current debt service payments to project capital spending burdens related to new development is clearly wrong in a period when prices are rising. Also analysts have begun to account for the possibility that the marginal costs of retrofitting existing infrastructure systems of roads and sewers often exceed the average costs. For example, the cost of adding two lanes to an existing two-lane road may be greater than the cost of building the initial two lanes.

The methodological changes can be illustrated by two fiscal impact studies carried out for Montgomery County, Maryland, in 1969 and 1989 (as described in Altshuler and Gómez-Ibáñez, 1993). The 1969 study shows that each of eight types of business property (all types other than three tax-exempt categories) generates revenues far in excess of the additional spending required to serve it. White-collar office buildings, such as corporate headquarters, head the list by generating $9.81 in revenues per dollar of additional spending. The net benefits fall significantly when the analysts include the fiscal effects of additional workers who might live in the county. Nonetheless, the study supports the conventional wisdom: to maximize the favourable fiscal impact of new development on established residents, the county should try to attract regional office complexes but avoid housing their employees, especially those with low or moderate incomes and school-age children.

The 1989 study of Montgomery County was more limited. It focused on office buildings alone, looked only at highway costs, and ignored the potential of new workers. The findings provide a striking contrast to the 1969 study. In particular, the 1989 study indicates that, per office worker, a new office building would generate $411 in annual tax revenue and would cost the county $347 annually to build and maintain the roads needed to get the worker to the job. The slim margin makes it unlikely that this category of development would generate enough revenue to cover needed infrastructure (which includes more than just highways). Altshuler and Gómez-Ibáñez attribute the differing results to the more careful attention to full capital costs in the second study. While they acknowledge that the true costs could have been higher in 1989 than 1969, they also suggest that the 1969 results might have been misleading: conceivably, office development never paid its fiscal way.

At a minimum, the new emphasis on capital costs is likely to alter estimates of the relative fiscal profitability of commercial and residential development. The conventional wisdom that residential property is more burdensome than commercial property emerged in part from the emphasis on current spending, the major component of which is education. A more careful accounting of capital costs is likely to increase the estimated costs of servicing commercial property relative to residential property.

Criticisms of Fiscal Impact Analysis

Although widely used by planners for 50 years, fiscal impact analysis is open to many criticisms. Three methodological problems are particularly noteworthy (Altshuler and Gómez-Ibáñez, 1993). First is the challenge of determining the baseline alternative. That is, what would have happened in the absence of the new development? Second is the challenge of calculating the true *marginal* costs, especially for infrastructure.

The third problem – how to deal with redistributive social services – raises more fundamental issues about fiscal impact analysis and its use. Implicit in the use of fiscal impact analysis as a decision tool is the view that new development should be permitted only if it pays its fiscal way. However, that raises basic questions about financing public services at the local level. One view is that living in a community automatically entitles a household to the public services of that community and that, to achieve equity, the costs should be distributed among taxpayers, not in line with benefits received but rather in line with their ability to pay. Another is that local governments should undertake no redistribution at all and that all services should be financed by benefit taxes. That is, everyone should pay taxes only for the benefits they receive. The situation is complicated further if an ability-to-pay standard applied in the past, but a benefit standard is applied to new residents. In that case the new residents pay some of the costs of the infrastructure built for established residents (in the form of property tax payments for debt service on outstanding bonds) as well as the full fiscal costs that they impose on the community. This scheme unfairly double taxes the new residents. More generally, to the extent that responsibility for redistributive services (such as education) is lodged at the local level, the imposition of a benefit standard of financing seems inappropriate.

Fiscal impact analysis can also be criticized as a tool for local decision-making on the grounds that, in contrast to social benefit–cost analysis, it takes an extremely narrow view of benefits and costs. Benefits of development are measured only as the additional revenues that accrue to the local government. Similarly, costs include only those that affect the local government budget. This local budgetary perspective does not even include all the fiscal effects of new development. For example, consider a project that increases the need for state-financed highways and generates state sales tax revenue. Neither of these fiscal flows would be included in the analysis because they do not directly affect the local budget. In addition, the perspective ignores the non-fiscal effects of economic development. For example, a new retail outlet may make shopping more convenient for local residents or may result in noise pollution. Neither of these non-fiscal effects would be included in the fiscal impact analysis. Thus even from the parochial perspective of local residents, fiscal impact analysis provides only a partial analysis of how the new development will affect them.

In sum, most economists agree that fiscal impact analysis is a bastardized form of benefit–cost analysis, and consequently cannot by itself provide appropriate signals about whether new development should be allowed, even in the absence of equity concerns about the people who are excluded. Because local residents care so much about their tax burdens, however, such analyses will often be requested. At best, fiscal impact analysis should be regarded as an input to a more comprehensive analysis of the benefits and costs of new development.

REGRESSION-BASED APPROACH TO MEASURING THE FISCAL EFFECTS OF POPULATION GROWTH

In a series of papers, Helen Ladd (1992, 1993, 1994) uses a different approach to explore the effects of development – as measured by population growth – on local spending and tax burdens. Based on data for 248 large counties throughout the country, her regression analysis indirectly sheds new light on whether development pays its way. The sample represents all the counties or county equivalents for which complete data on spending and taxes were available for the years 1978 and 1985, where public sector spending and taxes for each county are aggregated over all local governments within the county boundary.[6]

The primary goal of Ladd's research is to improve our understanding of how population growth affects per capita local public spending. Economic theory yields no clear prediction (Ladd, 1994). On the one hand, population growth may reduce pressures on spending as jurisdictions take advantage of economies of scale in production or economies of density. In addition, to the extent that public services are characterized by non-rivalry in consumption, increased population may permit lower per capita spending. On the other hand, a larger population may increase the costs of providing public services through its impact on the harshness of the environment in which the services are produced. For example, a larger population in a fixed land area means higher density and consequently greater congestion, which in turn may require more spending on police services and traffic controls for the jurisdiction to provide a given level of public safety. Additionally, population growth may place special pressure on capital spending and debt service costs, especially if prices and interest rates are rising. Finally, population change may be correlated with changes in other variables, such as income and employment, which also put upward pressure on spending.

While it seems reasonable to presume that population growth increases total spending, its impact on spending per capita is unclear. Hence empirical work is needed to determine its effects. Ladd's methodology is straightforward. First, she regressed the (1978–85) percentage change in various categories of per capita spending and taxes only on the percentage change in population (and the percentage change squared to allow the relationship to be non-linear). Then she added to each regression various other control variables that might be correlated with population growth and that also might affect spending. The first set of descriptive regressions measures the impacts of population growth on spending, accounting for all their direct and indirect effects, including the effects of variables such as income growth that might be correlated with population growth. The second set measures the impact of population growth, controlling for changes in employment, income, age distribution of the population and intergovernmental fiscal relations.

Impacts of Population Growth on Spending

For total current account spending, Ladd finds a U-shaped relationship between the growth in per capita spending and the rate of population growth (based on the regression with no control variables). The estimated quadratic equation suggests that per capita spending declines (but only very slightly) at very low growth rates, to a minimum at a population growth rate of 7 per cent (less than 1 per cent per year) and then rises at an increasing rate. The marginal impact of a percentage point increase in population at a 30 per cent growth rate (3.8 per cent annual rate) is 0.22; that is, a 10 percentage point positive difference in population growth (around this starting point) is associated with a positive difference in *per capita* spending of roughly 2.2 percentage points. Stated differently, for seven–year growth rates greater than 7 per cent, total current spending increases faster on average than population, leading to rising per capita spending.

The addition of variables to control for changes in income, employment, age distribution of the population, and the division of intergovernmental responsibilities modifies the results somewhat. Population change still exerts a statistically significant U-shaped impact on current spending, but the minimum point of the curve now occurs at a higher rate of population growth. Only when population is growing at a rate greater than 3.8 per cent per year is faster population growth, controlling for other factors, associated with higher per capita spending. Detailed analysis suggests that the major determinant of the difference between the results with and without controls is the change in the local share variables, not the income and age composition variables. In other words, the upward pressure in spending in moderately- and fast-growing counties largely reflects the failure of state governments to maintain their share of state–local spending in the face of local population growth.

To service a growing population, localities need to increase their investment in roads, water and sewer systems, and public buildings. Such investment differs from current spending in that it is designed to yield services to residents over an extended period of time. Moreover, in growing areas, capital projects must often be designed to serve not only the current residents but also the anticipated future residents. Not surprisingly, population growth exerts a relatively large impact on capital spending. According to the preferred non-linear specification, the impact on spending increases throughout most of the relevant range of population growth, but at a decreasing rate. The impact reaches a maximum at a growth rate of about 40 per cent; counties that grew by 40 per cent over the seven-year period (equivalent to a 4.9 per cent annual rate) faced increases in per capita capital outlays of 24 per cent, while counties having no growth averaged a 3 per cent decline in per capita capital outlays. The addition of control variables has little effect on the estimates.

Because capital outlays typically are financed not out of current taxes but rather through bonds or intergovernmental grants, a better indicator of the impact of capital spending on current local tax burdens is their impact on interest outlays. Rising capital outlays in fast-growing counties, combined with high interest rates during the 1978–85 period, produced tremendous pressure on interest outlays. A county that grew by 50 per cent during the period (equivalent to a 6 per cent annual rate) experienced an average increase in per capita interest costs of 151 per cent. Once again, the picture is similar with the addition of controls.

With respect to the control variables, the most relevant results emerge for the growth in jobs and in income variables. Holding constant a county's rate of population growth, growth in current account spending is negatively associated with growth in per capita income, but positively associated with growth in the number of jobs in the county per resident. In other words, economic development that increases the income of county residents is fiscally beneficial; it apparently reduces fiscal pressure primarily by reducing spending on social services. However, except to the extent that it increases the income of county residents, additional employment in the county adds to spending pressures.

Impact of Population Growth on Tax Burdens

The final question in the Ladd analysis is how population growth affects revenue sources and tax burdens (defined as taxes relative to personal income). Even after growth in income and jobs, changes in the age distribution of the population and changes in intergovernmental responsibilities are controlled, for population growth apparently exerts large and significant impacts on per capita taxes and tax burdens. For example, the burden (defined as revenues divided by income) of own-source revenues is estimated to increase by 4.3 percentage points with a 10 percentage point increase in population. Part of this increase apparently reflects the fact that fast-growing localities turn increasingly to miscellaneous non-tax revenue sources. Part, however, represents an increasing burden of local taxes, including the local property tax. Ladd's results show that population growth at rates above 1 per cent per year typically raise both property tax and total tax burdens. Only in very slow-growing or declining counties does more population reduce tax burdens.

For any given rate of population growth, growth in the income of county residents reduces tax burdens (both by increasing the denominator of the burden measure and also by reducing spending pressures), while growth in county jobs per resident increases 'other' tax burdens (taxes that in some cases may apply directly to firms), with little impact on tax burdens for other categories of taxes. This analysis applies at the county level. Chapter 10 provides a new, more detailed look at the effects of business development on the tax burdens of local residents at the more disaggregated level of the local municipality.

Implications for Land Use Policy: Does Development Pay its Way?

Ladd's study provides some new indirect evidence on whether new residents in growing areas pay their fiscal way. Ideally, one would like to know if the taxes paid by new residents are sufficient to finance the additional spending associated with the growth in population. Because Ladd's study does not distinguish between new and established residents, it cannot provide a direct answer. Nonetheless, the results suggest that new development, as measured by population growth, may not pay its way when population growth is rapid.

The first piece of evidence is that in rapidly growing areas, population growth increases *per capita* spending levels. Hence even if new residents paid the average costs per resident of providing services in the absence of growth, the new revenues would not be sufficient to cover the higher per capita spending associated with that growth.[7] This statement needs to be qualified only to the extent that the higher per capita spending reflects higher services for residents. However, Ladd argues that the higher spending probably reflects higher costs of providing public services rather than increased services. (One such cause of higher costs is the higher density associated with having more people in a fixed land area which is discussed below.)

Second, and related, is the finding that both per capita taxes and average tax burdens increase with population growth in rapidly growing areas. Because broad-based taxes such as property and sales taxes generally apply uniformly to both established and new residents, higher average tax burdens overall also imply higher average tax burdens for one segment of the population, the established residents. The observation that this finding emerges even when the growth in jobs per resident is included in the equation suggests that the higher tax burdens cannot be dismissed simply as the result of higher taxes on non-resident taxpayers such as the owners of business property.

The U-shaped relationships, it should be noted, imply that not all population growth imposes fiscal burdens. Starting from a situation of declining or stable population, additional people could well decrease per capita spending and reduce tax burdens on established residents.

COSTS OF DIFFERING PATTERNS OF DEVELOPMENT: IS DENSER DEVELOPMENT FISCALLY CHEAPER THAN LESS DENSE DEVELOPMENT?

Fiscal considerations also play a role in planners' decisions about the most desirable density of development. The foreword to a recent survey of the relevant literature begins:

> One primary premise of modern urban planning is that compact development promotes efficient use of infrastructure, and conversely, that urban sprawl increases costs for public facilities and services ... The concept appears instinctively correct: development spread out requires more miles of roads and sewer and water pipes than development clustered in a smaller area. Yet the thesis rests on a frail foundation of empirical and theoretical research (Frank, 1989).

Early Studies of Planners

Many engineering and planning studies investigate the link between population density and public sector costs. Typically, these studies develop cost estimates for hypothetical developments of differing densities and other characteristics. One of the earliest, the study by Wheaton and Schussheim (1955), was initially widely interpreted as providing evidence that higher density development reduces public sector costs. However, as noted by Kain (1967) in an unpublished survey, the authors' conclusions relate more to the placement of the development than to density.

The most widely cited study of this type, the Real Estate Research Corporations' (1974) study, *The Costs of Sprawl*, reports significant savings for the local public sector from high density planned development. The data show that compared with low density development, high density development significantly decreases both the capital and operating costs of the police, fire and solid waste collection and disposal services, water supply, sanitary sewers and storm sewers, but not schools (based on an analysis of the data in the *Costs of Sprawl* carried out by Downing and Gustely in 1977). These findings, however, are based on the assumption of a given number of people and a fixed amount of land which produce a constant average density (see Windsor, 1979); indeed the 'high density' development might more accurately be labelled 'compact development plus open space'. In addition, the findings focus quite narrowly on the costs of servicing the residential site alone, with little attention to the costs of providing public services such as roads for all the activities, such as jobs, shopping and relaxation, that accompany residential development.[8] Finally, the findings refer to the costs of providing intermediate outputs, such as waste collection, rather than final outputs, such as a sanitary environment.

Regression Studies by Economists

An alternative approach involves the use of regression analysis. With this approach, the analyst typically uses cross-sectional data to examine the relationship between per capita local public spending and density, controlling for other determinants of public spending. This approach is advantageous in that it can pick up all the effects of density, not just those on the costs of providing direct outputs. Moreover, it provides a more comprehensive view by extending the analysis beyond the typically site-specific perspective of the engineering studies just described.

Several recent regression analyses of the cost of providing public services in cities offer evidence to support the view that, savings through the production of direct outputs notwithstanding, higher average density *increases* the costs of providing the final outputs that citizens value (Bradbury *et al.*, 1984; Ladd and Yinger, 1991). The mechanism through which this outcome occurs can be understood in terms of the harshness of the environment. For example, compared with an area with low population density, higher density may require more traffic lights and traffic control officers to achieve a given level of traffic safety or traffic flow. Similarly, higher density may raise the social costs of inappropriately disposed waste and, therefore, may require more waste collection and disposal. Higher density may also provide an environment more conducive to crime which requires more police services to achieve a given level of protection from crime.

In the regression study based on county data alluded to earlier, Ladd (1992) provides additional evidence that, except in sparsely populated counties, population density may lead to higher public sector costs. Her results are based on a cross-section regression analysis of per capita current account spending and public safety spending by all local governments in each county using 1985 data for 247 large U.S. counties.[9] In each equation, a set of density variables is embedded in a fully specified model of per capita spending that includes demand, cost and taste variables; intergovernmental relations variables; and population change variables as control variables. No functional form is imposed on the density variables so that the data are allowed to determine whether the relationship between spending and density (controlling for other determinants of spending) is linear or U-shaped or some other form.

She concludes that population density exerts a U-shaped impact on both current account and public safety spending by local governments. The lowest current account spending (and hence costs) occurs at a density of about 250 people per square mile. For densities between 0 and 250 people per square mile, lower density raises costs. For example, costs in a sparsely populated county with a density of only 125 people per square mile are predicted to exceed the minimum by about 14 per cent. This finding is consistent with the planners' view that public sector costs are high at very low densities. However, costs in counties with densities above 250 people per square mile also exceed the minimum. Counties with densities of 1 250 people per square mile are estimated to have costs that exceed the minimum by 19 per cent, and extremely dense counties to have costs that exceed the minimum by up to 43 per cent. These findings directly counter the conventional wisdom from engineering and planning studies.

The difference between Ladd's findings and that of earlier studies by planners rests partially on the distinctions between capital and current costs and, more importantly, between direct and final outputs. In contrast to the earlier studies, Ladd focuses on current, rather than capital, costs on the grounds that current costs are quantitatively much larger than capital costs.[10] The distinction between direct and final outputs emerges in the observation that population density apparently creates a harsher environment for providing public services and therefore requires more direct outputs, such as police patrols, to provide a given level of final output, such as public safety.

In the planning literature, analysts focus on the narrow question of the costs of servicing residential developments of different densities. As already noted, such studies typically hold both population and land area constant. In other words, these studies focus on the fiscal effects of differing distributions of a given number of people in a given area. In contrast, Ladd's study focuses on the fiscal effects of differing average densities, where the averages are calculated over a relatively large geographic area, the county.

Although counties are quite large and diverse, Ladd argues that, nonetheless, they are a reasonable unit of observation for investigating how density affects public sector costs. Each county is big enough to include a variety of land uses. This variety is desirable because public sector activities serve people in their capacity not only as residents but also as employees, commuters and recreationists. Hence a complete measure of the costs of financing patterns of development should extend beyond the residential patterns alone to include the public sector costs of the other activities in which residents engage.

In summary, the conventional wisdom from the planning literature which claims that higher density development can be served at lower public sector costs than less dense development, may be incorrect. If one accepts Ladd's argument that counties are a reasonable unit of observation for examining how density affects costs, then her study implies that public sector costs are a U-shaped function of population density.

CONCLUSION

Much of the blame for fiscally motivated zoning has been placed on the local property tax. Not only is the property tax the most widely used tax at the local level, its clear relationship to the use of land makes it relatively easy for land use planners to influence property tax collections through restrictive land use policies. At the same time, the role of the property tax should not be overstated. If local governments are allowed to use a sales tax, they have strong incentives to encourage the development of commercial malls within the locality (but preferably near the boundary to minimize adverse effects), and if they employ an income tax they have fiscal incentives to try to zone out households with low income. Thus fiscally motivated zoning is more correctly viewed as the result of our spatially fragmented governmental system – in which substantial responsibilities for public spending, taxes and land use are lodged at the local level – than to the property tax *per se*.

This review suggests a number of areas for additional research. First, there is room for research on the extent to which localities engage in fiscally motivated land use policies. The first research goal would be to design a study that would allow one to isolate fiscal considerations from other considerations that might affect land use and growth controls. A secondary goal would be to determine the characteristics of localities that lead to fiscally motivated zoning and to explore what, if any, policy levers might be used to reduce the amount of fiscally motivated zoning.

Second, the welfare effects of restrictive zoning deserve additional attention. Despite many studies of the price effects of zoning, only one (Peterson, 1974) tries to weigh the gains to the winners against the losses to the losers. More work is needed on determining the aggregate changes in land value associated with restrictive zoning.

Third, more work is needed on how development affects local spending and taxes. Some of this research should focus on a single county, some on local development pressures across a state, and some across the country. Focusing on a particular county or state avoids the problem of variation in fiscal institutions across states. Also a narrow focus may allow the research to define the key variables more precisely than otherwise. For example, in research based on the tax records of a single county, the research may be able to examine the effects of non-residential growth on residential tax burdens, or possibly even of other types of growth on the fiscal burdens of established residents. Chapter 10 provides an excellent example of this type of research.

Fourth, the last word has not yet been written on how density affects public sector costs. While the site-specific approach of the engineering and planning studies may be too narrow, the county-specific analysis of Ladd may be too broad. More empirical research would be helpful.

NOTES

1. Land use controls of the type discussed here tend to be used less frequently by central cities, most of which are trying to encourage, rather than limit, growth. Recent stringent controls in San Francisco are an exception to this generalization. Similarly, they are less common in rural areas or, more generally, in towns outside of metropolitan areas, which also typically are more interested in promoting than in limiting growth.
2. As noted by Hanushek and Quigley (1990), controls on non-residential property are harder to justify in terms of rational behaviour on the part of voters. Their figures suggest that the main beneficiaries of controls on commercial development in San Francisco are probably the owners of existing commercial property rather than the residents who voted for the controls.
3. In addition to being denied the opportunity to attend good suburban schools, Fischel (1985, p. 317) also notes that the poor may have to pay high central city taxes for public services, that they are denied the advantages of living in safer, more pleasant neighbourhoods, that they are denied convenient access to suburban jobs, and that they may face higher housing prices.
4. Presumably, however, the same problem would arise with a local income tax: families with low income would receive more in public services than they would pay in taxes.
5. An alternative solution to the problem of fiscally motivated zoning is to increase federal and state financing for local public services. The disadvantage of this solution is the reduction in welfare that comes from the loss of local control. However, aid targeted to local jurisdictions that are fiscally disadvantaged or aid that increases with the community's openness to low income housing could potentially reduce some of the fiscal pressures for exclusionary zoning.
6. Although the sample represents only 8 per cent of the counties in the country, the large size of the counties included means that the sample includes more than 59 per cent of the nation's population. The years were chosen to minimize the effects of the national economy on the data; both 1978 and 1985 are three years into the expansion phase of the national economic cycle. Within the sample, the mean increase in population during the seven-year period was 9.5 per cent and the median 5.8 per cent. Population change ranged from a 9 per cent decline in St Louis City to increases of more than 74 per cent in Gwinnett, Georgia and Fort Bend, Texas. A quarter of the sample experienced population increases of more than 15 per cent, but only 8 of the 248 large counties experienced increases greater than 40 per cent.
7. This statement is based on the spending equations without controls. Only if the state–local division of spending responsibilities can be held constant in the face of local population growth are the no-controls equations the relevant ones.
8. A recent survey of this literature by Frank (1989) concludes that, 'none of the studies are free of technical problems. None, furthermore, reach unassailable conclusions. The studies represent stimulating but faulty and ultimately unsatisfying attempts to define efficient patterns of development' (p. 1).
9. See note 6 for a description of the sample.
10. Ideally, she would like to examine the sum of current costs plus the annual cost of using capital, but the latter is not available in the Census of Governments. Following standard government accounting practices, the Census accounts for capital spending when it occurs rather than on an annual cost-of-capital basis.

REFERENCES

Altshuler, Alan A. and José A. Gómez-Ibáñez (1993), *Regulation for Revenue: The Political Economy of Land Use Exactions*, Washington D.C: Brookings Institution and Cambridge, MA: Lincoln Institute of Land Policy.

Bradbury, Katharine L., Helen F. Ladd, Mark Perrault, Andrew Reschovsky and John Yinger (1984), 'State aid to offset fiscal disparities across communities', *National Tax Journal*, **37** (2), 151–70.

Brueckner, Jan K. (1990), 'Growth controls and land values in an open city', *Land Economics*, **66** (3), 237–48.

Buchanan, James M. (1965), 'An Economic Theory of Clubs', *Economica*, **32** (February), 1–14.

Burchell, Robert W. and David Listokin (1978), *The Fiscal Impact Handbook: Estimating Local Costs and Revenues of Land Development*, New Brunswick, NJ: Center for Urban Policy Research.

Burchell, Robert W. and David Listokin (1992), 'Fiscal impact procedures and state of the art: the subset question of the costs and revenues of open space and agricultural lands', prepared for *Does Land Conservation Pay?*, sponsored by the Lincoln Institute of Land Policy, Cambridge, MA (May).

Cason, Forrest M. (1981), 'Land-use concomitants of urban fiscal squeeze', *Urban Affairs Quarterly*, **16** (3), 337–53.

Chapman, Jeffrey I. (1988), 'Land use planning and the local budget: a model of their interrelationships', *Public Administration Review*, July/Aug., 800–806.

Downing, Paul B. (1977), 'Suburban nongrowth policies', *Journal of Economic Issues*, **11** (2), 387–400.

Downing, P.B. and R.D. Gustely (1977), 'The Public Service Costs of Alternative Development Patterns: A Review of the Evidence', in P.B. Downing (ed.), *Local Service Pricing Policies and Their Effect on Urban Spatial Structure*, Vancouver, BC: University of British Columbia Press, 63–86.

Fischel, William A. (1985), *The Economics of Zoning Laws: A Property Rights Approach to American Land Use Controls*, Baltimore, MD: Johns Hopkins University Press.

Fischel, William A. (1992), 'Communication: property taxation and the Tiebout Model: evidence for the benefit view from zoning and voting', *Journal of Economic Literature*, **30**, 171–7.

Fischel, William A. (1995), *Regulatory Takings: Law, Economics, and Politics*, Cambridge, MA: Harvard University Press.

Frank, James E. (1989), *The Costs of Alternative Development Patterns: A Review of the Literature*, Washington, DC: Urban Land Institute.

Hanushek, Eric A. and John M. Quigley (1990), 'Commercial land use regulation and local government finance', *AEA Papers and Proceedings*, **80** (2), 176–9.

Kain, John F. (1992), 'The spatial mismatch hypothesis: three decades later', *Housing Policy Debate*, **3** (2), 371–460.

Kain, John F. and Joseph J. Persky (1969), 'Alternatives to the gilded ghetto', *The Public Interest*, (Winter) 74–88.

Ladd, Helen F. (1992), 'Population growth, density, and the costs of providing public services', *Urban Studies*, **29** (2), 273–95.

Ladd, Helen F. (1993), 'Effects of population growth on local spending and taxes', in R.D. Norton (ed.), *Structuring Direct Aid: People vs. Places*, Greenwich, CT: JAI Press, Research in Urban Economics, Vol. 9, pp. 181–224.

Ladd, Helen F. (1994), 'Fiscal impacts of local population growth: a conceptual and empirical analysis', *Regional Science and Urban Economics*, **24**, 661–86.

Ladd, Helen F. and John Yinger (1991), *America's Ailing Cities: Fiscal Health and the Design of Urban Policy*, updated edition, Baltimore: Johns Hopkins University Press.

Mills, Edwin S. (1979), 'Economic analysis of urban land-use controls', in P. Mieszkowski and M. Straszheim (eds), *Current Issues in Urban Economics*, Baltimore, MD: Johns Hopkins University Press, 511–41.

Mills, Edwin S. (1990), 'An evaluation of community growth controls,' prepared for Urban Land Institute under agreement with NCI Research, April, (unpublished).

Peterson, George E. (1974), 'Federal tax policy and land conversion at the urban fringe', in George Break (ed.), *Metropolitan Financing and Growth Management Policies: Principals and Practice*, Madison, WI: University of Wisconsin Press, 51–78.

Pogodizinski, J. Michael and Tim R. Sass (1990), 'The Economic Theory of Zoning: A Critical Review', *Land Economics*, **66**, (3), 294–314.

Real Estate Research Corporation (1974), *The Costs of Sprawl: Environmental and Economic Costs of Alternative Residential Development Patterns at the Urban Fringe*, Washington, DC: US Government Printing Office.

Wheaton, William L. C. and Morton J. Schussheim (1955), *The Cost of Municipal Services in Residential Areas: A Study Prepared for the Housing and Home Finance Agency*, Washington, DC: US Department of Commerce.

White, Fred C. and Bill R. Miller (1978), '"Comparison of property tax circuitbreakers applied to farmers and homeowners". Reply', *Land Economics*, **54** (3), 397–9.

White, Michelle (1978), 'Self-Interest in the Suburbs: The Trend Towards No–Growth Zoning', *Journal of Urban Economics*, **5** (4), 485–504.

Windsor, D. (1979), 'A Critique of the Costs of Sprawl', *Journal of the American Planning Association*, **45** (31), 279–92.

Windsor, Duane (1990), 'Chapman's fiscal impact model: extensions and caveats', *Public Administration Review*, September/October, 546–56.

COMMENT

Dick Netzer

Ladd provides an excellent summary of the extensive literature on the question of the fiscal effects of alternative land use regulation policies in the United States, something that has been actively discussed by planners for 50 years and by urban economists for about half as long a period. Prior to World War II, suburban residential development in the form of small, independent political jurisdictions was largely occupied by households with relatively high incomes. Fiscal zoning, as a response to residential development occupied by people of more modest means, accompanied the revolution in mortgage financing and construction techniques that made possible mass suburbanization of the less-than-affluent.

Both planners and economists, whatever their views on the merits or demerits of fiscal zoning, tend to assume that the practice is very widespread indeed; sometimes articles read as if the practice is ubiquitous. It is worth paying some attention to this issue, and not only because the policy relevance of the discussion depends on the prevalence of fiscal zoning and whether it is increasing or decreasing. If the practice is not universal, then the examination of the variables that determine its presence may be productive. The first issue discussed in this commentary is the extent to which the local governments that are responsible in the United States for implementing them in practice do base their land use decisions heavily on expected fiscal effects, rather than on other externality considerations.

Second, do those land use regulations have the expected fiscal effects? Ladd does discuss this issue fully, but an added caveat about the empirical evidence is in order.

Third, if the fiscal effects are as expected, what are the welfare consequences? What are the equity consequences? This, too, is fully discussed by Ladd, but only briefly touched upon in this commentary.

How Widespread is Fiscal Zoning?

A number of subordinate questions arise with regard to the prevalence of fiscal zoning. As several writers have pointed out, there can be a variety of different motivations for exclusionary or restrictive zoning, zoning that is effective in preventing development that is otherwise permitted by law and for which there is a market (for example, Bogart, 1993). Some of these motivations are legitimate and have respectable welfare and equity effects. For example, Bogart notes these categories: fiscal zoning (people are excluded if they pay less in taxes than the costs of the services provided to them);

public goods zoning (people are excluded if their presence increases the unit costs of producing local public goods); consumption zoning (people are excluded if they impose negative consumption externalities on the decisive residents); and political economic zoning (people are excluded if their demands for local public services differ from those of the decisive residents). The trouble is that, empirically, one cannot determine which of the motivations is at work: the results look the same. And because overt fiscal zoning (for example, a requirement that a new house must involve a minimum dollar investment) can be, and has been held to be, unconstitutional, it is difficult to conduct surveys that honestly sort out motivations *ex ante*.

A number of the large-scale metropolitan area planning studies that were popular in the 1960s did demonstrate that restrictive zoning, usually in the form of large minimum-lot-size zoning, was common in suburbs in the major Northeastern and Midwestern metropolitan areas. For example, a 1962 study in the New York area which carefully mapped zoning rules for vacant land throughout the 22-county region and compared the zoning with actual development in the immediately preceding years, found that most of the vacant land was zoned for much larger lot sizes than the sizes of lots on which the great bulk of development was then occurring. This meant that the zoning rules, if effective over time, would produce solutions that were inconsistent with market forces (Regional Plan Association, 1962).

However, that study also showed that minimum lot sizes tended to be smaller, the larger the geographic extension of the local planning jurisdiction.[1] It was also noteworthy that reports of fiscal zoning and large minimum lot sizes were uncommon in states in which the zoning powers were exercised by counties – large-area jurisdictions – compared with states in which smaller municipal units were the land use controllers. County land use controls are common in the South and in Western states as well. So fiscal zoning has never been as ubiquitous as much of the literature implies.

The existence of fiscal zoning in the United States – and in no other country – would seem to depend on the simultaneous existence of the following four conditions, which is widely the case only in this country:[2]

1. Local governments are responsible for the provision of many public services and for a substantial share of the financing of those services.
2. Most local governments get a large portion of own-source revenues from a tax whose yield is directly linked to the land development that occurs over time within that jurisdiction: the property tax.
3. Those same local government units are the ones who exercise most land use controls, notably zoning.
4. Local government units outside the central cities are, in many states, small in geographic size and population.

Given the existence of these conditions, fiscal zoning seems inevitable. In the absence of any one of the conditions, the reason for fiscal zoning is not clear. If local governments have very limited powers or revenue-raising responsibilities (as in, say, Australia), it would hardly seem worthwhile to control land use for fiscal reasons. If the main sources of local revenue are tied only loosely to the nature and extent of land development or directly reflect the public service costs of each type of development (for example, marginal cost-based user charges), the same is true. If the local government unit is large in area, the likelihood is that the development of the small fraction of the land area that occurs within a few years will not have much fiscal impact, or that, over time, the jurisdiction will attract diverse types of development, including some that clearly 'pay their way'. And if zoning powers are not exercised by the conventional small local government at all, there is no reason to expect fiscal zoning to begin with.

It is not clear that the prevalence of fiscal zoning – as contrasted with *writing* about it – has increased over time. It is true that fiscal zoning in the form of overall growth controls has increased over the past 20 years, but it may be that fiscal zoning in the form of minimum lot sizes has not, in part because so much development is occurring in jurisdictions that are relatively large in area.

The size of suburban jurisdictions is a subject on which there has been some good recent research. One recent paper concludes that the character of the demand for local public services has a strong influence on the mean size of municipalities and school districts across metropolitan areas, in addition to the influence of various political, institutional and structural economic characteristics (Fisher and Wassmer, 1994). The number of jurisdictions within a given metropolitan area tends to increase with the extent of variation in demand variables, which would suggest that the possibility of fiscal zoning should play a part in fostering the creation of new jurisdictions. Thus it is plausible to predict that fiscal zoning will become more, rather than less, prevalent over time.

The Fiscal Effects of Land Use Regulation regimes

The empirical research reviewed by Ladd shows that increased population, above a fairly low level, does tend to increase the unit costs of local government services, so the fiscal effects are negative unless the marginal revenue that accompanies the additional population is higher than the average revenue per household, an unlikely prospect in most cases in the absence of fiscal zoning. So growth controls should be a good thing in fiscal terms. The fiscal impact of density is more equivocal, as Ladd's review shows. The extensive literature purporting to show that low density is associated with higher local

government costs, *ceteris paribus,* is seriously flawed in a number of respects. Moreover, there is some reason to believe that the empirical reality is
the economist's beloved U-shaped curve.

However, there is a conceptual problem here, related to X-inefficiency.
When we write of economies or diseconomies of scale, we are usually refer-
ring to the inherent nature of a productive process or industry, on the assumption that producers are operating at the production possibility frontier, not at
some technically inefficient point well within the frontier. But nearly all the
writing about economies of scale with respect to population size or density in
the production of local government services ignores that fine point, implicitly
assuming that producers are in fact operating as efficiently as they can be
expected to operate. Thus actual data with respect to public spending per
capita (or some other measure of unit costs) can be used to estimate true
returns to scale.

It can be argued that this is a valid assumption: if nearly all very densely
populated places have high per capita costs, but we know that nearly all of
them operate far from the production possibility frontier (for example, with a
far higher ratio of labour to capital inputs than is technically appropriate), it
is conceivable that there are such powerful political and institutional barriers
to efficiency that the X-inefficiency should be viewed as an inherent property
of high density places. But would we as economists be persuaded that there
are, inherently, decreasing returns in agriculture with respect to size of farm
by the strong evidence that crops yields per acre decline sharply with size of
farm in Russia? I doubt it very much. We would want some theory that
explains why the barriers to achieving technical efficiency are invulnerable to
change. But the widely cited studies that seem to verify the urban planner's
intuition that low density suburban residential development is costly are
firmly based on the presumption that nothing can be changed except density.

In the Real Estate Research Corporation's 1974 study, *The Costs of Sprawl,*
it was found that the per household cost of all services that are directly
provided to housing units (rather than to persons) vary directly with residential lot sizes, over the range of densities that are conventional in the suburbs
in large American metropolitan areas. In fact, the empirical relationship is
amazingly uniform over densities and services, and seems almost magical:
doubling lot sizes (say, from one-half to one acre) increases unit costs by
close to 44 per cent, that is, from 1.00 to 1.44, or the square root of 2. But as
John Kain pointed out nearly 30 years ago, this is largely a function of the
fact that engineering standards and operating practices are essentially uniform over the conventional range of densities: if every residential street is of
the same width and pavement thickness, then the per-housing-unit costs of
street construction, maintenance, cleaning, snow removal and so forth, *must*
increase rapidly with lot size (Kain, 1967).

No doubt it is convenient for local officials to post physical standards that do not vary with density. But it is obvious from past history and the variations in standards over cities in this country and throughout the world that the uniformity is a matter of convenience, not physical law. To accept engineering 'requirements' as essential economic properties of the provision of public services is not that different from accepting long-traditional management practices in Russian agriculture as essential economic properties of agriculture, and determining optimal farm size from those data.

It would seem obvious that congestion must be an explanation for Ladd's finding that unit costs rise with average county density, above the very lowest density levels. But here, too, we ought to be concerned with the extent to which this finding is based on the institutional fact that the congestion of public services and facilities is almost never priced. Would the relationships be so one-sided if the public sector did apply congestion charges, as we economists have urged time and again? Should we really accept the proposition that higher density is a fiscally bad proposition, if unpriced congestion is the real problem?

The data indicate that public service costs are especially high in the large cities with the highest densities. Is this really worth worrying about? What are the relevant policy questions? Are the measures truly significant? Isn't each large city fairly distinctive, with high costs in some functions but not in others, or with different combinations of inputs? For example, for some years Baltimore city had very high ratios of employees to population for most functions, but relatively low payroll per employee. It would seem strange to relate Baltimore's position with respect to costs among large cities to something inherent in density. Planners these days tend to stress, as the main case for higher density of new development, one set of costs which may be real but are not fiscal costs. Higher density is positively associated with greater use of public transportation.[3] New York City and London (the 32 London boroughs) have about the same populations, but London's area is about twice that of New York; the percentage of journeys to work in central London by public transportation is far lower than is the case for the Manhattan central business district. However, the evidence is fairly overwhelming that it requires very large increases in density to produce much of a modal shift, the widespread construction of new light rail notwithstanding (Downs, 1992).

On the question of whether non-residential development is fiscally beneficial, doesn't this necessarily depend on jurisdiction size, in two respects? First, the larger the jurisdiction, the less likely it is that the possibly higher marginal costs of providing public services and facilities to the new entrant will have a perceptible effect on average costs over the entire jurisdiction. Second, the larger the jurisdiction, the more likely it is that most of the local public costs and benefits from the new development will be internalized. That is, a large jurisdiction can capture all of the positive effects on local revenues, including second- and subsequent-round effects. Because in a large jurisdiction it is unlikely that all existing local public services are being used at capacity, it seems highly probable that any specific new non-residential use must impose added costs far below the added revenue (unless that development has been elicited by substantial local tax concessions).

Welfare Costs of Controls are not Obvious

If fiscal zoning works as predicted, the negative equity consequences are fairly obvious. As some of the above comments suggest, the welfare costs in the form of negative externalities that planners write about are less obvious. I offer only one comment about this. Planners emphasize the transportation consequences of low-density development. Granted that low density zoning ('sprawl') does result in more vehicle miles of travel and perhaps in more time spent in travel (which is not necessarily the case, if low density permits higher average speeds), is this a welfare loss? It does seem that, in the United States, wages are quite low – relative to the regional averages – in a good many especially low density urban areas in the Sunbelt. Examples include Tucson, Colorado Springs, Abilene, Waco, Tallahassee, the Norfolk–Hampton Roads area in Virginia, and Columbus, Georgia.[4] This implies that the time costs of travel will be relatively low in such areas, despite the additional vehicle miles travelled.

Finally, there is the whole issue of whether land use control powers *should* be exercised by small local government units. It has never been evident that this is inherently equitable or efficient, unless we are dealing with a pure Tiebout world. There is also the question of legitimacy, which we are probably not professionally entitled to address.

Notes

1. Because the local governments with planning powers tended to be larger in area the further one moved from the centre of the region, the average minimum lot size required by zoning was relatively small in the furthest reaches of the region. This is hardly consistent with an Alonso-type urban model.
2. I first made this point in Netzer (1962).
3. See, for example, the Meyer and Gómez-Ibáñez (1981) comparison of Phoenix and Boston.
4. There is a weak, but statistically highly significant, positive relation between the density of the 200 largest cities (in 1990) and average annual payroll per employee in the central counties of the metropolitan areas that contain these cities. The relationship is somewhat stronger if the Northeast and Midwest are excluded and the comparison confined to the Sunbelt, with a dummy variable for the main regions within the Sunbelt.

References

Bogart, William T. (1993), '"What Big Teeth You Have!": identifying the motivations for exclusionary zoning', *Urban Studies*, **30**, 1669–81.

Downs, Anthony (1992), *Stuck in Traffic*, Washington, DC: Brookings Institute and the Lincoln Institute of Land Policy.

Fisher, Ronald G. and Robert W. Wassmer (1994), 'Economic influences on the structure of local governments in US metropolitan areas', mimeo.

Kain, John (1967), 'Urban form and the costs of urban services', mimeo, Cambridge, MA: MIT–Harvard Joint Center for Urban Studies.

Meyer, John R., and José A. Gómez-Ibáñez (1981), *Autos, Transit and Cities*, Cambridge, MA: Harvard University Press.

Netzer, Dick (1962), 'The property tax and alternatives in regional development', *Papers and Proceedings of the Regional Science Association*, **9**, 190–97.

Real Estate Research Corporation (1974), *The Costs of Sprawl*, Washington, DC: US Government Printing Office.

Regional Plan Association (1962), *Spread City. Projections of Development Trends and the Issues they Pose: The Tri-State New York Metropolitan Region, 1960–1985*, New York: Regional Plan Association.

4. Effects of taxes on economic activity

Helen F. Ladd

Any tax that affects economic activity may affect land use. For example, a 7 per cent retail sales tax in the state of Connecticut would reduce retail activity in the state even if no consumer responded to the tax by purchasing consumer goods in other states. Consumers would simply cut back on their consumption of taxed goods, which in turn would force some retailers out of business and reduce the size of others. The impact of the Connecticut sales tax on economic activity and land use would be even larger if some Connecticut consumers tried to avoid the tax by shopping in other states. In general, taxes will exert larger effects on land use patterns when the tax induces movement outside the taxing jurisdiction than when it does not.

Analogously, other taxes also have effects on land use, so that the overall effect of taxes on a state's land use depends on the composition of the state's taxes. Moreover, because neighbouring communities are likely to be better substitutes for the residential, shopping and working needs of households than are neighbouring states, the impacts on land use of decisions about the mix and level of taxes are likely to be even greater at the local than at the state level.

Most of the controversy about the land use effects of taxes relates to the effect of taxes on the location and investment decisions of firms. On the one hand, legislators and city council members throughout the county are frequently induced to reduce business taxes or provide generous tax abatements to particular firms in response to the (often vocal and well financed) claims of business firms that high taxes will lead them to invest elsewhere. On the other hand, economists have, until recently, been surprisingly unified in their view that taxes do not matter very much, and that tax abatements are typically tax giveaways. However, a spate of new studies has recently challenged the conventional wisdom of economists.

The effectiveness, or lack thereof, of explicit attempts by state or local governments to influence economic activity through tax policy tools such as abatements or enterprise zones is reserved for a later chapter. This chapter focuses research about the *unintended* effects of state or local tax decisions on economic activity. While the distinction between tax policies that have unintended effects and those that are explicitly designed to affect land use impact may not always be clear, my intent is to recognize that some tax policies are motivated primarily by the desire to raise revenue while others are specifically designed to influence economic behaviour and, in particular, the use of land.

The literature on the location and investment effects of state and local taxes is now extensive and is documented in several good surveys. To review once again all the individual studies would be redundant. Hence my approach in this chapter is to use the surveys as an indicator of the changing conventional wisdom about the effects of taxes on economic activity.

OVERVIEW

In his 1961 survey of the literature on the location of industry, John Due concluded that: 'While the statistical analysis and study of location factors are by no means conclusive, they suggest very strongly that the tax effects cannot be of major importance' (Due, 1961, p. 170). By 1991, the conventional wisdom had changed, as evidenced by Timothy Bartik's conclusion that, 'state and local taxes have much stronger effects on the economic development of states, metropolitan areas, and small jurisdictions than was once believed' (Bartik, 1991, p. 102).

A close look at the Due and Bartik reviews plus three reviews published in intervening years – by William Oakland in 1978, Michael Wasylenko in 1981, and Newman and Sullivan in 1988 – provides a reasonably clear picture of what we know about the effects of taxes on economic activity and how we know it.

The starting point for most theoretical models of firm location decisions is profit maximization and the observation that a firm's profits vary by location. Location can affect both revenue or sales and the costs of producing the good. On the cost side, the firm is affected by labour market conditions such as the cost, availability and productivity of labour; the proximity and price of transportation; the availability and price of energy and immobile inputs such as water or coal; the price of land; and the taxes the firm must pay relative to the public services it receives. Because tax differentials are likely to be imperfectly correlated with service differentials, taxes are likely to affect profits and, hence, the firm's location decision.

Economic theory suggests that taxes operate through a substitution effect and an output effect. An increase in a taxed input, say capital, induces firms to substitute away from the taxed input in favour of other inputs. The higher tax also raises the costs of producing output and thereby induces the firm to produce less output in the taxed region (the output effect). The size of the substitution and output effects will vary with the characteristics of production functions, the mobility of factors of production and the price elasticity of demand for output, where price elasticity refers to the responsiveness of consumers to changes in the price of the good. For example, the easier it is for firms to substitute labour for capital, and the more responsive are consumers to price differentials, the larger is the predicted impact on business activity of a regional tax on capital. The impact will also be greater the greater is the capital intensity of production in the taxing region and the more mobile are factors of production, including labour. Unfortunately, these theoretical considerations are often hard to incorporate directly into empirical studies. However, they are sometimes useful in guiding the empirical work (for example, encouraging researchers to focus on firms that sell in a national market and consequently have little control over the price of the good) or in interpreting results for different industries.

The reviews discussed here all distinguish between the effects of taxes on intrametropolitan location and investment decisions and those on interstate or interregional decisions. This distinction makes sense for various reasons. First, factors other than taxes, such as labour market conditions and access to markets, may well dominate in interstate, but not intrametropolitan, decisions. Second, tax burdens are often easier to measure for jurisdictions within a metropolitan area than for states. In the latter case, measuring tax burdens is complicated by the variety of tax bases used by different states and the

Table 4.1   Effects of taxes on business activity

	Intrametropolitan	Interstate or Interregional
Due (1961)	Taxes may matter, but impact is likely to be small	Negligible impact
Oakland (1978)	No good evidence	NA*
Wasylenko (1981)	Taxes may matter, but are of secondary importance	Negligible impact
Newman and Sullivan (1988)	Taxes may matter, but evidence is still limited	Mixed results
Bartik (1991)	Among suburban jurisdictions, taxes have powerful effects on business activity	Substantial evidence of negative impact of state and local taxes

Note: *Not applicable because Oakland limits his review to intrametropolitan studies. However, Oakland fully concurs with Due's conclusion that taxes have virtually no effect on interstate or interregional location decisions.

variation within states of local tax burdens. Third, intrametropolitan studies often suffer from lack of generalizability and from limited data.

Table 4.1 summarizes the main conclusions of the five reviews. Of most interest is how the conclusions have changed in recent years.

JOHN DUE (1961): TAXES DO NOT MATTER

After surveying the literature of the 1950s, John Due was firmly convinced that state and local taxes do not have much effect on firms' location and investment decisions. Moreover, he expressed outrage at misleading propagandizing by business firms about the location effects of taxes. At the end of his survey he advocated more research by state tax agencies and unbiased research organizations to 'ascertain the actual effects of taxation on location decisions', research that he believed, 'is almost certain to explode the widely used arguments about the disastrous effects of taxes on location' (p. 172).

Due based his conclusion on his analysis of three types of research: statistical studies based on simple correlations, interview studies and studies that examine the importance of taxes relative to other costs. The statistical studies of the 1950s were relatively unsophisticated in that researchers typically simply correlated growth in manufacturing employment or investment with per capita state and local tax collections or growth in tax collections. Typically, the expected negative correlation between taxes and investment did not emerge. Correctly criticizing these studies for their lack of statistical controls, the crudeness of their tax measures and their insufficient attention to the firms for which taxes might be decisive, Due nonetheless pointed out that in any case they provided no support for the view that taxes adversely affect location and investment decisions.

Nor did the interview approach provide any support for the hypothesis that taxes affect location decisions. Interviews that ask about the factors that affect location decisions typically find taxes far down on the list – an unsurprising finding given the variety of demand and cost considerations that influence a firm's profits and hence its location decision. For example, a 1958 *Business Week* study found that out of 747 references to location factors, only 5 per cent referred to taxes. Not surprisingly, interview studies that explicitly asked about taxes provided a somewhat different picture. A study by the Federal Reserve Bank of Boston, for example, reported that of 196 manufacturing firms, 16 per cent indicated that local taxes and 19 per cent that state taxes had influenced their location decisions. However, Due discounted this and other comparable studies by pointing out that Massachusetts was a high tax state and that, 'the anti-tax attitude of many business men conditions them to stress the tax factor, as does the belief that their answers may influence the conclusions of the survey and thus ultimately bring lower taxes' (p. 167).

Finally, Due argued that taxes are inconsequential because they account for such a small portion of total costs. With reference both to studies that used data of actual firms operating in more than one state and to those that used data for hypothetical firms, he provided evidence that taxes represent a small portion of total costs. While he acknowledged that differences in taxes would have a bigger effect on profits than on costs, and therefore could conceivably affect location and investment decisions, Due downplayed that possibility by pointing out that firms may be able to shift some of the tax burden to others, that wage differences are likely to be far more important than tax differences, that the burden of state and local taxes is reduced by their deductibility for purposes of federal taxation, and that firms consider governmental services as well as taxes in making location decisions.

Due's conclusions defined the conventional wisdom among economists for the next two decades. His first conclusion was that tax effects 'cannot be of major importance'. The second was that the siting decision within a metropolitan area was more susceptible to the influence of taxes than the choice of region or state, but that, 'state and local taxes represent such a small percentage of total costs that the cases in which they are controlling cannot be very significant'. As Oakland (see below) subsequently pointed out, Due may have overstated his case, especially for intrametropolitan location decisions where differences in non-tax factors such as wages play less of a role. In particular, Oakland showed that tax differentials between cities and suburbs might plausibly account for 10 per cent of profits. He also showed that the deductibility argument was bogus,[1] and pointed out the absence of evidence to support the possibility of tax shifting.

As will be seen, the tone of Due's review differed from that of subsequent reviews. Instead of simply suggesting that the jury was still out, Due chose to use much stronger language, presumably to counter what he viewed as outrageous claims by business firms that state and local taxes had big impacts on their location decisions.

WILLIAM OAKLAND (1978): NO CONVINCING EVIDENCE

In his 1978 review of the effect of local taxes, William Oakland accepted without question the conventional wisdom from John Due that taxes have little effect on interstate or interregional location decisions. Less clear, however, was whether local taxes have much impact on the spatial distribution of firms within a metropolitan area. Unwilling to accept without evidence Due's assertion that tax differentials are likely to have a negligible impact even at the local level, Oakland turned to recent statistical studies to resolve the issue. The paucity of careful studies generated his main conclusion, namely that economists knew almost nothing about whether local taxes have any effect on intrametropolitan local decisions.

Oakland bases this conclusion on the only three empirical studies that he could find: one by Beaton and Joun in 1968, one by Fox in 1973 and one by Schmenner in 1973.[2] He summarily dismissed the Beaton and Joun study based on some of its peculiar results. He also found Fox's study, which implied that a 10 per cent increase in property taxes would decrease industrial investment in Cleveland by 44 per cent, at best suggestive. Finally he was unpersuaded by Schmenner's conclusion that income tax differentials affected the location of firms in Cleveland because many of the estimated coefficients from Schmenner's 1973 comprehensive study of both property tax and income tax differentials had the wrong sign and were statistically insignificant.

Oakland concluded that additional studies of the same ilk were unlikely to increase our knowledge. Instead he argued for empirical studies based on a firmer theoretical foundation. In particular, he advocated that researchers, 'incorporate the fact that industrial location is *jointly* determined by the behavior of firms and host communities' (p. 23).

MICHAEL WASYLENKO (1981): TAXES ARE NOT VERY IMPORTANT

Wasylenko reviewed both the interregional and the intraregional literature on the location effects of taxes. I begin with the intraregional literature because some of the papers Wasylenko discussed directly heeded Oakland's plea for researchers to pay attention to the host community's willingness to supply sites for business development.

Intraregional Location Decisions

Fischel (1975) provided an important conceptual underpinning by showing that residents in some communities might rationally want to restrict the amount of industrial activity in the community. In making their zoning decisions, local communities trade the fiscal benefits from industrial property against the harm to the environment that it might cause. Because communities with strong environmental preferences might find the trade-off unacceptable, they would have an incentive to exclude industrial, and also possibly some forms of commercial, property, from the community. If this behaviour were common, including such communities in a study of firm location could make it appear that tax levels had no effect on business activity when in fact high taxes depressed such activity in the more relevant set of communities, those that welcomed industrial development.

In addition to reviewing some of the more standard attempts to isolate the intraregional location effects of taxes, Wasylenko referred to two studies of the late 1970s that incorporated this refinement: Fox (1981) and Wasylenko (1980). The strategy of both authors was to compare the effects of fiscal factors that emerge from a regression model estimated with a sample that included all suburban jurisdictions in the relevant metropolitan area with those that emerge from a smaller sample that excluded the jurisdictions that zoned out industrial property. The results were striking in both cases. In Fox's Cleveland sample, the larger sample yielded statistically insignificant fiscal effects and the smaller sample indicated that taxes had a negative and statistically significant impact. In Wasylenko's study of firms that moved from Milwaukee city to its surrounding suburbs, the exclusion of communities that zoned out industrial property produced statistically significant negative effects of the property tax variable for manufacturing and wholesale trade firms, but not for retail, finance and service firms which, reasoned Wasylenko, were more concerned about accessibility to consumers than about costs.

These two studies illustrate the potential gains from more careful modelling of the process of firm location, a theme to which I shall return. Although the studies are not flawless (see Newman and Sullivan, below), they represent clear progress in our understanding of the effects of intrametropolitan tax differentials.

Despite the statistically significant findings from these two studies, Wasylenko downplayed the adverse effects of local taxes. The statistical significance of taxes as a determinant of industrial location notwithstanding, he argued that taxes were still less important predictors of intraregional location decisions than labour supply considerations and agglomeration economies (p.184). However, he also suggested that taxes might influence firm location indirectly through their effects on household location. If, for example, fiscal factors are a consideration, as argued by Bradford and Kelejian (1973), in the movement of households out of central cities into the suburbs, and if firms follow people, then taxes indirectly affect the location of industry.

Interregional location and investment decisions

Wasylenko fully supported Due's conclusions with respect to interregional location decisions. Because they are dominated by factor and product market considerations, tax differentials do not have much impact. Support for his position came from additional survey results similar to those cited by Due and from some new statistical studies.

The new statistical studies made use of Dun and Bradstreet micro data on the birth of new firms, on-site expansions and contractions, and locations of new branch plants. Use of these data allows the researcher to ground the empirical analysis in the microeconomic theory of firm behaviour. Wasylenko highlighted various 1977 papers by Carlton[3] which focused on firm births in three different industries by metropolitan area. Because taxes emerged as statistically insignificant, Carlton – and also Wasylenko – concluded that taxes are unimportant.

One explanation for the small impact of taxes that emerged from both the surveys and the statistical studies could conceivably be that tax burdens did not vary much across states. Relative uniformity of tax rates would obtain if states specifically tried to keep tax rates on firms in line with those of states with which they competed for business. To counter this view, Wasylenko provided data on state and local taxes as a share of state personal income or relative to population to show that tax burdens varied significantly across states. Unfortunately, Wasylenko's measures of tax burden are not very relevant to firms. More useful would have been a measure of the effective tax rate they face in each state. Only more recently have researchers focused on how best to measure the tax burden on firms.[4]

ROBERT J. NEWMAN AND DENNIS H. SULLIVAN (1988): TAXES MAY HAVE SOME EFFECTS

During the 1980s, statistical studies of the effects of taxes on industrial location proliferated and became more sophisticated. Newman and Sullivan's review was timely in that it categorized the various studies and looked closely at their statistical validity. With respect to intrametropolitan studies, they concluded that taxes probably did matter, but that the evidence was still limited. With respect to interstate studies, they concluded that the evidence was mixed. This softening of the conventional wisdom reflected their observation that significant tax effects emerged when models were carefully specified.

Newman and Sullivan distinguished three types of empirical study. First are equilibrium models. In such models, the observed locations of firms are treated as equilibrium responses to current locational variables such as wage and tax rates.[5] Specifically, researchers try to explain cross-sectional variation in measures of business activity as a function of current product market and cost variables. The challenge of such studies is to include as control variables all the other determinants of business activity that might be correlated with the tax variables. Otherwise one might attribute to taxes the effects of other factors that were not included in the model.[6] The data requirements for equilibrium studies of this type are daunting, especially at the interstate level.

More common are disequilibrium models in which firms are assumed to be out of equilibrium at the beginning of the period. Changes in their behaviour are then modelled as a function of beginning-of-the-period location factors. One must be careful, however, to measure correctly the initial disequilibrium. For example, in looking at the effect of wages one needs to control for the level of productivity. High wages in the initial period may not repel labour-intensive firms if they are offset by high productivity.

The third approach treats *changes* in the existing distribution of locations as the response to *changes* in the inter-area distribution of site characteristics. This approach is advantageous in that locational determinants that do not change over time can be omitted. However, adjustment lags complicate the specification. A slightly different approach is to focus on differential growth rates rather than simply on changes.

Intrametropolitan Studies

Like Wasylenko, Newman and Sullivan began by focusing on the contributions of Fox and Wasylenko, both of whom adjusted their samples for zoning by host communities. They faulted Fox's equilibrium model for its unrealistic assumptions and its statistical limitations.[7] Wasylenko's focus on *movers* is superior and more in the spirit of disequilibrium models; moving is a way of responding to the initial disequilibrium (or, in Wasylenko's model, mid-period disequilibrium). Newman and Sullivan praised Wasylenko's econometric technique and his focus on six disaggregated types of business. They noted that he finds significant repelling effects of the property tax for relocating manufacturing and wholesale firms, but not for other types of firm.

Newman and Sullivan also commended a study by Charney (1983) based on manufacturing firms in Detroit. Like Wasylenko, Charney focused on movers. Although she did not specifically control for restrictive zoning, she addressed the issue in part by scaling many variables by land area. She concluded that the number of firms relocating in a jurisdiction per acre of usable land was not responsive to the local income tax, but was significantly responsive to the property tax rate.

In sum, Newman and Sullivan concluded that taxes may affect intrametropolitan location decisions, but that the evidence was still quite limited.

Interstate Decisions

With respect to interstate tax decisions, Newman and Sullivan departed from the conventional wisdom by concluding that the evidence was mixed. While some studies indicated no effect of taxes, some of the more sophisticated studies indicated some effect.

Studies during the late 1970s by Carlton on firm births (see above), and also on branch plant locations, yielded no tax effects. However, these studies were based on a small sample of industries and required strong assumptions.[8] Greater credence can be placed on Bartik's (1985) study of plant locations because he used an edited version of the Dun and Bradstreet data, added a set of regional indicator variables to loosen the assumptions of the model, and constructed an appropriate set of effective tax rates as the ratio of tax collections and business tax bases as estimated by the Advisory Commission on Intergovernmental Relations. Bartik found negative effects of both the corporate tax rate and the property tax rate, but only the effects of the corporate rate were statistically significant.

Several other studies also yielded some significant impacts on business activity of either the property tax or the corporate rate. These studies include one by Hodge (1981) (based on regional investment patterns for four industries) and one by Gyourko (1987) (a long-run equilibrium model of factor intensity). Newman and Sullivan discounted Plaut and Pluta's (1983) finding that fiscal variables exerted no major effects on manufacturing growth between 1967 and 1972 on the grounds that the inclusion of a tax effort variable complicated the interpretation of the other tax variables and that their five-year disequilibrium model ignored major cyclical disruptions of manufacturing during the period.

Studies by Newman (1983) and Helms (1985) also provided evidence that taxes matter. Newman modelled employment growth in 15 two-digit manufacturing industries as a function of changes in relative tax rates across states. He found that changes in employment were affected by changes in relative corporate tax rates in five industries, that capital-intensive industries were more sensitive than labour-intensive industries to changes in rates, and that rapidly expanding industries were more sensitive to changing tax differential than slower-growing or declining industries. Each of these findings is plausible, but the study was somewhat incomplete. First, his focus on employment growth as a measure of capital mobility ignored consideration of the potential substitutability between capital and labour. Second, he did not include changes in labour taxes, local property taxes, or state and local government spending.

Government spending was explicitly modelled in Helms's 1985 study. Helms's introduction of a government budget constraint permitted him to interpret the tax coefficients as the effects of increasing tax receipts to finance

transfer payments, holding other public services constant. In his pooled time-
series model of growth in state personal income, Helms also included both
year variables and shift parameters for each state. These variables account for
time-specific factors, such as secular and cyclical effects, and for state-specific
characteristics, such as climate and available land, that might otherwise bias
the estimates of the fiscal effects. He found that tax increases retarded economic growth when the revenues were used to finance transfer payments.
However, when tax increases were used to finance other public services, such
as education or infrastructure, they made a state more attractive to both firms
and households.

Newman and Sullivan concluded that the tax impact on industrial location,
'should be treated as an open rather than a settled question' and they predicted that new data sets and more sophisticated econometric models, 'will
permit work in this area to proceed at an accelerated pace' (p. 232).

TIMOTHY BARTIK (1991): TAXES MATTER

Newman and Sullivan's prediction was correct. Both in terms of quality and
quantity, work in this area took off in the late 1980s and early 1990s. For
example, Timothy Bartik listed 33 new studies of interstate or interregional
tax effects published after 1986.[9] Together with the 24 studies published
between Carlton's seminal work in 1979 and 1986, Bartik reviewed 57 empirical interstate studies. In addition, he reviewed 25 intrametropolitan or
intrastate studies.

The large number of studies permitted Bartik to take a different approach
from the other authors. Instead of dwelling on the results and limitations of
each individual study, he looked at them in the aggregate and in groups.
Although he acknowledged potential criticisms of individual studies, he con-
vincingly argued that some systematic flaw would have to cut across all
studies for the consensus results to be invalid. In striking contrast to previous
reviewers, he concluded that taxes have quite large and significant effects on
business activity.

Interstate and Interregional Studies

Bartik's analysis is summarized in Table 4.2 (reproduced from Table 1 of
Bartik (1992)). As shown in the first row, 70 per cent of the 57 inter-area
studies reported at least one statistically significant negative effect of taxes on
one measure of business activity, such as employment, output or business
capital. This observation alone suggests that the conventional wisdom that
taxes do not matter deserves to be questioned.

Table 4.2   Summary of results from various types of recent study of state and local taxes on the economic activity of a state or metropolitan area

Type of Study	Percentage of studies with at least one negative and statistically significant tax effect	Mean elasticity of economic activity with respect to taxes (standard error of mean)	95% confidence interval for mean
All studies	70% (57 studies)	−0.25 (0.053) (48 studies)	−0.14 to −0.36
Studies with public service controls	80% (30 studies)	−0.33 (0.085) (25 studies)	−0.15 to −0.51
Studies with fixed effect controls	92% (12 studies)	−0.44 (0.106) (11 studies)	−0.20 to −0.68
Studies with both public service and fixed effect controls	100% (7 studies)	−0.51 (0.134) (6 studies)	−0.17 to −0.85

Note: Figures in parentheses are the number of studies used in calculations. This table is derived from Table 2.3 in *Who Benefits From State and Local Economic Development Policies?* (Bartik, 1991). The elasticity numbers used are the long-run percentage effects on each study's measure of local business activity (employment, and so on) of a 1 per cent increase in all state and local tax measures used in the study. The calculation of the mean elasticity includes all studies in which such an elasticity can be calculated, including studies in which taxes had a positive effect. Studies with public service controls include as a control variable at least one measure of the level of public services for each state or metropolitan area. Studies control for fixed effects by differencing all variables from the previous year's value or the sample mean for that state or metropolitan area, or by including a set of dummy variables for each state or metropolitan area.

Reproduced from Timothy Bartik 1992, Table 1.

To determine the magnitude of the effects, Bartik calculated for each study the implied long-run elasticity of a change in taxes. This elasticity indicates the percentage change in total business activity associated with a given percentage change in all state and local taxes included in the study. This calculation was performed for all studies for which data were available, regardless of whether the tax coefficients were positive or negative or whether they were statistically significant. As reported in column 2, the average elasticity based on 48 studies is −0.25. This result implies that a 10 per cent difference in all state and local taxes is associated with a 2.5 per cent difference in business activity, all other factors held constant. For example, if employment in a state with average taxes was predicted to grow by 20 per cent over a 20-year period, a 10 per cent reduction in all its taxes would increase the predicted growth rate to 22.5 per cent.[10]

In support of the conventional wisdom that taxes do not affect location and investment decisions, people often argue that the repelling effects of taxes are offset by the attracting effects of the public services financed by taxes. Even accounting for the fact that the offset might be imperfect, the failure of researchers to control for differences in services is likely to bias the coefficient of the tax variable towards zero. Support for this view emerges in the second row of Table 4.2. In the 25 studies that control for public spending or services (and for which the elasticity can be calculated), the average elasticity with respect to taxes is –0.33. In other words, as expected, the estimated response of business firms to taxes is greater when services are held constant than when they are not.

Many studies can be criticized for omitting other potential determinants of the location decisions of firms. If these omitted variables are correlated with tax variables, their omission will bias the coefficients of the tax variables. This problem of bias is a particularly serious problem for cross-sectional equilibrium studies because of the difficulty of controlling for all relevant variables given that some of them may be unobserved or unmeasurable. The standard way to avoid the problem is to use panel data – that is, cross-section data from more than one time period – and to include indicator variables for each area represented in the data. Another way to control for the 'fixed effects' associated with each area is to difference all variables from their means or from the previous period's level for each area.

In general, studies that control for the unobservable fixed effects are preferred to those that do not. As shown in the third row of Table 4.2, the average elasticity across the 11 studies that control for fixed effects is –0.44. In other words, more sophisticated studies tend to yield larger estimated responses than less sophisticated studies. The largest average elasticity, –0.51, emerges from the six studies that control for both public services and fixed effects. Based on those studies, we would conclude that a 10 per cent difference in taxes, not accompanied by a difference in services, would, in the long run, change business activity by about 5 per cent.

Adding to the plausibility of Bartik's conclusion is that several recent studies yield additional results that are generally consistent with theoretical expectations. For example, some of the studies indicated that the long-run response of manufacturing employment was much larger than that for non-manufacturing (see Wasylenko and McGuire (1985) and Testa (1989)), as would be predicted given that manufacturing property is typically more footloose and independent of the local market. In addition, Newman (1983) indicated that the negative effect of the corporate tax on employment growth was greater for more capital-intensive industries.

In sum, researchers made tremendous progress during the 1980s in determining the impacts of taxes on economic activity. This new research renders obsolete the old conventional wisdom among economists that taxes have negligible impacts on interstate location decisions. Indeed, taxes appear to have quite large impacts.

Intrametropolitan Studies

Bartik distinguished between two types of intrametropolitan study. The first looks at how taxes affect the relative growth of individual jurisdictions within a region. The second focuses on how taxes affect the growth of the central city compared with the suburbs.

Based on seven studies published since 1979, Bartik concluded that taxes have extraordinarily large effects on the growth of individual jurisdictions. While central cities are included in some of the studies, Bartik argues that the results apply most clearly to suburban jurisdictions. He calculates an average elasticity with respect to the property tax of −1.91.[11] This estimate implies that a 10 per cent cut in local property taxes would increase business activity by 19.1 per cent, which is large enough to generate additional revenue. The small number of studies, plus the great variability in the estimates (from −4.43 to 0.62), suggests that one should not put too much credence on the precise estimate. In addition, one should bear in mind that the cut would be predicted to have this large an impact only if all other factors were held constant, including service levels and tax burdens in surrounding communities. If several communities within a metropolitan area simultaneously reduced their tax rates, the predicted effects of a tax cut in any one community on business activity in that community would be a lot smaller.[12]

Studies that focus on how taxes affect the movement between central cities and suburbs typically yield negligible effects.[13] Only one of four studies (one by Luce and Summers (1987)) finds a statistically significant effect. One explanation for the negligible effect is that central cities may not be very good substitutes for suburban communities. If these results hold up in future studies, they suggest that cities, which need economic development the most, may be the least able to use business tax reductions to achieve it.

A few additional studies of the effects of taxes in big cities are worth noting. Two studies in the 1970s by Ronald Grieson (Grieson *et al.* (1977) and Grieson (1980)) indicated that over a four- to five-year period manufacturing jobs in New York City fell by about 3.5 per cent in response to a 10 per cent rise in taxes and that in Philadelphia both manufacturing and non-manufacturing jobs were quite responsive to the city wage tax – he concluded that jobs in both sectors would fall by about 3–3.5 per cent in response to a 10 per cent increase in taxes. However, subsequent experience in Philadelphia and re-estimation of Grieson's models indicate that he significantly overestimated the effect of taxes on jobs in that city. A subsequent study indicated that a 10 per cent rise in Philadelphia's taxes would lead to a 1–2.5 per cent loss of jobs (see Gruenstein, 1980).

Focusing not on a single city but rather on the experiences of 86 large cities over time, Bradbury and Ladd (1988) shed additional light on the effects of city taxes. Their focus is not on jobs, but rather on the size of the city's property tax base. Their analysis indicates that a 10 per cent increase in property taxes would in the long run reduce city property tax bases on average by 1.5 per cent. Moreover, they found that increases in local income taxes and taxes used by overlying jurisdictions would also reduce the size of a city's property tax base and thereby would reduce revenues from the property tax. Further evidence of the effect of city taxes on city economic activity is reported in Robert Inman's commentary on this chapter.

CONCLUDING REFLECTIONS

During the past 30 years, economists' views about how state and local taxes affect business location and investment decisions have changed quite dramatically. Three hypotheses about the reasons for the change are worth exploring. The first two hypotheses posit a change over time in objective circumstances or in behaviour. The third posits a change in economists' ability to measure behaviour that has remained relatively constant over time.

Possible Explanations

First is the possibility that the change in economists' views reflects greater variation in tax rates in recent years compared with prior years. If tax differentials across relevant locations are small, firms are unlikely to cite taxes as a major determinant of location decisions. This response need not mean that tax differentials would never influence location decisions, only that the existing variation in tax rates was insufficient to influence the location decision. Similarly, small variations in tax rates might lead to statistically insignificant coefficients on tax variables in statistical studies. The standard statistical tool of ordinary least squares yields more precise results when the explanatory variable exhibits wide variation than when it exhibits limited variation. If tax rate differentials were greater in the 1980s than in the 1950s and 1960s, statistical studies based on recent data might yield more precise estimates.

However, tax rate differentials appear to have been declining over time. This conclusion emerges from data on the tax effort made by each state, where tax effort is computed as revenues divided by potential tax bases, for total taxes, corporate income taxes and property taxes for the period 1979 to 1991.[14] Unfortunately, only the corporate tax burden measures business taxes explicitly. Nonetheless, trends in the other two categories are likely to be highly correlated with trends for business burdens. If Alaska and Hawaii are set aside on the grounds that they differ from the other states in significant ways, the coefficient of variation (which measures the variation across states relative to the mean tax effort) declined for each of the three categories of taxes. Specifically, between 1979 and 1991, the coefficient of variation for total taxes declined by 31 per cent, for corporate income taxes by 10 per cent and for total property taxes by 10 per cent. A similar picture emerges across nine regions of the country. In 1979, the average tax effort in the region with the highest average total tax effort exceeded that for the region with the lowest tax effort by 77 per cent; in 1991, the highest region exceeded the lowest region by only 38 per cent. For corporate income taxes, the comparable figures were 248 per cent in 1979 and 153 per cent in 1991. For property taxes, the difference fell from 202 per cent in 1979 to 126 per cent in 1991. My guess is that tax rate differentials within metropolitan areas have also decreased over time as a result of increased intergovernmental aid. Compared with the 1960s and the 1970s, states provided much more aid for local governments, especially for schools, in the 1980s, and much of this aid was designed to equalize fiscal resources across communities.

A second hypothesis is that over time firms may have grown more responsive to tax differentials. This changed response to tax differentials might reflect increased spatial mobility of firms and smaller location-specific differentials in other determinants of location. For example, as markets for certain types of firm expanded from local to national or global markets, firms would be less dependent on local demand conditions. Similarly, changes over time in the types of good produced might reduce the importance of transportation costs or proximity to specialized factors of production such as coal or water. With lower location-specific profits (or in economists' jargon, rents), taxes are more likely to influence behaviour rather than simply to capture location rents. Although the importance of this explanation is hard to gauge, it probably has some validity.

The third and most plausible hypothesis is that the greater sophistication of recent studies makes them more suitable than early studies for determining the location effects of taxes. Clearly, most of the early survey studies were not very effective at eliciting information about effects at the margin, such as how a 10 per cent difference in taxes would have affected the firm's location decision. Moreover, because survey responses do not commit firms to specific behaviour, firms may have incentives to provide strategic responses. The increased emphasis on statistical studies has the advantage of linking taxes to actual decisions of firms.

Early empirical studies were hampered by the absence of a theoretical foundation and various statistical problems. The most dramatic example of how theory matters emerges from the intrametropolitan studies. When no attention was paid to the willingness of communities to permit industrial activity, taxes appeared not to matter. With the addition of that consideration, taxes appeared to matter a lot. A variety of statistical problems hampered the early interstate or interregional studies, especially those based on equilibrium models estimated with cross-sectional data. These problems include the difficulty of measuring many key location factors including taxes, the desirability of accounting for past decisions given the durability of capital and the importance of agglomeration economies, the endogeneity of many key explanatory variables, and the presence of important unobservable characteristics of regions, states and local areas (see Bartik, 1991, pp. 30–36). The increasing capacity of computers and the development of panel data sets have now made it possible for researchers to overcome many of these statistical problems. As noted by Bartik, the more sophisticated studies, particularly those that control for unobservable fixed effects, tend to generate larger tax elasticities than less sophisticated studies.

What Does the New Consensus Mean?

Bartik's elasticities indicate the long-run responses of various forms of business activity to changes in state and local taxes. By themselves, the elasticities tell us little about the relative importance of taxes as a determinant of the spatial distribution of business activity. That is, they do not answer the question: how much of the current spatial distribution of business activity can be explained by tax differentials? To answer that question the information on elasticities would need to be combined with information on the variation in tax rates.

The new consensus that taxes affect location decisions is more directly useful for understanding the behaviour of state policy-makers. The greater the elasticity of firm response, the greater is the incentive for states to keep their tax rates similar. Somewhat ironically, similarity in tax rates across jurisdictions probably indicates not that taxes do not matter, but rather that they matter a lot.

Finally, the new consensus suggests that, contrary to the old conventional wisdom of economists, state tax policies designed to promote economic development could potentially be effective in some situations. However, as discussed in the next chapter, their effectiveness is not assured. It depends on how such programmes are structured, how other jurisdictions respond and on the costs of such programmes relative to their benefits.

NOTES

1. Because all costs are deductible from federal taxable income, net taxes are the same share of net costs as gross taxes are of gross costs.
2. Oakland's survey was originally presented at a 1974 conference. Consequently, he ends the literature survey in 1974, not in 1978 as might be indicated by the year of publication.
3. The reference here is to various unpublished reports for the Center for Mathematical Studies in Business and Economics, University of Chicago. Subsequent reviews refer to his 1979 and 1983 published papers.
4. See Wheaton (1983) for measurement of business tax burdens. Also see the discussion in Fisher (1996, pp. 613–17). As emphasized by Bartik (1991, p. 33), failure to measure business tax burdens correctly tends to bias their coefficients in statistical studies towards zero.
5. The locations are equilibrium locations only in the sense that the costs of moving are greater than the gains from moving. The existence of transactions costs suggests that the resulting pattern would differ from the pattern that would be made *de novo*.
6. In addition, one must worry about the statistical problem of simultaneity that occurs when an explanatory variable, such as a tax rate, is affected by the dependent variable, the level of business activity.
7. In particular, they criticized the assumption that industrial sites were elastically supplied and noted that the equations were not statistically identified.
8. The models require the strong assumptions implicit in a conditional logit model.
9. I chose 1986 as the cut-off date because Newman and Sullivan's article was completed in 1986 even though it was not published until 1988.
10. The standard error of 0.053 implies that if additional studies were undertaken, the probability is 95 per cent that the mean elasticity will fall in the range from –0.14 to 0.36.
11. This figure is reported in Bartik (1991) Table 2.3. It differs slightly from the –1.76 figure reported in Bartik (1992). The –1.91 average is consistent with the elasticities reported for individual studies in Bartik (1991, Appendix 2.2).
12. For evidence that communities may mimic the tax policies of surrounding jurisdictions, see Ladd (1992).
13. This paragraph is based on Bartik (1992, p. 108).
14. The following figures are based on data by state calculated by the US Advisory Commission on Intergovernmental Relations (ACIR, various years). The potential tax base for each tax for each state measures the size of a uniformly defined tax base in the state and is independent of how the state defines the tax base. Since tax effort is calculated as the ratio of revenues to the potential tax base rather than to the actual tax base, it measures the average effective tax burden in the state. Because states vary in how broadly they define specific tax bases, use of the ratio of revenues to the actual tax base or, alternatively, of nominal tax rates, would give a misleading picture of the variation in tax burdens across states.

REFERENCES

Bartik, Timothy J. (1985), 'Business location decisions in the United States: estimates of the effects of unionization, taxes, and other characteristics of states', *Journal of Business & Economic Statistics*, **3** (1), 14–22.

Bartik, Timothy J. (1991), *Who Benefits from State and Local Economic Development Policies?*, Kalamazoo, Michigan: W. E. Upjohn Institute for Employment Research.

Bartik, Timothy J. (1992), 'The effects of state and local taxes on economic development: a review of recent research', *Economic Development Quarterly*, February, 103–11.

Beaton, Charles R. and Young P. Joun (1968), *The Effect of the Property Tax on Manufacturing Location*, Fullerton, CA.: California State College.

Bradbury, Katharine L. and Helen F. Ladd (1988), 'City property taxes: the effects of economic change and competitive pressures', *New England Economic Review*, July/August, 22–36.

Bradford, David F. and Harry H. Kelejian (1973), 'An econometric model of the flight to the suburbs', *Journal of Political Economy*, **81** (3), 566–89.

Carlton, Dennis W. (1979), 'Why do new firms locate where they do?: an econometric model', in W.C. Wheaton (ed.), *Interregional Movements and Regional Growth*, Washington, DC: The Urban Institute.

Carlton, Dennis W. (1983), 'The location and employment choices of new firms: an econometric model with discrete and continuous endogenous variables', *Review of Economics and Statistics*, **65** (3), 440–49.

Charney, A.H. (1983), 'Intraurban manufacturing location decisions and local tax differentials', *Journal of Urban Econometrics*, **14**, 184–205.

Due, John F. (1961), 'Studies of state–local tax influences on location of industry', *National Tax Journal*, **14**, 163–73.

Fischel, William A. (1975), 'An evaluation of proposals for metropolitan sharing of commercial and industrial property tax base', *Journal of Urban Economics*, **3**, 253–63.

Fisher, Ronald C. (1996), *State and Local Public Finance*, Chicago: Irwin.

Fox, William F. (1973), *Property Tax Influences on Industrial Location within a Metropolitan Area: A Report for the Department of Economics and Community Development*, Columbus: State of Ohio.

Fox, William F. (1981), 'An evaluation of metropolitan area tax base sharing: a comment', *National Tax Journal*, **34**, 275–9.

Grieson, Ronald E. (1980), 'Theoretical analysis and empirical measurements of the effects of the Philadelphia income tax', *Journal of Urban Economics*, **8**, 123–37.

Grieson, Ronald E., William Hamovitch, Albert M. Levenson and Richard D. Morgenstern (1977), 'The effect of business taxation on the location of industry', *Journal of Urban Economics*, **4**, 170–85.

Gruenstein, John (1980), 'Jobs in the city: can Philadelphia afford to raise taxes?', *Business Review*, Federal Reserve Bank of Philadelphia, May/June, 3–11.

Gyourko, Joseph (1987), 'Effects of local tax structures on the factor intensity composition of manufacturing activity across cities', *Journal of Urban Economics*, **22**, 151–64.

Helms, L. Jay (1985), 'The effect of state and local taxes on economic growth: a time-series-cross section approach', *The Review of Economics and Statistics*, **67** (4), 574–82.

Hodge, J.H. (1981), 'A study of regional investment decisions', in J.V. Henderson (ed.), *Research in Urban Economics*, Vol. 1, Greenwich, CT: JAI Press.

Ladd, Helen F. (1992), 'Mimicking of local tax burdens among neighboring counties', *Public Finance Quarterly*, **20** (4), October, 450–67.

Newman, Robert J. (1983), 'Industry migration and growth in the South', *Review of Economics & Statistics*, **65**, 76–86.

Newman, Robert and Dennis Sullivan (1988), 'Econometric analysis of business tax impacts on industrial location: what do we know and how do we know it?', *Journal of Urban Economics*, **23**, 215–34.

Oakland, William H. (1978), 'Local taxes and intraurban industrial location: a survey', Chapter 1 from *Metropolitan Financing and Growth Management Policies*, Proceedings of a Symposium Sponsored by the Committee on Taxation, Resources and Economic Development (TRED) at the University of Wisconsin, Madison, pp. 13–30.

Plaut, T.R. and J.E. Pluta (1983), 'Business climate, taxes and expenditures, and state industrial growth in the United States', *Southern Economic Journal*, **49**, 99–119.

Schmenner, Roger W. (1973), 'City taxes and industry location', *1973 Proceedings National Tax Association–Tax Institute of America*, Columbus, Ohio: NTA–TIA.

Summers, Anita A. and Thomas F. Luce (1985), *Economic Report on the Philadelphia Metropolitan Area*, Philadelphia: University of Pennsylvania Press.

Testa, William A. (1989), 'Metro Area Growth from 1976 to 1985: Theory and Evidence', Working Paper, Federal Reserve Bank of Chicago (January).

Wassmer, Robert (1994), 'Can local incentives alter a metropolitan city's economic development?', *Urban Studies*, **31** (8), 1251–78.

Wasylenko, Michael J. (1980), 'Evidence of fiscal differentials and intrametropolitan firm relocation', *Land Economics*, **56** (3), 339–49.

Wasylenko, Michael (1981), 'The location of firms: the role of taxes and fiscal incentives', *Urban Affairs Annual Reviews*, **20**, 155–89.

Wasylenko, Michael and Therese McGuire (1985), 'Jobs and taxes: the effect of business climate on states' employment growth rates', *National Tax Journal*, **38** (4), 497–511.

Wheaton, William C. (1983), 'Interstate differences in the level of business taxation', *National Tax Journal*, **36** (1), 83–94.

COMMENT

Robert P. Inman

Taxes impose burdens on households and firms and discourage economic activity. Helen Ladd's survey chapter summarizes the latest estimates of these adverse effects of state and local taxes on economic activity, finding that the effects within a single political jurisdiction are often significant, both statistically and quantitatively. Contemporary evidence that taxes negatively affect economic activity appears strongest and most convincing for suburban jurisdictions within a metropolitan area and for states. Ladd's survey notes that convincing evidence on the effects of taxation in large cities is largely lacking. What evidence that does exist generally shows only small effects.[1]

As part of a larger study of fiscal policy in large US cities, Steven Craig, Andrew Haughwout, Thomas Luce and I have completed estimates of the effects of taxes on economic activity within three cities: Houston, Minneapolis and Philadelphia.[2] Like recent studies for states and suburbs, our large-city studies find potentially significant negative effects of taxes on economic activity.

Philadelphia raises revenues from three taxes: (1) a uniform property tax on business and household property; (2) business taxes on business gross receipts and business profit income; and (3) a wage tax on wages earned by residents and by non-residents working within the city. Houston and Minneapolis raise most city tax revenues from two taxes: a property tax on residents and a separate property tax on business property. Separate tax base equations were estimated for each city, based on available data from the late 1960s to the early 1990s. For each city, variations in city tax base were explained by a structural time trend in economic activity, by annual economic activity within the city – unemployment in Philadelphia, population growth and the oil shock in Houston, and unemployment and a period of (exogenous) downtown development during the 1980s in Minneapolis – and by the level of city tax rates in the previous fiscal year. Each tax base equation was estimated to correct for possible serial correlation over time in the omitted factors affecting city tax bases. Each estimated tax base equation revealed a statistically significant negative effect of lagged city tax rates on the level of affected economic activity within the city. Are the estimated effects important economically?

To answer this question, revenue hills relating tax rates to tax revenues per capita were specified from the estimated tax base equations for each tax in each sample city. Figures 4.1 to 4.3 report the estimated revenue hills for each city and the tax rate which can produce the maximum revenue for the city, specified for the last year of each city's sample. Actual tax rates for each tax in that last sample year are also reported in Figures 4.1 to 4.3.

a: Wage tax revenue

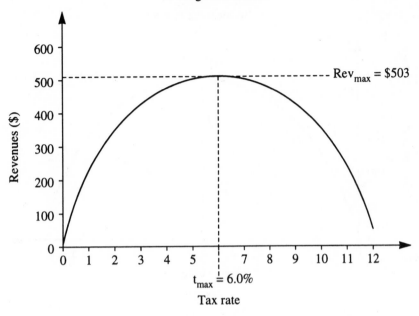

b: Property tax revenues

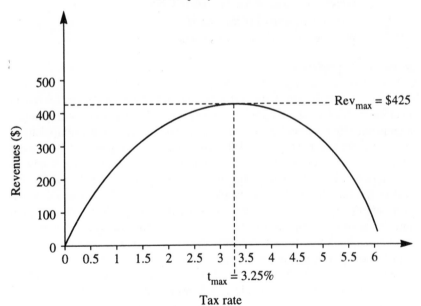

Figure 4.1   Revenue hills for Philadelphia

c: Business tax revenues

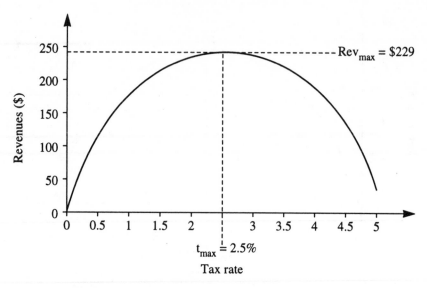

FY 1990 tax rates
Weighted average wage tax rate = 4.765
Effective property tax rate = 2.48
Weighted average business tax rate = 1.50

Figure 4.1   continued

Figures 4.2 and 4.3 illustrate that Houston and Minneapolis have room to manoeuvre fiscally; these cities can increase their tax rates and still generate significant city revenues in the long run. Figure 4.1 shows that Philadelphia in 1990 could not. Facing a projected fiscal deficit in fiscal year 1991 of $204 million, the city was estimated to be able to raise (in equilibrium) only an additional $135 million through tax increases (Inman, 1992). Given this reality, the fact that Wall Street would not finance the $204 projected deficit with additional short-term borrowing was hardly surprising. The city went into 'state receivership' as a consequence. While there are several causes of the Philadelphia fiscal crisis, certainly the 19 tax increases over the previous 15 years did not help (Inman, 1995).

Our time-series results summarized here show a significant negative effect of tax rate on tax base in three large US cities and illustrates the validity of Ladd's three conjectures for the observed growing importance of taxes on tax base. First, the last 30 years have shown significant changes in the economic

a: Resident property tax revenues

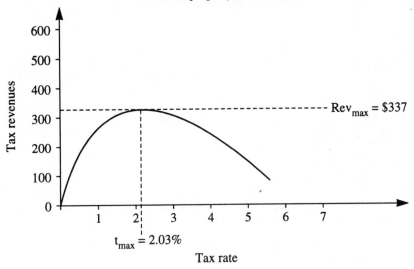

b: Business property tax revenues

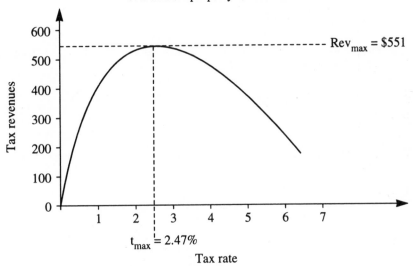

FY 1993 tax rates
Effective residential property tax rate = 2.28
Effective business property tax rate = 2.28

Figure 4.2   Revenue hills for Houston

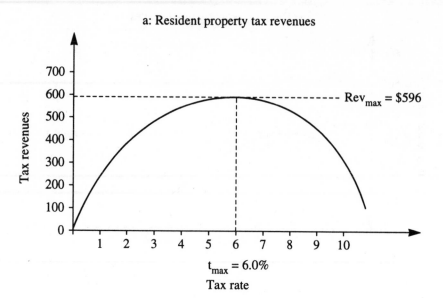

a: Resident property tax revenues

$t_{max} = 6.0\%$

$Rev_{max} = \$596$

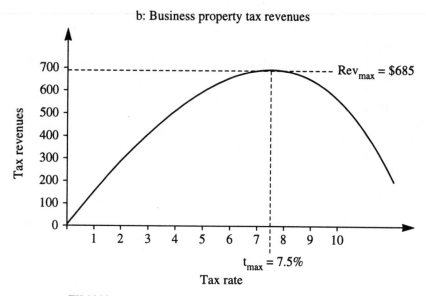

b: Business property tax revenues

$t_{max} = 7.5\%$

$Rev_{max} = \$685$

FY 1992 tax rates
Effective residential property tax rate = 1.48
Effective business property tax rate = 5.15

Figure 4.3   Revenue hills for Minneapolis

fortunes of large US cities. If public services demands are inelastic with respect to income, tax rates must change. The consequence has been significant variations in tax rates over the past 30 years, sufficient to reveal an underlying sensitivity of economic activities – most likely those of businesses and upper income households – to tax changes. Second, Ladd suggests that firms' investment and location decisions may have become more sensitive to taxation in recent years. This certainly seems reasonable for large cities as the service and communication 'revolutions' have reduced the agglomeration advantages of large-city locations. Finally, Ladd notes the failure of previous econometric studies of tax effects to control adequately for important cross-state, cross-region or cross-location variations in zoning laws, and other 'unobservables' may conceal the true effects of taxes on economic activities within a given locality. The within-city time-series analyses in our study are one attempt to minimize these problems. It is encouraging that our estimated effects of tax rates on tax base reported here are well within the elasticity bounds reported in the 1991 survey by Bartik and summarized in Ladd's review. Perhaps there is a consensus emerging on this important issue after all.

Notes

1. Ladd's survey does not include three studies, by Grieson *et al.* on New York City (1977) and Philadelphia (1980) and by Gruenstein (1980) on Philadelphia, each of which finds a significant effect of business taxes on business activity.
2. A longer research paper detailing our estimates is available upon request. In that paper we report preliminary estimates of the effects of tax rates on tax base for New York City as well. Though preliminary, the New York City results appear consistent with the conclusion from Philadelphia, Houston and Minneapolis that tax rates do have adverse effects on the levels of economic activity within the city.

References

Bartik, Timothy (1991), *Who Benefits from State and Local Economic Development Policies?*, Kalamazoo, Michigan: Upjohn Institute for Employment Research.
Grieson, Ronald E. (1980), 'Theoretical analysis and empirical measurements of the effects of the Philadelphia income tax', *Journal of Urban Economics*, **8**, 123–37.
Grieson, Ronald E., William Hamovitch, Alfred M. Levenson and Richard D. Morgenstern (1977), 'The effect of business taxation on the location of industry', *Journal of Urban Economics*, **4**, 170–85.
Gruenstein, J. (1980), 'Jobs in the city: can Philadelphia afford to raise taxes?', *Business Review*, Federal Reserve Bank of Philadelphia, May/June, 3–11.
Inman, Robert P. (1992), 'Can Philadelphia escape its fiscal crisis with a tax increase?', *Business Review*, Federal Reserve Bank of Philadelphia, September/October, 5–20.
Inman, Robert P. (1995), 'How to have a fiscal crisis: lessons from Philadelphia', *American Economic Review*, **85**, 378–82.

COMMENT

Michelle J. White

Chapter 4 discusses how the conventional wisdom concerning the effects of taxes on economic activity has changed over the period between John Due's survey article of 1961 and Timothy Bartik's survey article of 1992. Due argued that taxes don't affect the location of industry, while Bartik argued that taxes do matter. The idea that firm location has become more sensitive to taxes over the past 30 or 40 years is intuitively appealing. The essential reason is that first-order effects on firm location – such as wages and the cost of land – vary less across locations now than they did in the past. Because firms have become more 'footloose' since the 1940s and 1950s, second-order effects – such as taxes – probably have become more important. Thus both Due and Bartik may be correct.

This comment tells several stories about why firms have become more footloose over time, making firm location more susceptible to the influence of tax differentials. Influences on *intra*metropolitan location of firms are addressed first, and influences on *inter*metropolitan location of firms second. The final section discusses how agglomeration effects make taxes a more potent influence on firm location.

Factors Affecting Firms' Intrametropolitan Location Choice

Firms have become more footloose within metropolitan areas because, over the past 50 years, workers have shifted from commuting by public transportation to commuting by car. In addition, the cost of goods transportation has fallen. Consider a metropolitan area in which all workers initially commute via a fixed rail transit system. The transit system consists of a set of radial lines running from the central business district (CBD) to the suburbs. A firm located in the CBD is considering moving to the suburbs of the same metropolitan area. Normally, when firms move out of the CBD, they benefit from both lower land costs and lower wages. However, since all workers commute by rail, the firm must remain within walking distance of a rail station. But land near rail stations is relatively scarce and expensive, so that the firm will not benefit very much from lower land prices by moving out of the CBD. In addition, workers are only willing to work for lower wages if they save on commuting.

In Figure 4.4, suppose the firm moves from the CBD to a location five miles south of the CBD along the southern rail line. Workers who live along the southern rail line but more than five miles from the CBD save ten miles of round-trip commuting each day if they work for the firm at its suburban location. These workers, who live in the region denoted *AB* in Figure 4.4, are

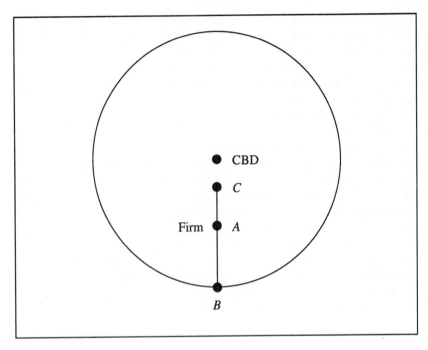

Figure 4.4   Commuting region – rail only

willing to work for the firm for a daily wage equal to their wage at the CBD minus the cost of commuting ten miles per day.

However, relatively few workers live in the region *AB*, so that the firm may wish to hire additional workers. In order to do so, it must raise its wage. Raising its wage slightly causes a few workers who live along the southern rail line but closer to the CBD than the firm to be willing to out-commute to the firm. Thus the firm's commuting region increases from *AB* to the slightly larger *CB* in Figure 4.4. But if the firm wishes to hire even more workers, then it must pay enough to make workers who live along other rail lines willing to commute inward to the CBD and then outward along the southern rail line to the firm. Since changing lines is time-consuming, the firm is likely to have to pay an even higher wage than the wage at the CBD in order to induce workers who live along other rail lines to commute to it. Thus unless firms are small, they get little or no benefit in terms of lower wages when they move out of the CBD. If large firms move to the suburbs, they are likely to have to pay wages that are higher than CBD wages in order to attract enough workers.

Now suppose some workers shift to commuting by car. This means that suburban sites which were inaccessible by public transportation become potential locations for firms because workers can reach these sites by car. As a result, the number of sites suitable for use by firms rises and the cost of suburban sites therefore falls. (The opportunity cost of suburban sites becomes its value for residential use, not its value for use by other firms.) Since workers commute to the firm by car rather than by rail, the firm's commuting region increases in size.

In Figure 4.5, suppose first that the firm again locates five miles south of the CBD, at point *D*. If the firm pays a daily wage equal to the wage at the CBD minus the cost to workers of commuting ten miles, then workers again will only be willing to commute to the firm from the commuting region *DE*, since only workers living in the region *DE* save ten miles of commuting by working at the firm. But now suppose the firm raises its wage. Then its commuting region spreads out in all directions to cover a region such as *FEH*. As the firm continues to raise its wage, its commuting region spreads out even further in all directions. Thus when commuting is by car rather than by public transportation, workers living in a larger geographic region are willing to commute to the suburban firm at location *D* for any given wage, and a given increase in the suburban firm's wage causes a larger increase in the number of workers willing to work at location *D*. As a result,

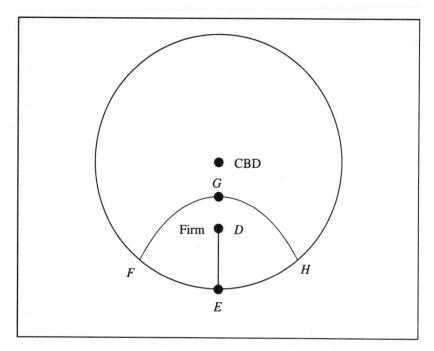

Figure 4.5   Commuting region – rail and car

suburban wages fall and moving to the suburbs becomes more attractive to firms.[1]

Further, these two trends are self-reinforcing. As more workers commute by car, firms have a greater incentive to locate at suburban sites that aren't accessible by public transportation. However, as more firms locate at sites that aren't accessible by public transportation, workers who still commute by public transportation have a greater incentive to shift to commuting by car. Over the postwar period, there has been a major shift from workers commuting by public transportation to commuting by car. Between 1950 and 1990, the number of trips by public transportation fell by half, from 17.2 million to 8.9 million trips per year. Over the same period, the number of miles of travel by car in urban areas increased more than seven-fold, from 184 to 1410 billion miles per year.

A similar story applies to movement of goods in cities. In the past, the cost of transporting goods was higher than the cost of transporting workers, which made it economically efficient for firms to locate at the CBD and workers to locate around the firms. Over time the cost of transporting both goods and workers has fallen, but the former has probably fallen more than the latter, which tends to make it economically efficient for firms to decentralize. In addition, goods that are imported to, or exported from, cities previously moved by railroad and ship, which made it efficient for firms to locate at the CBD where the port and the railroad terminal are. But today goods move by road and by air, and freeways and airports are located in the suburbs. Thus firms benefit from lower costs of goods transportation when they move out of the CBD.[2]

The result of these shifts is that firms have become footloose – they can locate anywhere within metropolitan areas where local zoning permits. By moving to the suburbs, firms benefit from lower land prices and lower wages. However, they can get these benefits anywhere in the metropolitan area. So the decision as to where to locate can depend on secondary concerns such as the level of taxes.

Factors Affecting Firms' Intermetropolitan Location Choice

An analogous story suggests that firms have become more footloose in terms of moving between metropolitan areas as well as within metropolitan areas. The main reason is that metropolitan areas outside the Northeast and Midwest are generally more like suburbs than central cities. Thus just as many firms found it profitable to move from the CBDs to the suburbs of older metropolitan areas in the Northeast and Midwest, they also now find it profitable to move from these older metropolitan areas to large and small urban areas in other regions.

Other factors have also reduced the advantages to firms of locating in the older metropolitan areas and made firms more footloose generally. One of these is the reduction in the real cost of air conditioning. Air conditioning has made the metropolitan areas of the Sunbelt – regions with basically unbearable climates in pre-air-conditioning days – bearable and even desirable.

Another is the revolution in telecommunications and computing. Cheap long-distance calls, overnight mail, faxes and video conferencing make it less important for firms to locate near their bankers, their lawyers and their advertising firms. Even if firms' headquarters remain in the central city, cheap and fast data transmission allows firms to move their back office bookkeeping operations out of their expensive headquarters locations and to the suburbs, to other metropolitan areas or even overseas.

The vast increase in the movement of goods by road and air is an additional factor. When railroads, barges and ships were virtually the only ways to transport goods, it was best for firms to locate in the cities of the Northeast and Midwest, which mostly are either ports or on navigable rivers and are served by a dense railroad network. But freeways and airports are much more evenly distributed. Thus firms can move to smaller cities and still have good access to freeways and an airport. They may even find that the cost of goods transport falls because there is less congestion. Similarly, newer metropolitan areas are less likely to have well-developed public transportation systems. In the past, when most workers commuted by public transportation, this was a disadvantage. But when workers commute by car, the lack of a public transportation system is no longer a drawback.

Fourth, the older metropolitan areas in the Northeast and Midwest have strict zoning and many environmental regulations, both of which add to firms' costs of production. In contrast, newer metropolitan areas in the Sunbelt usually have less regulation, so that costs of production are lower.

Agglomeration Economies, Taxes and Firm Location

The stories already discussed suggest that the agglomeration economies which result from firms locating in the central cities of older metropolitan areas have diminished over time, thus reducing firms' incentives to remain in central locations. However, agglomeration economies have not disappeared entirely and they still affect firm location patterns. For example, firms in the computer business benefit from locating in the Silicon Valley area because they can hire experienced computer scientists and programmers without having to bear the cost of training them. However, firms can benefit from these agglomeration economies without locating in close physical proximity – Silicon Valley covers a large area. This means that firms can potentially locate in many different communities while benefiting from the Silicon Valley area agglomeration economies.

The existence of agglomeration economies makes firm location patterns subject to problems of multiple equilibria and, as a result, firm location may be quite strongly responsive to taxes. This encourages individual communities within a metropolitan area to engage in tax competition in order to attract firms choosing locations within a metropolitan area, and also encourages states or cities to engage in tax competition to attract firms choosing locations across regions.

To be concrete, suppose there are two firms, 1 and 2, and two locations, A and B. The two locations are assumed to be in different communities, but the communities could be located in a single metropolitan area or in different metropolitan areas or regions. Firm 1 and firm 2 are both assumed to be better off if they locate at the same place than if they locate at different places. (For example, firm 1 might be a supplier to firm 2, so that they benefit from locating near each other.) Table 4.3 gives firm 1's and firm 2's profit for all four possible location patterns. Agglomeration economies make the two firms' combined profits higher if both locate at the same place than if they locate at different places, but agglomeration economies are stronger in community A than community B. Thus combined profits are 8 if both firms locate at A, 7 if both firms locate at B, and only 4 if either firm locates at A and the other at B. The most efficient outcome is for both firms to locate in community A. (Note that either firm 1 or firm 2 could be viewed as representing several firms rather than a single firm.)

Table 4.3   Profits by location

		Firm 2	
		Community A	Community B
Firm 1	Community A	5,3	2,2
	Community B	2,2	3,4

Now suppose firm 1 chooses its location first. Suppose that firm 1 chooses location A since its highest profit occurs there. Firm 2 chooses its location second and, given that firm 1 has already chosen A, the best strategy for firm 2 is also to choose location A. Thus the location pattern in this case is economically efficient. But now suppose that firm 2 chooses first. Suppose that firm 2 chooses location B since its highest profit occurs there. Firm 1 chooses second and, given that firm 2 has already chosen *B,* the best strategy for firm 1 is also to choose *B.* Thus the location pattern is less efficient, since combined profits are lower at *B* than at *A.* In the absence of taxes, there are two equilibria to the location game: both firms locating at *A* and both firms locating at *B.* If the game is played many times, sometimes firms such as firm 1 will choose first and the outcome will be efficient, while sometimes firms such as firm 2 will choose first and the outcome will be less efficient. But the least efficient outcomes, in which the two firms locate in different communities, never occur.

Now introduce taxes and interjurisdictional competition into the model. Because of agglomeration economies, communities have an incentive to compete for firms by offering tax breaks, and the location pattern is likely to be sensitive to these inducements. Consider three scenarios.

In the first, firm 2 chooses its location first. Without a subsidy, suppose that it chooses location *B.* But now suppose that community *A* offers firm 2 a subsidy of 1 or more, in which case firm 2 will choose location *A* rather than location *B.* Then firm 1 will also choose location *A,* assuming that no community offers it a subsidy. Thus the effect of tax competition is to cause both firms to locate at *A* rather than at *B.* Since the tax subsidy causes both firms to move from *B* to *A,* it improves economic efficiency.

However, tax competition may also cause worse rather than better outcomes to occur. In scenario 2, suppose firm 1 chooses first. Firm 1 will choose location *A* if there is no tax subsidy, but it will choose location *B* if community *B* offers a subsidy of 2 or more. If firm 1 chooses *B,* then firm 2 will also choose *B,* assuming that no tax subsidies are offered. Thus in this case tax competition causes both firms to move from *A* to *B,* with a resulting loss in economic efficiency.

Finally in the third scenario, firm 1 chooses first and locates at *A,* but then community *B* offers firm 2 a tax subsidy of 1 or more to locate at *B* rather than *A.* Now the outcome is that the two firms separate: firm 1 locates at *A* and firm 2 locates at *B.* As a result, combined profits fall from 8, if both located at *A,* to only 4 if firm 1 locates at *A* and firm 2 locates at *B.* The loss in profits is greater than in the previous example because there are no agglomeration economies if the two firms separate. An important result in this case is that a tax subsidy which costs community *B* as little as 1 causes the two firms to incur a combined loss of profits of 4. This is because firm 2 and community *B* ignore the large loss of profits suffered by firm 1 as a result of firm 2 locating elsewhere.

Why does community *B* act as a spoiler in this scenario? In reality, location games are played out repeatedly rather than just once. Thus when community *B* offers a tax subsidy to firm 2, its officials may view themselves as playing a different game than that depicted in Table 4.3. They view themselves as playing a game with some other community, *C,* in which communities *B* and *C* are both competing to attract their first firm in order to start themselves on the road to establishing agglomeration economies within their communities. These examples, simple as they are, capture important aspects of why communities engage in tax competition. Because of agglomeration economies, a relatively small tax subsidy to the first firm to locate in a particular community may result in many other firms choosing the same community, even if no subsidies (or only small subsidies) are offered to later firms. Thus communities have an incentive to subsidize early firms to locate within their borders in the hope of establishing agglomeration economies which will attract later firms. These effects were captured in the first and second scenarios just discussed and they showed that tax competition may either enhance or reduce efficiency. However, in the third scenario, tax competition prevents agglomeration economies from ever developing because competing communities that have few firms offer tax subsidies to attract their first firms. The resulting competition causes firms to spread out over multiple locations, even though they would all be better off if they concentrated in a few locations. Thus tax competition may prevent agglomeration economies from ever developing.

Notes

1. See White (1988, 1996) and Wieand (1987) for further discussion.
2. See Mills (1972) and Fujita and Ogawa (1982) for models which determine the optimal spatial location of firms and households in cities. White (1996) contains a review of this literature.

References

Fujita, M. and H. Ogawa (1982), 'Multiple equilibria and structural transition of nonmonocentric urban configurations', *Regional Science and Urban Economics,* **12,** 161–96.

Mills, E.S. (1972), *Studies in the Structure of the Urban Economy,* Baltimore, Maryland: Johns Hopkins University Press.

White, M.J. (1988), 'Urban commuting is not "wasteful"', *Journal of Political Economy,* **96,** 1097–1110.

White, M.J. (1996), 'Urban areas with decentralized employment: theory and empirical work', in Paul Cheshire and Edwin S. Mills (eds), *Handbook of Applied Urban Economics,* Amsterdam: North-Holland.

Wieand, K. (1987), 'An extension of the monocentric urban spatial equilibrium model to a multi-center setting: the case of the two-center city', *Journal of Urban Economics,* **21,** 259–71.

5. Tax policies to promote economic development

Helen F. Ladd

Tax instruments are frequently used as explicit tools of land policy. As discussed in Chapter 7, the goal is sometimes to limit development to preserve open space. In other situations the goal is to promote more intensive use of the land by encouraging economic development. This chapter focuses on two of the strategies used by local governments to promote local economic development, particularly in metropolitan areas.[1] One strategy is to provide tax abatements to new or expanding firms for a specified period of years. A second, related, strategy is to target the tax relief to spatially defined areas, often referred to as enterprise zones. Other tax policies to promote development include reducing the property taxes on improvements relative to taxes on land, a strategy currently used only by Pittsburgh and a few other Pennsylvania cities, and financing the public infrastructure needed for economic development from the tax increments generated by the development. These two strategies are described and evaluated in Chapters 6 and 9.

TAX ABATEMENTS

Tax abatements can be viewed as 'tax expenditures' in that the same economic development goals could be achieved through the expenditure side of the budget. For example, giving a firm a tax abatement is comparable to taxing the firm at the full tax rate and then appropriating money to subsidize the firm's investment decision. Typically, tax expenditures receive less public scrutiny than comparable subsidies appropriated as expenditures. This lack of scrutiny may help to account for the widespread use of tax abatements by local governments despite the conventional wisdom of economists that many of them are not very effective.

In principle one should judge the effectiveness of tax abatements in the same way one would judge the effectiveness of any economic development strategy, namely by comparing the costs of the abatement with the benefits.

The difficulty arises in identifying and measuring the benefits. A natural starting point is to ask whether the programme has any impact on investment and jobs in the local community. The technical challenge here is to isolate the impacts that can be attributed to the programme from those that would have occurred without the programme. Depending on the goals of the programme, a second task often involves translating these impacts into effects on residents in the targeted area. An increase in local economic activity need not improve the welfare of disadvantaged local residents. It may simply provide new jobs to non-residents or may show up in higher land prices.

Third, one might want to ask the most difficult question of all, namely whether the programme has a net positive impact from a national, in contrast to a local, perspective. To the extent that it simply transfers economic activity from one area to another, it may provide no net benefits to the nation. However, as Bartik (1991, pp. 191–2) and others have argued, a movement of activity from a high to a low employment area may be beneficial since the social costs of losing a job from a tight labour market may be less than the social benefits of gaining a job in a market with a surplus of labour. Although this national perspective is clearly important for federal policy-makers considering programmes such as nationally supported enterprise zones, further discussion of the national perspective is outside the scope of this review.

Most of the studies summarized below focus on the local impacts. While none of the studies performs a full benefit–cost analysis, some of them provide useful information on the cost-effectiveness of the programmes by reporting, for example, the cost per job created. Somewhat surprisingly, a number of the studies take a much narrower perspective and focus on budgetary impacts alone.

The effects of tax abatements on jobs and investment are often hard to detect. The main problem is that tax abatements often apply to such a small fraction of the city's economic activity that their effects are likely to be too small to discern from aggregate data. When abatement programmes are targeted to small geographic areas, the detection problem becomes less severe in that impacts could be sufficiently large relative to total economic activity in the target area to be observable. The challenge in this case becomes one of determining what would have happened in the absence of the abatement programme. (See below for evidence on the success of enterprise zones).

An alternative to examining outcomes in specific areas is to make inferences about the success of tax abatement strategies from the evidence on the location and investment effects of firms (as summarized in Chapter 4). Thus one could take the estimated long-run elasticities of the effects of taxes on local economic activity and determine what they imply for the cost per job. Bartik's calculations (Bartik, 1992, p. 106) suggest a cost of $1906 to $10 800 per job per year, costs that are not out of the feasible range. One would need to determine the value of a new job and to compare the costs of alternative ways of achieving it. While a useful first step, this approach is limited in that it provides at best average impacts. The evaluation of a particular programme would require more specific estimates of effects.

Ironically, Bartik's finding of large tax elasticities at the intrametropolitan level (among suburban jurisdictions only) implies that tax abatements are not an appropriate tool for suburban jurisdictions to use to influence the location decisions of firms. The potential response of firms is sufficiently large that action by one suburban community is likely to induce retaliatory responses from other communities, with the net effect of the competition for jobs through the tax code being lower taxes in the metropolitan region as a whole. While these lower taxes could encourage some additional investment in the region, the response is likely to be sufficiently low that the cost per new job is likely to be high.

Interestingly, many of the empirical studies of specific tax abatement programmes focus not on the broad social benefits from the subsidies, but rather only on their fiscal effects.[2] Consistent with the theoretical model of fiscal zoning, the idea is that communities seek industrial property specifically to increase tax revenue. From this narrow pecuniary perspective, an abatement programme is deemed successful if the revenue generated by the induced investment and higher land values (net of the cost of providing additional services) exceeds the revenue loss from the abatement.

Illustrative of this approach is a 1986 study of Ohio's Community Reinvestment Tax Exemption Law (Morse and Farmer, 1986). By comparing expected net revenues with and without an abatement, the authors found that the abatements would be self-financing if 8.8 per cent or more of the local investment could be attributed to the abatement. Based on survey data from firms receiving abatements, they concluded that 25 per cent of all investments were affected by abatements. Hence they concluded that the use of abatements by Ohio communities was rational in that it increased net revenue (ignoring, however, any increased costs of providing public services). However, as they point out, the required 8.8 per cent response depends crucially on the institutional fact that Ohio's state school aid formula rewards communities using abatements with more school aid. Without such aid, the 25 per cent observed response rate would have fallen short of the 41.7 per cent impact on investment that would have been required to make the abatements rational.

Although Wolkoff (1985) paid lip-service to a variety of potential benefits from abatements, he, too, based his main policy conclusions on consideration of revenues alone. Using data for Detroit between 1970 and 1979, Wolkoff estimated various equations from which he simulated the effects of tax abatements given to firms in that city. Specifically, for four different investment series, he estimated the response of investment to the user cost of capital, and then used the estimated elasticity to simulate the effect of a 100 per cent property tax abatement. Based on an elasticity of –0.5 (the middle of his estimated range), he found that full abatement of property taxes would increase capital investment in Detroit by only 2 per cent. In addition, he found that property tax abatements had at most a small impact on the probability that investment would occur. These small impacts imply that the costs of across-the-board abatement awards cannot be justified in terms of the additional revenue that they generate. This conclusion led Wolkoff to argue that the city should tailor abatements by firm, with larger abatements being targeted to the firms more likely to be responsive to the tax break. His calculations suggest that if Detroit had tailored its abatement programme to the most responsive firms, the city could have induced the same level of additional investment at a cost of $15 000 less per firm than its current abatement budget.

However, giving local officials the discretion to vary abatements by firms is potentially dangerous in that it provides an incentive for firms to engage in wasteful (and possibly corrupt) activities to obtain abatements (see Coffman, 1993). This undesirable behaviour, labelled by economists as 'rent-seeking', occurs whenever governments create an artificial scarcity of something of value. If the overall abatement budget is fixed, firms will try to obtain abatements by preparing detailed documents supporting their applications and lobbying public officials, activities that are wasteful from a social perspective (Coffman, 1993, p. 595). Based on this critique, Coffman argues that instead of fine-tuning tax abatements, city officials simply should not use them at all.

An additional argument for not using abatements is that they are likely to become increasingly ineffective over time, as use by one city is likely to lead other cities to adopt them as a defensive policy.[3] Cities with the most undesirable location characteristics have the greatest incentive to offer local tax abatements. However, firms may well use the offer of an incentive from such a community to get a similar incentive from another community that has more favourable characteristics. Only if state policy-makers restricted use of incentives to the first type of community would incentives serve to redirect economic development to declining areas.

ENTERPRISE ZONES: A SPATIALLY TARGETED ECONOMIC DEVELOPMENT STRATEGY[4]

In contrast to general tax abatements, the enterprise zone approach to local economic development concentrates tax abatements and other subsidies in small geographic areas. Based on a model developed in England in the 1970s, the original idea in the US was to promote local development in distressed areas by reducing regulatory barriers. Opposition from unions and environmentalists, however, quickly shifted the emphasis to tax reduction. By 1993, at least 37 states, plus the District of Columbia, had some form of enterprise zone programme. Interest in enterprise zones at the national level started with the Kemp–Garcia Bill of 1980 and was finally implemented in modified form by the 1993 Budget Reconciliation Act.[5]

Enterprise zones are typically established in depressed or blighted areas to achieve two primary goals: revitalization of the local economy and the provision of employment to local residents.[6] To achieve these goals, a typical enterprise zone provides a combination of tax and financial subsidies for firms. As of 1985, a majority of the states with enterprise zone programmes included property tax abatements, new-job tax credits or grants, and sales tax exemptions for construction materials and machinery. Other incentives available in some states included investment tax credits, corporate income tax deductions or exemptions, and low interest loans. Two states (California and Indiana) included tax credits for zone employees.

In practice, it is difficult for enterprise zones to meet both goals. A programme that successfully revitalizes the local economy may provide jobs to non-residents rather than to low skilled residents of the zone. To counter this possibility, some zones require that a firm hire 50 per cent of its employees from the local area to be eligible for the tax concessions. Because zones are small and do not have the diversity of potential workers of larger areas, this requirement often puts too large a burden on firms and keeps them from participating. The challenge is to design a programme that generates jobs for low skilled local workers.

Proponents believe that enterprise zones have the potential to generate new jobs, not just move jobs around from one area to another. Towards this end, proponents favour small firms over large ones (Butler, 1991, pp. 32–7). Small firms are viewed as more likely than large firms to hire local residents and to unleash their latent entrepreneurial energy. Small firms are also preferred because of the greater likelihood that they can use existing buildings; large firms typically need to build their own customized facilities. Thus the small-firm strategy is attractive because it makes plausible the possibility that jobs will be generated that will increase the total output of the economy, that the new jobs may go to disadvantaged local residents, and that, because some of the residents will become owners of local firms, they will have a larger stake in the economic stability of the community.

In light of the logic of the small-firm strategy, it is somewhat surprising to find that many of the enterprise zones include tax abatements that are not particularly useful for small firms. For example, a reduction in corporate tax rates does not help small firms that are sole proprietorships or partnerships. Similarly, property tax abatements may not help small firms which rent, rather than own, their property.

In addition, many analysts have observed that, given the goal of increasing local employment, subsidies to capital make less sense than subsidies to labour (see, for example, Gravelle, 1992). A capital subsidy is attractive to capital-intensive firms and encourages firms to substitute away from labour in favour of capital. Only by reducing production costs and inducing more production can such a subsidy generate jobs. In contrast, a subsidy to labour would be more attractive to labour-intensive firms and would encourage more use of labour relative to capital. Leslie Papke (1993) uses a simulation model to develop this argument more fully. Based on a standard economic model of a local economy which produces some goods for export outside the community and some for consumption within the community, Papke has shown that if the overall demand for the produced goods is not very sensitive to price, a subsidy to *capital* reduces the wages paid within the zone. Thus the benefits of the subsidy accrue to the owners of the firms, or, in the context of a more complete model, in the form of higher land prices to the owners of local land. Consistent with economic theory, she shows that regardless of the responsiveness of consumers to prices, wages in the zone increase much less with a 10 per cent subsidy to capital than with a 10 per cent subsidy directly to labour. Thus assuming that the goal of the development strategy is more jobs, the research of both Gravelle and Papke provides compelling evidence that labour subsidies should be an important part of the incentive packages. Papke also shows that a labour subsidy targeted to zone residents increases zone wages by more than a general labour subsidy.

Empirical studies have yielded conflicting conclusions about the effectiveness of state enterprise zones. Studies from the early and mid 1980s generally found positive results, but raised some problematic issues and did not grapple fully with some important methodological issues. For example, positive effects on employment in Connecticut were not easily reconciled with the observation that many firms did not take advantage of the tax incentives (Eisinger, 1988, pp. 195–6). The two thorniest methodological issues are: (1) how can one distinguish the effects of the zone and its various incentives from what otherwise would have occurred in the zone; and (2) how can one determine whether the jobs in the zone are new or simply have been moved from nearby locations? The following sections summarize recent work on enterprise zones in Maryland, Indiana and New Jersey that grapple with these issues.

Maryland

A 1988 study by the US General Accounting Office provides one of the most pessimistic evaluations of any state's enterprise zone programme. The programme offers investment credits and also employment credits aimed at hiring disadvantaged and non-disadvantaged workers. Over a four-year period, employment by participating businesses in Maryland zones increased by a low of 8 per cent (63 workers) in one zone and a high of 76 per cent (555 workers) at another. However, factors other than the programme apparently accounted for these increases.

The study focused on three enterprise zones in the Maryland programme: Hagerstown, Cumberland and Salisbury. Using monthly data from the state's unemployment insurance programme by participating firms, the researchers examined trends over time to determine whether the level and growth of employment were affected by the implementation of the programme at each site.

The analysis of employment effects in Hagarstown illustrates the approach. The Hagerstown zone covers about 2000 acres which include the old central business district, several industrial areas and a large industrial park. In 1982, at the time of enterprise zone designation, about 3300 workers were employed in businesses with at least five employees. The initial analyses of employment by the 64 participating firms showed that employment increased in August and October 1984, eight and ten months after the programme was implemented. The question, then, was whether these employment jumps could be attributed to the programme. In fact, two new employers accounted for the two employment jumps. Interviews with both employers indicated that the programme was not the catalyst for the change. In one case the employer was not aware of the programme at the time of hiring. In the other case, the firm indicated that it would have located in Hagarstown without the programme. When data for these two employers were removed, the employment trends revealed no employment effect of the programme. Comparable results were found for the other two sites.

The absence of employment effects implies that the programmes would not pass a benefit–cost test. In effect the programme represented a transfer of resources from Maryland taxpayers to participating firms, or to local land-owners to the extent that the geographically targeted tax savings were translated into higher local land prices.

Indiana

The Indiana programme was established in 1983 to create and retain jobs in some of the state's most distressed urban communities. Zone size was limited to three square miles, and 14 zones had been created by 1990. Unlike most other states, the Indiana property tax includes business inventories as part of the local property tax base. In response to business criticism of this tax, the major tax incentive under the zone programme is a generous 100 per cent credit against the local inventory tax for all inventories in the zone. In addition, the legislation provides an exemption of all incremental income from the corporate income tax, a tax credit for lenders of 5 per cent of the interest income from loans from participating lenders, an income tax credit for hiring zone residents, and an income tax deduction for zone residents. Because of the generosity of the inventory credit, the revenue foregone by local governments accounted for about 85 per cent of state and local programme costs.

A programme evaluation of Indiana enterprise zones by the Indiana Department of Commerce in 1992 reported that total costs in 1990 were $20.6 million and that 2024 new jobs were created. Of the new jobs, only 19 per cent (395) were held by zone residents. Based on these official figures, the average cost per job in the Indiana programme was $10 178, and the cost per new job for a zone resident was $53 506.

In a more detailed study of a specific zone – the Evansville zone which was reputed to have been particularly successful – Rubin and Wilder attempted to sort out the new jobs that could be attributable to the programme from those that might have been created in the zone in the absence of the programme. Using the statistical tool of shift-share analysis, they attributed to the programme only the growth in jobs that could not be predicted by the average growth rate in the region or the industry-specific growth rates. This methodology generated an annual cost per job (including both local and state government costs) of only $1633 (Rubin and Wilder, 1989, as interpreted by Ladd, 1994, p. 205).

However, the study most likely grossly understates the cost per *net* new job in the region, as distinct from new jobs in the zone. As Rubin and Wilder note, about two thirds of the new jobs in the zone are related to warehousing, a not surprising outcome given the generous tax credit for inventories. Because it is highly likely that the warehouses would otherwise have located somewhere else in the region, most of the new jobs in the zone most likely represent simply the movement of jobs from one area to another. Adjusting the Rubin and Wilder figures downwards for this possibility leads to a cost per net new job of $8280 and a cost per new job per zone resident of as much as $43 579 (Ladd, 1994, p. 204).[7]

The Indiana programme has also been carefully studied by Leslie Papke (1991, 1993). Using standard statistical procedures to control for other unobservable determinants over time and by zone, Papke estimated the average effect of enterprise zones on each of three outcome measures. According to the simplest model, enterprise zones generated a 9.8 per cent decline in investment in machines and equipment, an 8.3 per cent increase in inventories, and a 25 per cent decrease in unemployment claims, where such claims include those from nearby offices as well as in the zones themselves. Models somewhat richer in the specification of the time variable and in the timing of the effects of the zone yield similar results. The findings for investment in inventories versus machinery and equipment were consistent with economic predictions: firms that benefit most from the tax incentives, mainly the warehouses, would replace those that receive fewer tax benefits from investing in a designated zone.

The most hopeful finding was the reduction in unemployment claims. To the extent that this reduction translated into increased output that otherwise would not have been produced, it represents a social benefit. A subsequent analysis (Papke, 1993, p. 37) using census data to compare changes in the well-being of zone residents with people in other areas of Indiana cities between 1980 and 1990, was less sanguine. Over the ten-year period, population loss was greater for the zones, and per capita income, which started at a lower level in 1980, fell in the zones while it increased in the other areas. Unemployment fell more in the zones than in the control groups, but the difference was small. On balance, the zones seem to have had little positive impact on the economic well-being of their residents.

New Jersey

Marilyn Rubin's 1990 article on New Jersey enterprise zones summarizes the results of a major survey-based study of that state's urban enterprise zone programme. Two specific characteristics of the study are noteworthy. First, she attempted to estimate indirect as well as direct effects of the programme. Second, she attempted to isolate the effects that are attributable to the programme. Somewhat surprisingly her overall evaluation of the programme is heavily based on a narrow budgetary perspective.

The New Jersey programme is based in ten cities selected by the state from 18 proposals. The programme provides eight major benefits to all qualified businesses: two involve reduced regulation, three provide incentives to businesses to hire workers with specific characteristics, and three provide general investment incentives. The costs of the programme are administrative costs plus foregone revenues associated with sales tax exemptions or rate reductions, corporate tax credits and rebates on unemployment insurance taxes.

The direct results of the programme were based on survey data collected during 1987 and 1988 from almost 500 participating firms. Based on the survey responses, grossed up to account for the non-respondents, Rubin reports that participating firms provided over 9000 new jobs, $242 million in new payroll, $1776 million in additional production and $803 million in investment.

Rubin argues that these direct effects produce indirect effects through a multiplier effect on the state economy. Indirect effects include those resulting from the increased spending of workers in zone businesses and those resulting from the increased spending by workers in industries that expanded to supply the needs of the firms in the zones. The magnitude of the estimated indirect effects were huge, both absolutely and relative to the direct effects. In particular, she estimated that 42.7 thousand jobs were indirectly generated, a number that is four times the number of new jobs in participating firms.

Rubin correctly recognized that not all the direct effects should be attributed to the enterprise zone programme. Indeed only 32 per cent of the businesses reported that zone benefits were the primary or only reason for their location or expansion decision. In light of this finding, Rubin repeated the analysis based only on the firms whose behaviour was affected by the programme. This adjustment reduced the total jobs generated to 16 280. Even this estimate represents an overstatement, because some of the job increase in these relocating or expanding firms presumably represents a response to the booming New Jersey economy rather than the enterprise zone programme.

Unfortunately, the case for adding indirect impacts is weak. Almost certainly, most of the second-round effects would be offset by reduced activity elsewhere in the state economy. The potential for offsetting reductions applies as well to the direct effects, but is potentially less compelling for them provided that jobs go to people who were otherwise unemployed or underemployed. This criticism implies that the study significantly overestimated the true effect of the New Jersey programme.

To provide an overall evaluation of the programme, Rubin concentrated initially on a narrow budgetary perspective. If the indirect effects were not counted, the additional taxes generated fell short of the costs of the programme. However, when the indirect effects were included, additional revenue exceeded costs by 90 per cent. Rubin prefers this latter result and concludes that the benefits of New Jersey's programme exceeded the costs. However, a more careful consideration of the displacement issue would have led to a far less favourable conclusion.

Rubin provided information on the economic effectiveness of the programme almost as an afterthought. Her estimates suggest that the cost per job was $13 070 if only the direct effects are considered and $3171 if both direct and indirect effects are included. Given the displacement issue, the higher figure is probably the more plausible. Even this figure, however, could substantially understate the true cost given Rubin's inability to rule out the employment growth that would have occurred anyway given New Jersey's booming economy at that time.

Support for applying caution in accepting Rubin's optimistic story for New Jersey is provided by a more recent empirical study based on municipal data (Boarnet and Bogart, 1996). In that study, the authors used data for nine years (1982–90) for 28 municipalities in the northern half of New Jersey. Of the 28, all of which were qualified to apply for an enterprise zone, 14 applied and 7 were granted the right by the legislature to establish zones during the period. A simple analysis of trends shows that for the two years prior to the start of the programme, the growth rate of employment in the municipalities granted zones exceeded that of the unsuccessful applicants. This suggests that the legislature tried to place zones in municipalities that were most likely to succeed. The authors' econometric analysis of the panel data set yielded no measurable impact of the New Jersey programme on jobs, wages or property values.[8]

Cost-Effectiveness of Enterprise Zone Programmes

The experience to date with enterprise zones provides a reasonably clear indication that the zones have not proven to be a cost-effective means of providing jobs. Cost-effectiveness estimates from the various studies, including some from England that were not discussed here, are summarized in Table 5.1. As shown, the basic estimates range from a low of $1633 for the Evansville programme to a high of infinity for the Maryland programme. However, as indicated in the right-hand column, various adjustments to these figures suggest that the true annual costs per new job fall into the $40–$60 000 range. The $60 000 figure for the English programme refers to the cost per net new job. Given the greater focus on zone residents in the US programmes, the preferred estimates for the state programmes refer to the cost per job for a resident of the zone. Unfortunately, lack of data on the number of jobs for residents makes it impossible to convert the New Jersey cost per job to the preferred measure of the cost per job for a zone resident. Nonetheless, the conclusion is clear: none of the programmes generates jobs in a cost-effective manner.

The preferred estimates in Table 5.1 are quite high, but not completely out of the question. They may be costs that states are willing to pay, especially if jobs for disadvantaged workers today have future effects on worker productivity. On the other hand, they are sufficiently high that they should force policy-makers to ask whether tax abatements are the best way to increase jobs, especially jobs for residents in depressed areas, and to explore cheaper methods such as more effective abatement programmes or alternatives such as training programmes.

Table 5.1   *Cost-effectiveness of enterprise zone programmes (annual cost per job or per job for zone resident)*

Programme or study	Basic estimate	Adjusted preferred estimate
England	$15 000 per job	$60 000 per job (assumes only one in four jobs attributable to the zone)
New Jersey (Rubin)	$13 070 per job[a]	>$13 070 per job[b] (no adjustment for growth of New Jersey economy)
Indiana Commerce Department	$10 170 per job $53 507 per job for zone residents	$53 506 per job for zone residents
Evansville (Rubin and Wilder)	$1633 per job[c]	$43 579 per job for zone residents (subtracts warehouse jobs and assumes 19 percentage of jobs accrue to zone residents)
Maryland	Infinite	Infinite (no new jobs)

Notes:
[a] Direct effects only for reasons given in the text.
[b] No reasonable way to estimate cost per job for zone resident.
[c] Adjusted upward to account for State share of costs.

Sources: Papke, 1991; Rubin and Wilder, 1989; Rubin and Richards, 1992; Rubin, 1990; and US General Accounting Office (GAO), 1988.

CONCLUSIONS

One surprising aspect of much of the research on abatement programmes and some of it on enterprise zones is the emphasis placed on the narrow budgetary perspective. Typically, expenditure programmes are not judged in this way. Instead one would look at the social benefits relative to the costs. Yet as noted earlier, even though they are implemented through the tax side of the budget, tax abatement programmes are similar to expenditure programmes.[9] For general tax abatement programmes, this budgetary perspective is somewhat understandable because the goals of such programmes are often quite vague. For enterprise zones, the budgetary perspective is less understandable because the goals of encouraging local economic activity and providing jobs to disadvantaged zone residents are typically quite clear. For these programmes, the research shows that the cost per new job per zone resident is quite high, and probably exceeds $40 000 per year.

Clearly, there is room for additional research on the effects of tax abatements and enterprise zones. One of the obvious dangers in evaluating programmes such as enterprise zones is that they are likely to be established in areas with unusually high unemployment or at times when unemployment is at a peak. As a consequence of these extreme starting points, the unemployment rate is likely to go down relative to other areas or over time even in the absence of the programme. This observation makes it particularly important that control groups be used in the evaluation. Ideally, the control group should be randomly chosen. For example, the state might randomly select areas for enterprise zone designation from among a number of areas applying for zone status. The areas not selected could then be used as control groups with which the outcomes in the participating zones could be compared. The use of comparable areas as controls will directly address the challenge of determining what would have happened in the zone in the absence of the tax abatement programme. However, it does not address the other thorny analytical question of whether the new jobs in the zone represent net new jobs for the metropolitan area or simply jobs that were transferred from nearby areas.

NOTES

1. See Chapter 8 for new work by William Fox and Matthew Murray on tax incentives designed to attract large new firms in rural areas.
2. One exception is the work by Robert Wassmer (see, for example, Wassmer, Urban Studies), who examines the impact of tax abatements and other local development strategies on business activity. He concludes that local fiscal incentives typically have little or no effect on local business activity as measured by employment or value added. Moreover, the effectiveness of such incentives appears to vary with the characteristics of the community. For example, Wassmer found that tax abatements for industrial property were more likely to induce additional manufacturing activity only in the communities that were the least desirable for manufacturing, namely those with high housing density and old capital stock. Whether his findings are generalizable to other metropolitan areas remains to be investigated.
3. For empirical evidence that communities emulate others with respect to the granting of abatements, see Anderson and Wassmer (1995). For the first 15 years of the abatement programme, municipalities in the Detroit metropolitan area became increasingly willing to end their spells of non-abatement to emulate their neighbouring communities.
4. This discussion draws heavily on Ladd (1994).
5. The Act authorizes the Secretary of Housing and Urban Development to designate six urban and three rural empowerment zones, and 65 urban and 30 rural enterprise communities. The goal of the programme is to build communities and empower residents of distressed areas so that they may prosper. The tax incentives include a 20 per cent tax credit covering the first $15 000 of wages and certain types of training that a business provides to

each employee who lives and works in the zone, as well as tax and financial incentives for investment in the zone. In addition, the programme creates a block grant that will direct money for social services to disadvantaged residents of the zone.

6. Ladd (1994) distinguishes economic development strategies of three types: pure people-oriented strategies, place-based people strategies and pure-place strategies. As initially developed in England, enterprise zones were essentially pure-place strategies. As implemented in the United States, however, enterprise zones focus on improving the situation of disadvantaged residents in the zones, as well as on economic development in the zone more generally. In this sense, US enterprise zones represent a cross of pure-place and place-based people strategies.

7. This figure assumes that 19 per cent of the non-warehouse and related jobs go to zone residents and that none of the warehouse jobs are given to residents. If some of the warehouse jobs accrue to residents of the zones, the cost per new job per zone resident would be lower than the $43 000 cited here.

8. The authors had no data on business investment. Hence it is conceivable, but unlikely, that the New Jersey programme increased business investment even though it did not increase employment or property values.

9. Revenue-generating effects also receive attention with respect to various other tax reduction strategies. For example, proponents of a reduction of the federal capital gains tax often claim that it will increase tax revenues.

REFERENCES

Anderson, John E. and Robert W. Wassmer (1995), "The decision to 'bid for business': municipal behavior in granting property tax abatements", *Regional Science and Urban Economics*, **25** (6), 739–57.

Bartik, Timothy J. (1991), *Who Benefits from State and Local Economic Development Policies?*, Kalamazoo, MI: W.E. Upjohn Institute for Employment Research.

Bartik, Timothy J. (1992), 'The effects of state and local taxes on economic development: a review of recent research', *Economic Development Quarterly*, Feb., 103–11.

Boarnet, Marlon G. and William T. Bogart (1996), 'Enterprise zones and employment: evidence from New Jersey', *Journal of Urban Economics*, **40** (2), 198–215.

Butler, Stuart M. (1991), 'The conceptual evolution of enterprise zones', in Roy E. Green (ed.), *Enterprise Zones*, Newbury Park, CA: Sage Publications, pp. 27–40.

Coffman, Richard B. (1993), 'Tax abatements and rent-seeking', *Urban Studies*, **30** (3), 593–8.

Eisinger, Peter K. (1988), *The Rise of the Entrepreneurial State: State and Local Economic Development Policy in the United States*, Madison WI: University of Wisconsin Press.

Gravelle, Jane G. (1992), 'Enterprise zones: the design of tax subsidies', Congressional Research Service Report for Congress, **92** STN, 110–15.

Ladd, Helen F. (1994), 'Fiscal impacts of local population growth: a conceptual and empirical analysis', *Regional Science and Urban Economics*, **24**, 661–86.

Morse, George W. and Michael C. Farmer (1986), 'Location and investment effects of a tax abatement program', *National Tax Journal*, **39**, 229–36.

Papke, Leslie E. (1991), 'Interstate business tax differentials and new firm location: evidence from panel data', *Journal of Public Economics*, **45**, 47–68.

Papke, Leslie E. (1993), 'What do we know about enterprise zones?', *National Bureau of Economic Research, Inc. Working Paper Series*, Cambridge, MA: No. 1817.

Rubin, Barry M. and Margaret G. Wilder (1989), 'Urban enterprise zones: employ-
    ment impacts and fiscal incentives', *Journal of the American Planning Association*,
    Autumn, 418–31.
Rubin, Marilyn (1990), 'Urban enterprise zones: do they work? Evidence from New
    Jersey', *Public Budgeting and Finance*, Winter, 3–17.
US General Accounting Office (1988), *Enterprise Zones. Lessons from the Maryland
    Experience*, Report to Congressional Requesters, December, Washington, D.C:
    US6PO.
Wolkoff, Michael J. (1985), 'Chasing a dream: the use of tax abatements to spur
    urban economic development', *Urban Studies*, **22**, 305–15.

PART II

Tax Policy as a Land Use Tool

6. The Pittsburgh experience with land-value taxation*

Wallace E. Oates and Robert M. Schwab

INTRODUCTION

Economists have had a long-standing interest in land taxation.[1] The physiocrats, Adam Smith, David Ricardo, James Mill, John Stuart Mill and, most notably, Henry George, all wrote extensively on the subject. They disagreed on many issues, but they were unanimous on one point: since the supply of land was perfectly inelastic, land taxes would be borne entirely by landowners and would not distort economic decisions. Despite this interest, our experience with land-value taxation is actually very limited. In the United States, virtually no governments use a pure land tax and only a small handful rely on a split-rate system where land is taxed more heavily than structures. Consequently, we have little idea about the actual consequences of a land tax.

We have tried to provide some evidence on this point by looking at a recent 'natural experiment' in Pittsburgh. In 1979 and 1980, Pittsburgh restructured its property tax system so that land was taxed at more than five times the rate on structures. The facts of the Pittsburgh case are both clear and dramatic. Pittsburgh enjoyed a boom in non-residential construction following the change in tax policy. Annual construction was on average 70 per cent higher in Pittsburgh during the 1980s than in the 1960s and 1970s. In sharp contrast, development fell sharply in most comparable, older, Rust Belt central cities. The interpretation of these facts, however, is far from clear. Some have argued that the graded land tax was the key factor behind Pittsburgh's build-

* Both authors are members of the Department of Economics, University of Maryland; Oates is also a University Fellow at Resources for the Future. For research assistance, we are grateful to James Heil, Jonathan Lewis, Dan Mussatti and especially to Janet McCubbin. For their help in obtaining required data, we thank Dina Silva-Decker at the Dun and Bradstreet Corporation, Ellen Ku of BOMA International and Stan Montgomery at the US Bureau of the Census. We also appreciate the help and patience of Dr Charles Blocksidge, the County Assessor of Allegheny County, Mark Gibbons, Chief Accounting Officer of the City Controller in Pittsburgh, and Michael Weir, Senior Research Associate of the Pennsylvania Economy League. Finally, we want to thank the Lincoln Institute of Land Policy for their extended support of this study.

ing boom. Many would disagree and would instead attribute the city's success to Pittsburgh's innovative urban renewal efforts and to the increased demand for office space stemming from the restructuring of the region's economy.

We have presented our analysis of the Pittsburgh experience in some detail in Oates and Schwab (1997).[2] Our goal here is to summarize our findings and to offer our views on this debate. The chapter has the following organization. We briefly look at the theory of land taxation in section 2 and then discuss land taxation in Pittsburgh in section 3. Section 4 presents a discussion of construction trends in Pittsburgh, and the final section includes a brief summary and conclusions.

THE THEORY OF LAND TAXATION

The literature on land taxation is often confusing and sometimes confused. The confusion has come in part as a result of a failure to distinguish between two experiments. First, suppose the increased revenues from a land tax are coupled with an expansion in the size of the public budget (what Musgrave (1959) has called a *balanced-budget* fiscal change). In this case, the overall fiscal effect depends both on the change in public expenditure and the effects of the change in taxes. In particular, we might want to look at the special case where the government returns the revenue to the citizens as lump-sum transfers. Assuming that we can safely ignore any income effects, the analysis of a tax in this case can proceed along familiar lines where we focus on the effects of the tax itself and ignore the consequences of the additional revenues. Second, we can view an increase in one tax as providing revenues that would allow the government to reduce a different tax while holding total revenue constant. For such a case of *differential* tax analysis, we compare the effects of the actual tax change *relative* to those of the revenue alternatives.

The analysis of a land tax in a static setting where we ignore the use of the additional revenue is straightforward. The supply of land is perfectly inelastic so that landowners can do nothing to escape the burden of the tax. A land tax thus does not distort economic decisions. It is neutral; it neither encourages nor discourages development. And this neutrality, of course, is part of its appeal.

If, on the other hand, we consider an increase in land tax where we use the revenues to reduce the tax on structures or other improvements, the economic consequences will be very different. A tax on structures reduces the intensity with which land is used. In the absence of a tax on structures, developers will choose a capital–land ratio such that the marginal product of capital is equal to the cost of capital; if we now introduce a tax on structures, they will choose a new, lower capital–land ratio where the marginal product of capital equals the sum of the tax and the cost of capital. Thus arguments that a tax on land can stimulate development turn in part on an implicit assumption that the revenues will be used to reduce the tax on structures. But let us be clear. In that sense, any tax will stimulate development as long as the negative effects of collecting the tax are less than the positive effects of reducing the tax on structures. Land taxes have no special claim as a tool to foster development. Almost certainly, for example, a nation-wide head tax would stimulate development in this sense.

Things become more complicated in a dynamic setting. Bentick (1979) and Mills (1981) have argued that land-value taxation need not be neutral with respect to the timing and nature of land development. In particular, the taxing of land values *may* distort the choice between earlier and later development of unused land parcels in favour of those projects that promise an earlier stream of net receipts. The implication of their models is that a movement in the direction of land taxation may hasten economic development, perhaps to an extent that is excessive purely on efficiency grounds. This effect, however, depends upon an important and controversial assumption concerning the way in which land is valued for tax purposes.

In Oates and Schwab (1997), we presented a simple example to illustrate the Bentick and Mills argument and to highlight the key issues. In that example, landowners can either devote their land to use A and earn \$1000 per period forever, or wait one period, develop their land in use B and earn \$1100 per period. Land use decisions can never be changed once they have been made. At a 10 per cent interest rate and with no taxes, landowners would be indifferent between these two options.

Now suppose the local government introduces a land tax. The impact of this land tax turns crucially on how it is administered. There are at least two possibilities. Bentik and Mills assume implicitly that the government would, in periods 2 and beyond, treat land developed in use A differently than land developed in use B. In their view, since land use decisions are irrevocable and the two land uses generate different land rents, land devoted to use B should be taxed more heavily than land devoted to use A. In this setting, all land would be developed in the first period. That is to say, the imposition of a tax on land would stimulate development.

At first blush, this line of argument seems compelling (and, to be truthful, we accepted it initially without reservation). But as David Wildasin (1982) and T. Nicolaus Tideman (1982) have pointed out, this form of a land tax is inconsistent with most peoples' view, including Henry George's, of a land tax. They would argue that, in the context of our example, the non-neutrality of land-value taxation results from the practice of taxing land on the value associated with its chosen use. If land were always assessed at each point in time for tax purposes on the basis of its 'highest and best' use, irrespective of any commitments to a particular use, then land-value taxation would indeed be neutral. Taxation at such a *standard value* (Vickrey, 1970) would be use-independent and hence neutral. In terms of our example, *all* parcels would be taxed as if they produced a rental income of $1000 in period 1 and $1100 in all subsequent periods. In this case all land is treated identically, and a land tax must clearly be neutral.

This is a difficult issue. It appears that the neutrality of actual land taxation turns on actual assessment practices. This suggests that any empirical study of the effects of land taxation must pay careful attention to existing assessment procedures.[3] We return to this issue when we discuss the Pittsburgh experience.

LAND TAXATION IN PITTSBURGH

In order to understand the effects of land-value taxation in Pittsburgh, it is important to place this tax reform in the context of the ongoing economic evolution of the city and metropolitan area.[4] Since the end of World War II, Pittsburgh has gone through a largely successful, though often painful, economic transition. The city was once a major manufacturing centre. As the steel and other heavy manufacturing sectors shrank, the Pittsburgh economy became more oriented towards white-collar jobs. The banking and other service sectors, for example, grew very quickly as Pittsburgh became the regional financial leader. In 1940, manufacturing employment in the four-county Pittsburgh Metropolitan Statistical Area accounted for almost half of the total work force; in 1985, manufacturing employment constituted only 16 per cent of total employment.

Pittsburgh has launched several major urban renewal projects. Renaissance I, initiated in the 1940s, was a major effort to revitalize the central business district through a public–private partnership. The project enjoyed a number of important successes. It was followed by a second major renewal effort in the late 1970s: Renaissance II. As before, the renewal effort involved an extensive partnership between public and private agents, with a major focus on continued development of the central business district. Several major corporations decided to expand their headquarters in Pittsburgh, and with public assistance constructed a series of major office complexes. The result was a striking surge in levels of commercial construction activity: there were commercial contract awards in 1980 for 9.5 million square feet of new space with (as we discuss below) continued high levels of building activity through most of the decade.[5]

Pittsburgh's Property Tax

Pittsburgh, along with a handful of smaller cities in Pennsylvania, has had a graded property tax system in place for many decades, a system under which land was taxed at a rate twice that of the structures on the land until 1979. As Table 6.1 indicates, Pittsburgh introduced a striking restructuring of the city's property tax in 1979 and 1980, raising the tax rate on land to about five times the rate on structures. This increased 'tilt' of rates has been maintained, and even increased slightly during the decade following the restructuring.[6]

Table 6.1 should be interpreted cautiously, however. Properties in the city of Pittsburgh are subject to taxation not only by the city government, but also by the county and the overlying school district. These latter two jurisdictions do not use a graded tax system but instead employ a conventional property tax that applies the same tax rate to land and structures. As the last column of Table 6.1 indicates, this results in *total* tax rates on land in the city of

Table 6.1   Pittsburgh property tax rates, 1972–91

	(a)	(b)	(c)	(d) School district	(e)	(f)	(g)
Fiscal year	Land tax rate (mills)	Structure tax rate (mills)	County tax rate (mills)	tax rate (mills)	Total land tax rate (mills)	Structure tax rate (mills)	(e) as a percentage of (f)
1972	53	26.5	15.5	23	91.5	65.0	141
1973	51	25.5	15.5	23	89.5	64.0	140
1974	51	25.5	15.5	23	89.5	64.0	140
1975	49.5	24.75	15.5	23	88.0	63.25	139
1976	49.5	24.75	15.5	29	94.0	69.25	136
1977	49.5	24.75	21.375	29	99.875	75.125	133
1978	49.5	24.75	21.375	29	99.875	75.125	133
1979	97.5	24.75	19.365	29	145.865	73.115	200
1980	125.5	24.75	23.0	29	177.5	76.75	231
1981	125.5	24.75	28.0	41	194.5	93.75	207
1982	133.0	32.0	29.0	36	198.0	97.0	204
1983	151.5	27.0	29.0	36	216.5	92.0	235
1984	151.5	27.0	29.0	40	220.5	96.0	230
1985	151.5	27.0	29.0	40	220.5	96.0	230
1986	151.5	27.0	31.25	40	222.75	98.25	227
1987	151.5	27.0	31.25	46	228.75	104.25	219
1988	151.5	27.0	31.25	46	228.75	104.25	219
1989	151.5	27.0	35.0	46	232.5	108.0	215
1990	184.5	32.0	36.5	46	267.0	114.5	233
1991	184.5	32.0	36.5	46	267.0	114.5	233

Source: Office of the City Controller, City of Pittsburgh.

Pittsburgh that are something more than twice the rate on structures. Properties outside the city are, in contrast, subject to conventional property taxation.

AN ANALYSIS OF THE PITTSBURGH EXPERIENCE

We have assembled time-series data on new building activity for a sample of 15 cities and metropolitan areas in the Rust Belt including Pittsburgh.[7] We have used data from two different sources, each of which has its own strengths and weaknesses. The Dun and Bradstreet data extend back to 1960 but provide little disaggregated detail. These data cover central cities only and thus do not allow us to look at suburban development; moreover, they do not separate residential and non-residential construction. The US Census data provide much more detail but unfortunately extend back only to 1974. The two data sources thus complement each other nicely and together offer an interesting perspective on development patterns during this period.

Table 6.2 presents figures for the real value of new building permits for the cities in our sample based on the Dun and Bradstreet data. The trends in

Table 6.2   Average annual value of building permits, Dun and Bradstreet data

	1960–79	1980–89	Per cent change
Akron	134 026	87 907	−34.41
Allentown	48 124	28 801	−40.15
Buffalo	93 749	82 930	−11.54
Canton	40 235	24 251	−39.73
Cincinnati	318 248	231 561	−27.24
Cleveland	329 511	224 587	−31.84
Columbus	456 580	527 026	15.43
Dayton	107 798	92 249	−14.42
Detroit	368 894	277 783	−24.70
Erie	48 353	22 761	−52.93
Pittsburgh	**181 734**	**309 727**	**70.43**
Rochester	118 726	82 411	−30.59
Syracuse	94 503	53 673	−43.21
Toledo	138 384	93 495	−32.44
Youngstown	33 688	11 120	−66.99
15-city average	167 504	143 352	−14.42

Note: All data are in 000s of constant 1982 dollars.

Table 6.2 are striking. In 13 of our 15 sample cities, construction was higher during 1960–79 than in 1980–89. In some cases the trends are dramatic: for example, construction fell by two-thirds in Youngstown and one-half in Erie. Columbus shows a slight rise. However, Pittsburgh is a remarkable outlier: the real value of building permits on an annual basis rose by some 70 per cent in the 1980s relative to the 20-year period preceding the tax reform!

The Census data tell a similar story.[8] The real annual value of total building permits is lower after 1979 than during 1974–78 in most cities. But Pittsburgh again stands out, with a dramatic increase of more than 250 per cent. The Census data point to two further interesting patterns. First, the Pittsburgh boom was a central city phenomenon; construction in the Pittsburgh suburbs was actually lower in the 1980s than in the mid and late 1970s. Second, virtually all of the increase in Pittsburgh construction was in the non-residential sector. Residential construction rose only slightly, while, in sharp contrast, commercial and industrial construction more than tripled in annual value.

The Role of the Land Tax in the Pittsburgh Experience

We now turn to the key question: what role did Pittsburgh's decision to increase the tax on land play in the city's construction boom? As we argued above, an increase in the land tax could stimulate development if land assessments for purposes of taxation are dependent on the particular use of a parcel rather than reflecting the highest and best use of a parcel irrespective of its current use. We have explored this issue with some care, including numerous discussions with the Director of Assessments for Allegheny County (of which Pittsburgh is part). The answer is far from clear. In principle, we learned, the assessed value of already developed land is driven by changes in value of undeveloped land, even if it would be impossible (or at least economically unfeasible) to change land use. Thus, in principle, assessed values reflect highest and best use. We also learned, however, that actual practice is often very different from stated principles. The assessment of large parcels typically involves complex negotiations, appeals and sometimes litigation. In the end, the outcome is often a 'compromise' in which numerous criteria are brought to bear. Thus it would not be at all surprising if, through one channel or another, existing patterns of land use had some impact on land assessments.

For this reason, Bentick–Mills types of timing effects cannot be ruled out categorically in the Pittsburgh case. However, it is our sense that such timing effects were probably not an important *direct* explanation of Pittsburgh's building boom. Some pieces of informal evidence support this conclusion. First, in their interviews with 'development experts', the Pennsylvania

Economy League (1985) found no evidence that the increase in rates of land taxation exerted a noticeable impact on construction activity.[9] Second, the League found that several of the major projects that were begun in 1981 were well along in the planning stages *before* the increase in the graded-tax ratio.

Third, it is clear that the dramatic changes in the Pittsburgh economy significantly increased the demand for office space but that the supply of office space was slow to respond. This excess demand for office space is apparent in data on office vacancy rates for Pittsburgh and some of the other cities in our sample. Vacancy rates in Pittsburgh ranged from less than 1 per cent to 3.5 per cent during 1978–82. The data suggest, moreover, that the construction of several massive new office buildings in the early 1980s effectively brought the market back towards equilibrium, as office vacancy rates rose sharply by the middle of the decade.

SUMMARY AND CONCLUSIONS

It is difficult to draw firm conclusions about the role of land taxation. Pittsburgh is the only major city in the United States that has had extensive experience with a graded tax system. We certainly cannot be certain that we have disentangled the impact of that city's tax policy from the impacts of the restructuring of the regional economy, the initiation of Renaissance II and a host of other quite plausible explanations of Pittsburgh's success. With these qualifications in mind, however, we can offer our interpretation of what we have found.

The basic data are clear on certain things. Pittsburgh experienced a dramatic building boom following the change in tax policy at the end of the 1970s. Over that same period, construction in other nearby, older Rust Belt cities fell sharply. Pittsburgh's success did not extend to its suburbs, all of which continued to tax land and structures at the same rate. The upsurge in construction was limited almost exclusively to the commercial sector and included a number of new major office buildings in the central business district.

How do we account for the Pittsburgh building boom? We would assign a major role to a fundamental imbalance between the supply and demand for office space generated by the growing importance of the financial and service sectors in the Pittsburgh economy and the commitment from a number of major corporations to the Pittsburgh central business district. Some proponents of land taxation may be disappointed by our conclusion, arguing that we have understated the importance of the change in tax policy. That would be a serious misinterpretation of our position. Assuming that the Bentick–Mills 'timing effects' were of minor importance, we are left with the view that, in accordance with traditional economic theory, a major increase in land-value taxation in Pittsburgh was (roughly) neutral. The critics of land-value taxation have suggested that the Pittsburgh tax reform was unimportant because it had little effect on development. The point here is that if land taxation is neutral, we would *expect* it to have no effects on any decisions. This is its very appeal: it does not distort economic choices! Thus the responses of those interviewed are fully consistent with the traditional view of the neutrality of land taxation. Land taxation should not, and apparently did not, in itself hasten development.

Does this mean that Pittsburgh's decision to increase the tax on land was irrelevant? The answer, we would argue strongly, is 'no'. What would have happened if the city had not decided to tax land more heavily? Pittsburgh was under severe fiscal pressure in the late 1970s, and some type of tax increase was virtually unavoidable. Had an increase in land-value taxation not been introduced, city officials would have turned to another form of taxation: perhaps higher taxes on structures, or (more likely according to contemporary reports) the introduction of a significant increase in the city's wage tax. Both theory and empirical evidence strongly suggest that such tax increases would have had a serious negative effect on the Pittsburgh economy. Bartik's (1991) summary, for example, shows that intrametroplitan area firm decisions are particularly sensitive to taxes. Moreover, existing evidence suggests that a sizeable wage tax can have a major detrimental impact on the local economy. Two econometric studies of the wage tax in Philadelphia find that the tax has resulted in large job losses in the city. Ronald Grieson (1980) estimates that a 1 percentage point increase in the wage tax in Philadelphia in 1976 led to a 10–15 per cent loss of employment in the city by 1980. A later study by Robert Inman (1992) turns up similar findings: Inman estimates that a potential increase in the Philadelphia wage tax from about 5 per cent to 6 per cent would result in a loss of over 80 000 jobs (or of 12.7 per cent from existing employment levels).[10]

It is against the backdrop of such alternatives that the tax on land values needs to be considered. The role of land-value taxation in Pittsburgh should be understood in a setting of *differential* taxation. The relevant issue here is how the effects of the land-value tax *compared* with those of the available alternative sources of tax revenues. It appears that a land tax did not cause a building boom in Pittsburgh, but that it did allow the city government to avoid policies that might have undercut that boom.

NOTES

1. See Tideman (1994) for an excellent discussion of the history of thought on land taxation.
2. There have been at least three earlier studies of the effects of land-value taxation in

Pittsburgh. Henry Pollakowski (1982) was unable to find much in the way of 'adjustment effects' as measured by the number of property transactions. However, his data extended only from 1976 to 1980. Steven Bourassa (1987) explored the effects of Pittsburgh's tax system on housing development. Using monthly data on the value of new residential building permits as his dependent variable, Bourassa found that the tax rate on improvements, but not the rate on land, was a statistically significant determinant of the level of residential building activity. Bourassa's findings, while of some interest, are limited in scope, for, as we shall see, the major impetus to development in Pittsburgh has been in the non-residential sector. Of more relevance to our concerns is an interesting study undertaken in the mid 1980s by the Pennsylvania Economy League (1985). At the request of Mayor Richard Caliguiri, the League examined the effects of the graded tax on both the development of the city and the equity of the tax system. Drawing both on extensive interviews with 'local development experts' and some quantitative analysis of the graded-tax ratio and development of different properties, the League concluded that: 'The graded tax has very little effect on development' (p. ii).

3. As Nicolaus Tideman has emphasized to us, the Bentick–Mills timing effect depends critically on the *systematic* association of land assessments with actual use. Simple random errors or inaccuracies in assessments will not in themselves compromise the neutrality property of land-value taxation.

4. For a useful description of the historical evolution of Pittsburgh with a focus on the renewal efforts under Renaissance I and II, see Shelby Stewman and Joel Tarr (1982).

5. The commercial building boom in Pittsburgh under Renaissance II has encompassed several major projects: PPG Place (six buildings, including a 40-storey office tower), One Oxford Center (a 46-storey office tower and retail complex), The Steel Plaza/One Mellon Bank Center (a 53-storey office tower and retail complex that includes the main station of the Light Rail Transit system), Allegheny International's headquarters, the Liberty Center, the Hillman Complex and several others.

6. The assessment–sales ratio in Pittsburgh is 0.25, so that the nominal tax rates appearing in Table 6.1 must be divided by 4 to obtain measures of effective tax rates.

7. See Oates and Schwab (1997) for a more detailed description of the sources and nature of our data.

8. We include an extensive set of tables based on the Census data in Oates and Schwab (1997).

9. Clearly, not everyone would agree with this assessment. Walter Rybeck (1991), for example, quotes the Pittsburgh City Council President as follows: 'I'm not going to say the land tax is the only reason a second renaissance occurred, but it's been a big help' (pp. 4–5).

10. There are, however, crucial differences between the structure of the income tax in Philadelphia and in Pittsburgh. In Philadelphia, the tax is a commuter tax; the suburbs around Philadelphia do not have wage taxes of their own. In contrast, in Pittsburgh the first claim on a person's income resides in his place of residence. So when the city of Pittsburgh raises the wage tax, suburbs tend to do likewise in order to get what, from their perspective, is essentially 'free money'. For this reason, the incentives for businesses to leave the city would be somewhat weaker in the Pittsburgh case than in Philadelphia. Nevertheless, higher wage taxes in the Pittsburgh metropolitan area could be expected to have a detrimental impact on economic growth in both the city and suburbs.

REFERENCES

Bartik, Timothy J. (1991), *Who Benefits from State and Local Economic Development Policies?*, Kalamazoo, Michigan: W.E. Upjohn Institute for Employment Research.

Bentick, Brian L. (1979), 'The impact of taxation and valuation practices on the timing and efficiency of land use', *Journal of Political Economy* , **87**, 859–68.

Bourassa, Steven C. (1987), 'Land value taxation and new housing development in Pittsburgh', *Growth and Change*, 44–55.

Grieson, Ronald E. (1980), 'Theoretical analysis and empirical measurements of the effects of the Philadelphia income tax', *Journal of Urban Economics*, **7**, 123–37.

Inman, Robert P. (1992), 'Can Philadelphia escape its fiscal crisis with another tax increase?', *Business Review* (Federal Reserve Bank of Philadelphia), 5–20.

Mills, David E. (1981), 'The non-neutrality of land value taxation', *National Tax Journal*, **34**, 125–9.

Musgrave, Richard A. (1959), *The Theory of Public Finance*, New York: McGraw Hill.

Oates, Wallace E. and Robert M. Schwab (1997), 'The impact of urban land taxation: the Pittsburgh experience', *National Tax Journal*, **50**, 1–21.

Pennsylvania Economy League (1985), *Development, Equity, and the Graded Tax in the City of Pittsburgh*, Pittsburgh, Pa.: Pennsylvania Economy League.

Pollakowski, Henry O. (1982), *Adjustment Effects of a Tax on Land: The Pittsburgh Case*, Cambridge, MA: Lincoln Institute of Land Policy, Lincoln Institute Monograph #82-8.

Rybeck, Walter (1991), 'Pennsylvania's experiments in property tax modernization', *NTA Forum*, 1–5.

Stewman, Shelby and Joel A. Tarr (1982), 'Four decades of public–private partnerships in Pittsburgh', in R.S. Fosler and R. Berger (eds), *Public–Private Partnership in American Cities: Seven Case Studies*, Lexington, MA: Heath, pp. 59–127.

Tideman, T. Nicolaus (1982), 'A tax on land value *is* neutral', *National Tax Journal*, **35**, 109–11.

Tideman, T. Nicolaus (1994), 'The economics of efficient taxes on land', in Nicolaus Tideman (ed.), *Land and Taxation*, London: Shepheard-Walwyn in association with Centre for Incentive Taxation, pp. 103–4.

Vickrey, William (1970), 'Defining land value for tax purposes', in D.M. Holland (ed.), *The Assessment of Land Value*, Madison: University of Wisconsin Press, pp. 25–36.

Wildasin, David E. (1982), 'More on the neutrality of land taxation', *National Tax Journal*, **35**, 105–8.

7. Property tax treatment of farmland: does tax relief delay land development?*

Adele C. Morris

INTRODUCTION

Regional planners and environmentalists have observed with concern the loss of productive farmland to urban development. As land values rise along urban fringes, the returns to developing land for housing or commercial enterprise exceed the returns to farming, and even some of the most productive agricultural areas become attractive sites for suburban settlement. Property taxes based on the fair market value of land could accelerate land development by increasing the cost of farming as land values rise. Since 1957, every state has responded to development pressures by allowing or requiring preferential property tax treatment of farmland, and in some states other open space land. Programmes vary from state to state, but the most common policy assesses the land at its value in its current agricultural or open space use (the use-value), as though the land had no speculative value for development. This study examines the policy issues behind farmland preservation programmes, reviews related research and examines the effect of tax relief policies on farmland retention using county-level panel data.

FARMLAND PRESERVATION AND PREFERENTIAL TAXATION

A landowner's property tax liability is determined by the basis to which the tax rates are applied (the assessment) and by the sum of the jurisdictional

*   The author is grateful to Helen Ladd and Karl Case for helpful comments on an earlier draft. Helen Ladd also contributed some unpublished background research. Thanks go to the excellent community of public finance economists at Princeton University and the participants at the TRED conference at the Lincoln Institute for valuable advice, and to the Center for Economic Policy Studies at Princeton for funding data acquisition.

rates that apply to the land, for example school district tax, city tax and library tax. These rates are usually determined locally rather than by state law.[1] The proportion of actual market value that a state uses as the property tax basis is known as the assessment ratio. These ratios vary widely across states, but are usually uniform within a state.[2] Almost all state programmes affecting farm property taxes work through the assessment because the overlapping mosaic of jurisdictions makes legislating rates too complicated.

Most people view special tax treatment of farmland as providing incentives to preserve farmland, and to many the preferential taxation of farmland is another government giveaway to a special interest group, shifting the tax burden on to everyone else. Indeed trying to distort the course of natural sectoral shifts in the economy is costly and probably fruitless in the long run in the absence of direct land use controls. Use-value assessment can also be a thorn in the side of strapped local governments, and political support for shifting taxes to non-farm property may be waning in some areas.

Possibly the most persuasive economic rationale for farmland preservation is the positive environmental externality associated with open space land, such as visually pleasing landscape, increased wildlife habitat and relief from congestion. In theory at least, use-value assessment only reduces tax burdens if there is pressure to develop the land, but development pressure does not necessarily correspond closely with the positive externality. If the primary policy goal is to preserve open space where it is enjoyed most, a programme targeted specifically at areas with the greatest social benefit might be more appropriate than non-targeted use-value assessment. Privately owned wilderness or otherwise idle land is not included in many tax relief programmes, in conflict with their ostensible goal of preserving open space land.

Another possible reason to tax farmland preferentially is to counteract implicit subsidies to development, such as construction of highways and airports in urban outskirts, and the deductibility of mortgage interest, which subsidizes large suburban plots. However, properly timed infrastructure investment has important economic benefits and may not create a land use distortion that should be counteracted. Some policy-makers may worry about a secure supply of food for future generations, although trends in technology and demographics make that argument uncompelling.

A lower tax burden on rural residents may be justified irrespective of broader land use considerations. Many of them pay privately for road construction and maintenance, sewage treatment, fire protection and other services, so rural landowners may consume fewer services per dollar value of land owned than residential or commercial landowners in the same taxing area. The benefit principle of property taxation would assign lower effective tax rates on rural land if its owners were relatively low users of the services that property taxes fund, and this would apply whether the land was used for farming or not.

For any of these reasons, state and local governments do mandate special tax treatment for farmland using a variety of approaches. Forty-nine states have included use-value assessment as part of their overall plan.[3] Along with preferential assessment, many states impose deferred taxes, also called rollback taxes, through which localities recapture previous tax abatements, sometimes with interest, when land is developed or otherwise loses its special status. Landowners in some states must sign long-term commitments or restrictive agreements not to develop in order to qualify for the tax break. Some states have a circuit breaker programme that targets tax relief to farmers whose property tax burdens are large relative to their income. In classified property tax systems, states apply different assessment ratios to different kinds of land (for example, residential, agricultural and industrial). The same tax rate applies to all land within a jurisdiction, but the tax basis of the land depends on its market value and the assessment ratio applied to its classification, with agricultural land generally receiving the lowest assessment ratios.

Land use zoning and purchasing conservation easements reduce property taxes indirectly by removing the development potential of the property, but direct land use controls pose several problems. They reduce assessments and property taxes on the targeted land, but nearby land without restrictions becomes more attractive for development. In fact, urban sprawl can leapfrog past protected areas, with the pockets of farmland in between becoming increasingly unviable for farming. Land use controls reduce the total tax base of a community, so either the tax burden must shift or revenue declines. Choosing parcels to protect efficiently is a difficult practical matter, and restrictive zoning may have takings implications. Innovative policy-makers may be able to exploit market forces in selecting parcels, perhaps through tradeable development rights.

Numerous authors have discussed the controversial issue of farmland preservation, though most approach the subject qualitatively. Gloudemans (1974) provides a comprehensive discussion of farmland preservation issues, and an interesting critique of relevant policies appears in Gardner (1977). Dunford (1980) and Barlowe *et al.* (1973) survey the different kinds of property tax relief programmes for farmland. Nickell (1994) discusses the extent of tax shifting caused by use-value assessment, and the statutes themselves are compiled in Aiken (1989). There are a few limited empirical studies of use-value programmes. A 1976 study of eight state programmes by the Regional Science Research Institute concluded that while differential assessment is a good way to reduce the tax burden on farmland owners, it is an inefficient and expensive tool for achieving land use objectives. Ferguson [1988] tests for a change in the trend of the proportion of land in a county devoted to farming with data from four Virginia counties near the Washington, DC area over the period 1920–80. He finds no significant effect of use-value assessment on development trends in three counties, while the fourth county showed a significant change in the trend of farmland loss after the policy was adopted. The current chapter includes close to 3000 counties and represents the first large-scale empirical study of the direct effects of the policy on land use.

While use-value assessment is the most common preferential tax policy for farmland, other schemes have received more attention in the literature. New York and California both have large programmes requiring restrictive agreements in order to qualify for special tax treatment. Conklin and Lesher (1977) discuss the New York policy of agricultural districts and contracts in two important agricultural counties. They point out that longer-term preferential tax agreements provide more incentive to undertake large farm-specific investments (for example, drainage, levelling and fencing), improving long-run efficiency. The contract programme established by the California Land Conservation Act, is known as the Williamson Act, is the oldest of the contract programmes and was studied quite carefully in the 1970s, with the main focus being the pattern of enrolments. Hansen and Schwartz (1975, 1976) find that under the Act, farmers who have little incentive to develop get substantial tax savings, and that farmers who might be prone to develop do not enrol in the programme. The authors conclude that while the lost revenue was substantial, there was no real impact on land use. Chicoine and Scott (1983, p. 2) cite evidence that states with lower income or a larger agricultural sector choose pure preferential assessment policies, and higher income, less property tax-dependent urban states combine preferential assessment with agricultural districts and restrictive agreements. Michigan and Wisconsin have circuit breaker programmes designed specifically for farmland (Gold, 1979, p. 103). One study of the Wisconsin circuit breaker programme, Barrows and Bonderud (1988), highlights the issue of defining income.

These studies are informative and useful, but leave important questions unanswered, particularly the direct impact of the policies on land use patterns. Even if planners and economists agreed (and they do not) that the government should be promoting farmland preservation, it remains to be shown whether property tax relief has worked. Clearly, if the difference between returns from farming and development is high enough, even zero taxation cannot preserve farmland indefinitely. The impact of a tax reduction can then only be to delay conversion of lands for which the disparity between farm and development returns is comparable with the tax reduction.

EMPIRICAL EVIDENCE ON THE IMPACT OF USE-VALUE ASSESSMENT ON LAND USE

To provide a bit of historical context, Figure 7.1 shows how many states adopted preferential tax policy in consecutive four-year periods. (See Table 7A.1 for the year and the type of special assessment policy that was adopted by each state.) While some states have modified their policies from time to time, in general the policies have remained fairly constant since they were adopted.

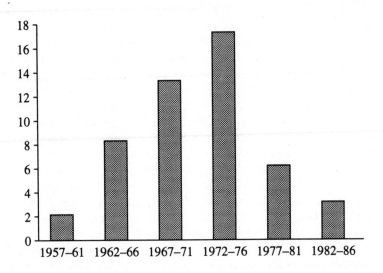

Figure 7.1   Number of states adopting use-value assessment in different time periods

The increased incidence of adoption of use-value assessment in the 1970s coincided with sharply increasing land prices and a general movement to reform assessment practices to conform with the law. Because farmland had tended to be systematically underassessed, some states may have adopted preferential tax policy to continue burdens unchanged in the wake of the reforms.

This study examines the effect of use-value assessment policy on farmland retention using county-level data from almost 3000 counties in 47 states from the years of the US Census of Agriculture 1959 to 1987 (1959, 1964, 1969, 1974, 1978, 1982 and 1987). This totals about 21 000 observations of county-year data. Table 7A.2 shows the number of counties from each state that were included in this study.[4] Table 7A.3 describes the variables used in this study, and Table 7.1 shows descriptive statistics for the proportion of land in a county that is agricultural, which is the dependent variable in the estimations that follow.[5] Changes in farmland share over time include farmland that is converted to and from other undeveloped uses as well as land lost to development.[6]

Table 7.1   County means (and standard deviations) of the dependent variable

County-level dependent variable	Year of the US Census of Agriculture						
	1959	1964	1969	1974	1978	1982	1987
Proportion of county land in farming	0.639 (0.276)	0.621 (0.285)	0.598 (0.300)	0.562 (0.300)	0.559 (0.303)	0.543 (0.297)	0.525 (0.303)
No. of observations	2963	2969	2957	2960	2957	2961	2939

In the estimations that follow, we ask whether counties in states with the policy lost significantly less farmland than counties in states that did not.[7] The first model specification is given by equation 7.1:

$$proportion\ farmland_{ct} = a_0 + \delta_1 polyr1 + \dots + \delta_{30} polyr30 + \beta_c + \gamma_t + \varepsilon_{ct} \quad (7.1)$$

The variable c represents the county and t equals the year of the observation. We want to allow different policy impacts in states that have had the policy for different lengths of time, so the empirical model includes a series of policy indicator variables, called *polyr1* to *polyr30*, that indicate the number of years the policy has been in place.[8] For each observation, we let a variable k_{ct} equal the number of years the use-value policy has been in place in county c in year t, where k_{ct} is zero if the policy has not yet been adopted. Then the indicator variable, *polyrk_{ct}*, equals one if county c in year t has had the policy for k years (no more, no less) and it equals zero otherwise. The series of coefficients δ_k on these variables trace out the cumulative effect of the policy over time without imposing a functional form.[9]

Year fixed effects are given by the γ_t in equation 7.1. These are important to control for year-specific unobservables, variables that do not depend on location but may have changed over time. For example, year indicators can control for the changing definition of a farm by the US Bureau of the Census. The 1974 and subsequent US Censuses of Agriculture required at least $1000 in sales to qualify as a farm, arbitrarily shrinking estimates of farmland acreage by a decreasing real amount. The year indicators represent 1964, 1969, 1974, 1978, 1982 and 1987, the last six of the seven years in the panel data.

County fixed effects, given by β_c in equation 7.1, control for local time-invariant unobservables, including all sorts of economic, demographic, policy, geographic and other characteristics associated with a given county that do not change significantly over time. In this model, then, the proportion of land in farming is the sum of the intercept,[10] the cumulative effect of the policy since it was adopted k years before year t, the county-specific factors, the year-specific effects and an error term. The second column of Table 7A.4 shows the ordinary least squares regression results for equation 7.1.

For comparison, we can impose a functional form on the cumulative impact of the policy. For instance, a linear function assumes that each additional year of the policy has the same effect. A quadratic form assumes that the effect of the policy accumulates over time, but potentially at a declining rate. If we assume a quadratic policy impact and let k_{ct} be the number of years the policy has been in place, the model becomes:

$$proportion\ farmland_{ct} = a_0 + a_1\ k_{ct} + a_2\ k_{ct}^2 + \beta_c + \gamma_t + \varepsilon_{ct} \qquad (7.2)$$

The third and fourth columns of Table 7A.4 show the regression results for linear and quadratic assumptions, respectively.[11] In the general model, the second column of Table 7A.4, a clear upward-trending pattern emerges in the *polyr* variables, implying that the policy has an increasing cumulative effect. Thus counties in states with the policy have clearly lost farmland at a lower rate than states without the policy. To visualize these results more easily, the regression coefficients on the policy year indicator variables are graphed (as squares) in Figure 7.2. The first year or two of adoption preserves about 2 percentage points more land in farming, and the cumulative effect increases significantly over time. After 20 years or so, we see about 10 percentage points more land in farming associated with the policy. This effect increases up to about 12 percentage points after 30 years, although the data contain few observations in that range.

The linear and quadratic models also show a positive trend in the impact of the policy over time, with a positive and significant coefficient on k, the age of the policy. The curve in Figure 7.2 shows the estimated policy impact from the quadratic model (equation 7.2) in column three of Table 7A.4. The negative coefficient on the quadratic term shows that the impact of the policy levels off gradually, to about 10 extra percentage points of land in farming after 30 years.

We now relax the assumption in the previous models that all versions of the policy had the same evolving impact. State policies clearly differ in

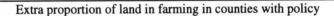

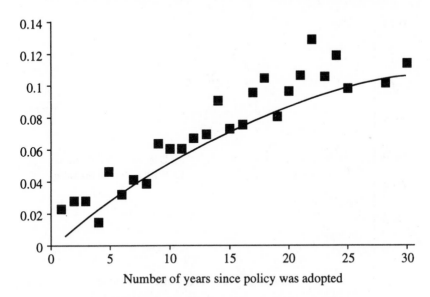

Figure 7.2 The impact of use-value assessment policy over time

whether they include deferred taxation, which allows local governments to reclaim some years of lost revenue when land use changes. The model in equation 7.3 allows counties in states with deferred tax to evolve differently. Again, the model includes variables *polyrk* (*k*=1...25, 28, 30), indicating whether the policy has been in place *k* years (no more, no less), but the model now also includes a number of additional variables, *dpolyrk*, that equal the *polyrk* only if there was a use-value assessment programme with deferred taxation in the counties and equal zero otherwise.[12]

$$\textit{proportion farmland}_{ct} = a_0 + \delta_1 polyr1 + ... + \delta_{30} polyr30 + \eta_1 polyr1$$
$$+ ... + \eta_{30} polyr30 + \beta_c + \gamma_t + \varepsilon_{ct} \qquad (7.3)$$

The regression results are listed in Table 7A.5. To visualize the results easily, refer to Figure 7.3, a graph of the policy effects with and without deferred taxation. The triangles are the coefficients on the *polyrk*, the indicator variables for the age of the policy, and the circles are the sum for each *k* of the coefficient on *polyrk* and *dpolyrk*, that is $\delta_k + \eta_k$.

We see from the estimation results and Figure 7.3 that counties in states with deferred taxation experienced significantly greater loss of farmland than

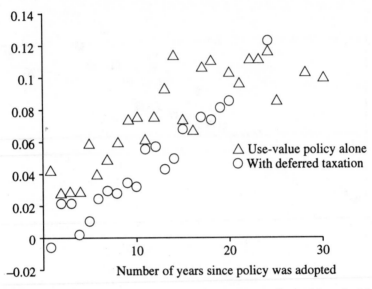

Figure 7.3 *The impact of use-value assessment policy, with and without deferred taxation*

counts with use-value assessment alone. After time the effects of the two implementations appear to converge somewhat, with some of the *dpolyrk* appearing insignificantly different from zero. If landowners must repay a portion of their tax abatement when the land is converted, then the disincentive to develop the land might have helped preserve farmland. We see no evidence of this. On the other hand, deferred taxation reduces the advantage to remaining in farming for the years of the tax recapture. If development pressure is building and the landowner expects that the next few years would only marginally put farming returns over returns to development, the loss of the preferential taxation may prompt earlier development. While at first glance we might think the lack of generosity inherent in deferred taxation could be behind the results of Figure 7.3, note that counties in states with use-value alone are already 4 percentage points different from those with deferred tax just one year into the policy. The results in Figure 7.3 suggest policy endogeneity if states that adopted deferred tax policies were the ones more prone to lose farmland. It seems plausible that areas where use-value assessment results in the biggest revenue loss would be more inclined to pass deferred taxation. These would be the areas where the disparity between the farming value and market value is highest, exactly the areas with the most development pressure.

Now we add other variables to the model, examine their influence on the dependent variable and determine the impact of the policy after controlling for them. Table 7A.6 describes the additional county-level explanatory variables, and their summary statistics appear in Table 7.2.[13] Population density has not gone up as much as one might have expected, and the market value of farmland and buildings peaked in the late 1970s – correlating closely with the value of farm products sold per acre. Property taxes per capita doubled from 1959 to 1987.

Table 7.2   County means (and standard deviations) of the explanatory variables

County-level variable (constant 1982 dollars)	Year of the Census of Agriculture						
	1959	1964	1969	1974	1978	1982	1987
Population density (population per acre)	146 (1176)	152 (1184)	128 (661)	127 (589)	149 (855)	160 (997)	173 (1055)
Market value of farmland and buildings ($ per farmland acre)	844 (6723)	1034 (8316)	942 (6271)	1163 (5158)	1479 (3362)	1288 (3560)	935 (2752)
Total property tax per capita	230 (158)	289 (193)	352 (231)	371 (257)	351 (264)	310 (252)	366 (300)
Value of farm sales ($ per farmland acre)	191 (1782)	183 (1167)	217 (1623)	314 (3214)	276 (1491)	244 (1615)	226 (1323)
No. of observations	2963	2969	2957	2960	2957	2961	2939

A quadratic specification is appropriate for population density because two kinds of county have very little farmland: mostly wilderness and mostly urban. If we had a measure of net returns to farming, we could find out how farm profitability preserved land in farming. Since county-level farm profit data are unavailable, we consider two possible substitutes: the average market value per acre of farmland and buildings, and the value of farm products sold per acre of farmland. Market values of farms will be high for two possible reasons: first because farming is profitable in that location, and second because there are pressures to develop that raise the market. The close correlation (0.81) of the market value of farmland and the value of farm produce supports the first explanation.

The effect of preferential tax policy probably depends on the overall property tax burden. If property taxes are not very high, then they are not a significant proportion of a farmer's production cost, and tax relief will not have much influence on a landowner's decision to sell out. We now interact a measure of the tax burden with the policy variable to find out how its impact varies with property tax levels in the county. It is not clear what measure would be best. Nominal tax rates are set very locally, so no one rate necessarily captures the county-level burden. In any case, nominal rates bear little resemblance to effective rates because of widely varying assessment ratios and classification systems. This study instead uses total property taxes per capita in the county. Taxes per capita are preferable to taxes per acre because they partially account for the greater share of structures in the tax base of densely populated areas. The tax variable is interacted with the policy by multiplying each of the indicator variables, the *polyrks*, with property tax per capita.

With the additional explanatory variables and the interaction terms (the η_i terms), the empirical specification becomes:[14]

$$
\begin{aligned}
\textit{proportion farmland}_{ct} = {} & a_0 + a_1 \ln(\textit{pop. density}_{ct}) + a_2 [\ln(\textit{pop. density}_{ct})]^2 \\
& + a_3 \ln(\textit{mkt. val. land}_{ct}) + a_4 \ln(\textit{prop. tax per capita}_{ct}) \\
& + a_5 \ln(\textit{value of produce}_{ct}) + \delta_1 \, \textit{polyr1} + \dots \\
& + \delta_{30} \, \textit{polyr30} + \eta_1 \, [\textit{polyr1}*\ln(\textit{prop. tax})] \\
& + \dots + \eta_{30} \, [\textit{polyr30}*\ln(\textit{prop. tax})] \\
& + \beta_c + \gamma_t + \varepsilon_{ct}
\end{aligned}
\tag{7.4}
$$

Table 7A.6 shows the results from the estimations of the enhanced model in equation 7.4, but without the interaction term. The second and third columns show the results for the linear and quadratic models of the policy effect over time for comparison with those models in Table 7A.4. After adding the other explanatory variables, the effect of the policy is still positive, significant and increasing over time, as easily seen in Figure 7.4. The evolving impacts do not seem to taper off as much as they did in the earlier models; in fact the quadratic term in column two in Table 7A.6 is statistically insignificant. For comparison, the line in Figure 7.4 shows the results of a linear policy effect model (third column of Table 7A.6).

As expected, the proportion of farmland and population density exhibit a strongly convex downward relationship. Two unexpected results are the negative relationships that market and produce values have with the proportion of land in farming, especially when controlling for population density. If those two variables are measuring the profitability of farming, then one would expect them to be positively correlated with the land in farming, especially since with the county indicators included we are measuring

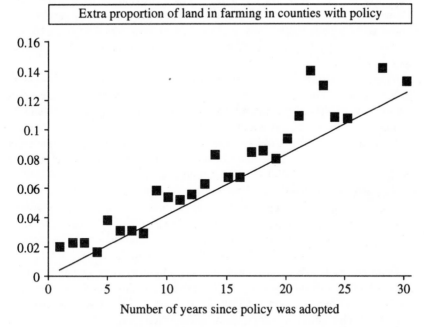

Figure 7.4   The impact of use-value assessment policy, controlling for other variables

everything relative to the county mean over time. Why would measures of farming profit not be positively related to farmland retention? One explanation could be that in counties with little farmland, perhaps it is the highest valued product that is the first to be produced or the last to be eliminated. It may also be that in areas with less farmland, fresh local produce receives especially high prices.

The interaction terms in Table 7A.7 have positive significant coefficients, suggesting that use-value assessment has more influence on land use when overall property tax burdens are higher, exactly what we expected. In the last column of Table 7A.7, the weighted totals of the policy and interaction term coefficients are computed; the interaction term is multiplied by the mean of the log of explanatory variables. That column is the full effect of the policy when interacted with the property tax levels, and we see a pattern very similar to the previous models.

These additional explanatory variables may be endogenous. For instance, the scale of agriculture in a county may affect farm returns, so the value of farm products sold (or any other similar measure) may be endogenous. Any measure of tax rates may be endogenous, because effective tax rates tend to be lower in rural areas, mostly because they provide fewer city services. Comparing the results from Table 7A.4, which did not include these variables, with those in Table 7A.6, we find consistent results for the coefficient on the policy variable. In every case, use-value assessment comes out positive and significant.

The policy itself may be endogenous, a standard econometric issue in policy analysis. In the context of this study, the concern would be that estimation results might not reflect the impact of the policy on land in farming, but rather the reverse. For instance, in states with a large share of land in farming, the farm lobby would be strong and successfully promote the adoption of the policy. First note that observations are county level and the policy is state level. With many counties in each state, the concern of endogeneity in the adoption of the policy is not as serious. Also, to get the results of Figure 7.1 through endogeneity of some kind, states would have to adopt the policy at a time when the individual counties in that state were already going to start losing farmland at a lower rate than they had before. There would have to be a change in the strength of the farm lobby or agricultural sector that made the beginning of a period of slower farmland loss coincide with the adoption of the policy, and this would have to be a fairly general phenomenon across states to produce the estimation results in this study. This does not seem to be a serious likelihood.

One final endogeneity concern may be that under a preferential assessment policy, landowners would have incentive to alter their behaviour in order for their land to become defined as 'agricultural' and be eligible, which would push up the measured proportion of land in farming. For instance, forest or idle land is not considered agricultural in some states unless a certain level of revenue is produced from it. A landowner may then sell a few Christmas trees or some firewood to pass the threshold and be eligible for the property tax benefits. That effect would better explain a big jump in the extra proportion of land in farming right after adoption, not the steadily increasing pattern in Figures 7.2, 7.3 and 7.4.

CONCLUSION

The estimations in this study suggest that preferential assessment of farmland can indeed delay the conversion of farmland to other uses. The policy produced a gradual but significant difference in the loss of farmland that after a 20-year period amounted to about 10 percent more of the land in a county being retained in farming than would otherwise have been the case. This is the first strong evidence of a long-term effect of use-value assessment on land use patterns. The results also predictably suggest that the policy may be more effective when property tax burdens are higher. While it would be useful to determine the effects of deferred taxation, the results here suggest that the choice of deferred tax policy implementation was endogenous.

While 10 per cent is a significant amount of land, several caveats are in order before the results of this study can be interpreted as an endorsement for the policy. First, this study has not demonstrated cost-effectiveness. Various studies (for example, Regional Science Research Council (1976) and Hansen and Schwartz (1976)) have concluded that use-value assessment does indeed relieve tax burdens on farmers,[15] implying some combination of lowered jurisdictional revenue and burden shifting. One way to get a simple measure of the potential revenue that communities lose would be to get data from states that require dual assessments for rollback taxation purposes. If states have to keep track of tax liabilities under both assessments, the difference would be a measure of the cost of the policy. Collecting a large sample of such data may not be simple because most tax records are kept locally and are often not in an easily accessed database. Even if a cost estimate could be determined, it still begs the question of whether or not the preserved land is worth the cost. The problems of monetizing the scenic amenities of open space are manifest, and measuring the externalities thoroughly would have to include the negative externalities to farming, such as agrochemical run-off and air quality impacts from dust and livestock.

Furthermore, it is not at all clear that preferential assessment should apply to all agricultural land, regardless of the value of the positive externalities it generates. If the amenity derives from open space generally, rather than farmland in particular, the common practice of targeting the programme solely to productive farmland does not follow. Finally, areas of urban sprawl cannot rely on preferential assessment, taking decades to accrue its potential impact on land use, to preserve open space when tax burdens are minor compared with potential returns to development.

NOTES

1. However, some states put upper limits on local rates.
2. Note that because assessment ratios differ, it is impossible to compare tax burdens in different states by looking only at nominal rates.
3. Use-value assessment exists in all states except Wisconsin, which has an income tax credit system for property tax relief and will be excluded from the empirical analysis in this chapter. While the principle of use-value assessment is quite simple, in practice it varies from state to state. One source of variation is in eligibility requirements. Some states have a minimum acreage requirement, usually about five to ten acres, and many have a minimum gross revenue requirement from the parcel, usually from $100 to $2500. New York requires revenue of $10 000 to qualify for agricultural districting. In theory, use-value is the capitalized value of net farm returns, but the owner's future income is difficult to capitalize when cost, price and yield are uncertain. Most states have a standard farm-value

formula based on the soil productivity rating, and some use state-wide average farm incomes in the computation of use-values, rather than the actual incomes for each farm. For a specific example of this computation, see Chicoine and Scott (1983), which outlines the formula used in Illinois. States also differ in the filing requirements, the number of years the land must be farmed before it is eligible, and the implementation of deferred taxation. Land use qualifications vary, but almost every ordinary agricultural production qualifies, and idle land that is part of crop rotation is generally included. Treatment of forest land and open space land that is not agricultural varies, and some states have separate statutes that cover timber land.

4.   Alaska and Hawaii have been excluded because early data were poor, and Wisconsin is excluded because it adopted a very different tax credit system. The data come from the Bureau of the Census, in particular the Census of Agriculture, the Census of Governments and the Census of Population and Housing. County-level data on land area, population and so on were obtained from computer tapes of *USA Counties* and the *County City Data Book*. All counties that appeared in each of the census data sources are included in this study. Some counties were excluded because their identifying numbers were not consistent over time, possibly because they were created or eliminated in the time period covered by this study. Independent cities were excluded because some Census of Agriculture data for them were unavailable. This represents a significant loss of data only for the state of Virginia, which has several dozen independent cities whereas only a handful of independent cities exist in the rest of the country. Some counties are excluded from the regression because of missing data, but these represent less than 2 per cent of the observations.

5.   When years for data from other censuses did not match up with the years of the Census of Agriculture, I interpolated between the available years. All dollar values are converted to 1982 dollars using the Consumer Price Index. The market value of farmlands and dwellings was determined by asking the operators their estimates of these values.

6.   Land defined as farming for census purposes may or may not qualify for a state's use-value programme, and vice versa. On one hand, the census classification is more strict because of the $1000 revenue requirement, somewhat higher than many states' eligibility requirements for use-value assessment. On the other hand, some states require land to have been engaged in farming for several years before it qualifies for use-value assessment, though the land would appear in the census figures. Data to untangle these problems are unavailable, so we use the term 'farmland' loosely to include both census and state statute definitions. For the census survey, the land in each farm was designated as being in the operator's principal county, the one where the largest value of agricultural products was produced. In a few, mostly agricultural, counties, this convention resulted in a figure for farmland acreage that was higher than the total acreage in the county. I dropped observations above 1.2 (163 out of about 21 000 observations) and truncated the rest to 1 (635 out of about 21 000 observations).

7.   As discussed earlier, not all states adopted identical policies, particularly those such as California and New York which had programmes involving agricultural districts and contracts. The regressions that follow were repeated without the four states with restrictive agreement programmes and the results were very similar.

8.   There are not many observations where k is greater than 25, and none for k equal 26, 27 and 29, so there are no variables *polyr26*, *poly27* and *polyr29*. The first column of Table 7A.4 shows the number of observations (for each k) for which *polyrk* is one.

9.   Note that this model assumes that the evolving impact of the policy does not depend on when it was adopted.

10. The intercept is the baseline proportion of farmland in counties without the policy in 1959, the first year of data in the sample, so all the other coefficients represent differences from that baseline.

11. County-level fixed effects explain much of the variation in the dependent variable, bringing the R^2 up to 0.975, from 0.0475 without county fixed effects. The regression coefficients are all statistically significant at a 0.1 per cent confidence level.

12. For some k there were no observations with deferred tax, so for those policy ages the

dpolyrk were dropped from the regression because they were perfectly colinear with the corresponding *polyrk* indicator variable.
13. When years for data from other censuses did not match up with the years of the Census of Agriculture, I interpolated between the available years. All dollar values are converted to 1982 dollars using the Consumer Price Index. The market value of farmland and buildings was determined by asking the operators their estimates of those values. The value of farm products sold may include wood products not covered by use-value programmes.
14. The model includes the log of the variables, so that the regression coefficients can be interpreted as partial elasticities. A percentage change in the explanatory variable will result in an a_i absolute change in the dependent variable.
15. Anecdotal evidence suggests that some formulae states use to determine use-value can lead to lower assessments even in the absence of development pressure.

REFERENCES

Aiken, J.D. (1989), 'State farmland preferential assessment statutes', Technical Report: University of Nebraska-Lincoln.

Anderson, John E. (1986), 'Property taxes and the timing of urban land development', *Regional Science and Urban Economics*, **16**, 483–92.

Anderson, John E. (1993), 'Use-value property tax assessment: effects on land development', *Land Economics*, **69** (3), 263–9.

Barlowe, R., J. Ahl and G. Bachman (1973), 'Use-value legislation in the United States', *Land Economics*, May, 206–12.

Barrows, R. and K. Bonderud (1988), 'The distributions of tax relief under farm circuit-breakers: some empirical evidence', *Land Economics*, **64** (1), 15–27.

Chicoine, D.L. and J.T. Scott (1983), 'Agricultural use-valuation using farm level data', *Property Tax Journal*, **2**, 1–12.

Conklin, H.E. and W.G. Lesher (1977), 'Farm value assessment as a means of reducing premature and excessive agricultural disinvestment in urban fringes', *American Journal of Agricultural Economics*, **59**, November, 755–9.

Dunford, R.W. (1980), 'A survey of property tax relief programs for the retention of agricultural and open space lands', *Gonzaga Law Review*, Spokane, WA: School of Law, Gonzaga University, **15**, 675–99.

Ferguson, J.T. (1988), 'Evaluating the effectiveness of use-value programs', *Property Tax Journal*, **7**, 157–65.

Gardner, B.D. (1977), 'The economics of agricultural land preservation', *American Journal of Agricultural Economics*, December, 1027–36.

Gloudemans, R.J. (1974), *Use-Value Farmland Assessments: Theory, Practice, and Impact*, Chicago: International Association of Assessing Officers.

Gold, S.D. (1979), *Property Tax Relief*, Lexington, MA: D.C. Heath and Company.

Hall G.E. and C.M. Slater (eds) (1993), *1993 County and City Extra, Annual Metro, City and County Data Book*, second edition, Bernan Press, Lanham, Maryland.

Hansen, D. and S. Schwartz (1975), 'Land owner behavior at the rural urban fringe in response to preferential tax treatment', *Land Economics*, **51**, 341–54.

Hansen, D. and S. Schwartz (1976), 'Prime land preservation: the California Land Conservation Act', *Journal of Soil and Water Conservation*, **31** (5), 198–203.

Heimlich, R.E., M. Vesterby and K. Krupa (1991), 'Urbanizing farmland: dynamics of land use change in fast-growth counties', Economic Research Service, US Department of Agriculture, Agricultural Information Bulletin No. 629, August.

Hsiao, C. (1986), *Analysis of Panel Data*, Econometric Society Monographs No. 11, Cambridge, New York and Melbourne: Cambridge University Press.

Keene, J.C. (1976), *Untaxing Open Space: An Evaluation of the Effectiveness of Differential Assessment of Farms and Open Space*, Regional Science Research Institute, Philadelphia.

Morris, A. (1995), 'Property tax treatment of farmland', PhD thesis in progress, Department of Economics, Princeton University.

Nickell, E. (1994), 'Tax issues arising from use-value assessment of agricultural lands', mimeo, Princeton University.

Rosen, H. S. (1992), *Public Finance*, Homewood, IL:Irwin, third edition.

Schwartz, S. I., D. E. Hansen and T. C. Foin (1975), 'Preferential taxation and the control of urban sprawl: an analysis of the California Land Conservation Act', *Journal of Environmental Economics and Management*, **2**, 120–34.

US Department of Commerce, Bureau of the Census, *Census of Agriculture*, Miscellaneous Years, US Government Printing Office, Washington, DC.

US Department of Commerce, Bureau of the Census, *Census of Governments, Volume 2 Taxable Property Values*, Miscellaneous Years, US Government Printing Office, Washington, DC.

Table 7A.1   State property tax policy for farmland

State	Tax Assessment Law			
	Preferential assessment only	Preferential assessment with deferred tax	Preferential assessment with restrictive agreements and deferred tax	Effective date for use-value assessment and/or contract programme
Alabama		x		1981
Alaska		x		1966
Arizona	x			1981
Arkansas	x			1969
California			x	1967
Colorado	x			1967
Connecticut		x		1963
Delaware		x		1969
Florida	x			1959
Georgia		x		1983
Hawaii			x	1963
Idaho	x			1970
Illinois	x			1972
Indiana	x			1963
Iowa	x			1969
Kansas	x			1977
Kentucky		x		1971
Louisiana	x			1978
Maine		x		1971

Table 7A.1   continued

State	Tax Assessment Law			
	Preferential assessment only	Preferential assessment with deferred tax	Preferential assessment with restrictive agreements and deferred tax	Effective date for use-value assessment and/or contract programme
Maryland		x		1957
Massachusetts		x		1974
Michigan			x	1976
Minnesota		x		1967
Mississippi	x			1975
Missouri	x			1983
Montana	x			1973
Nebraska		x		1976
Nevada		x		1975
New Hampshire		x	x	1973
New Jersey		x		1965
New Mexico	x			1967
New York			x	1973
North Carolina		x		1974
North Dakota	x			1973
Ohio		x		1974
Oklahoma	x			1976
Oregon		x		1963
Pennsylvania		x		1966
Rhode Island		x		1968
South Carolina		x		1976
South Dakota	x			1970
Tennessee		x		1977
Texas		x		1966
Utah		x		1972
Vermont		x		1978
Virginia		x		1973
Washington		x		1970
West Virginia	x			1985
Wyoming	x			1974

Sources: Aiken (1989); Gloudemans (1975, p. 16); Census of Agriculture (1987, Appendix C); Census of Agriculture (1982, Appendix C) and Census of Agriculture (1978, Appendix A, Table 3).

Tax policy as a land use tool

Table 7A.2   States and counties in the data set

State	No. of Counties (Total = 2963)	Percentage of Sample
Alabama	66	2.23
Alaska	0	0.00
Arizona	14	0.47
Arkansas	75	2.53
California	57	1.92
Colorado	61	2.06
Connecticut	8	0.27
Delaware	3	0.10
Florida	67	2.26
Georgia	159	5.37
Hawaii	0	0.00
Idaho	44	1.48
Illinois	102	3.44
Indiana	92	3.10
Iowa	99	3.34
Kansas	104	3.51
Kentucky	120	4.05
Louisiana	64	2.16
Maine	16	0.54
Maryland	23	0.78
Massachusetts	14	0.47
Michigan	83	2.80
Minnesota	87	2.94
Mississippi	82	2.77
Missouri	113	3.81
Montana	56	1.89
Nebraska	92	3.10
Nevada	16	0.54
New Hampshire	10	0.34
New Jersey	21	0.71
New Mexico	31	1.05
New York	61	2.06
North Carolina	100	3.37
North Dakota	53	1.79
Ohio	88	2.97
Oklahoma	77	2.60
Oregon	36	1.21
Pennsylvania	67	2.26
Rhode Island	5	0.17
South Carolina	46	1.55
South Dakota	66	2.23

Table 7A.2 continued

State	No. of Counties (Total = 2963)	Percentage of Sample
Tennessee	95	3.21
Texas	239	8.07
Utah	27	0.91
Vermont	14	0.47
Virginia	94	3.17
Washington	39	1.32
West Virginia	55	1.86
Wisconsin	0	0.00
Wyoming	22	0.74

Table 7A.3 Definitions and units of county-level variables in estimations

Proportion of land in farming	Proportion of county land area that qualified in census as farmland
Policy indicator variables *Polyrk*, where $k = 1,...,30$	Set of variables indicating whether the policy had been adopted k years (no more, no less) in a given state in a given year
Year indicators	Indicator variable = 1 if observation is for the given year, 0 otherwise
Population density	Population per acre of land area, logarithmically interpolated from Census of Population years
Market value of farm products sold	Average value per acre of all farm products sold (for example, livestock, crops)
Total property tax per capita	Total property tax revenues in the county divided by the interpolated population
Value of land and buildings	Market value of farmland and farm-related buildings per acre of farmland

Sources: Census of Agriculture: 1959, 1964, 1969, 1974, 1978, 1978, 1982, 1987. Census of Population and Housing: Census of Governments; 1993 County City Extra Data Book.

Electronic Data Sources: County and City Data Book Consolidated File, County Data 1947-1977; COSTAT 4; Census of Agriculture 1982, CD-ROM.

Table 7A.4   *OLS estimation results, model from equation 7.1*
              Dependent variable: proportion of county land in farming[1]

Explanatory variable	No. of observations where *polyrk* = 1, *k* = 1,...25, 28, 30	Model with all *polyr* indicator variables	Model with linear policy effect	Model with quadratic policy effect
polyr1 (1 if *k*=1, 0 otherwise)	794	.021		
polyr2	636	.027		
polyr3	580	.027		
polyr4	713	.015		
polyr5	818	.046		
polyr6	547	.031		
polyr7	520	.039		
polyr8	687	.037		
polyr9	653	.062		
polyr10	299	.059		
polyr11	804	.059		
polyr12	617	.066		
polyr13	422	.068		
polyr14	383	.090		
polyr15	464	.071		
polyr16	449	.074		
polyr17	193	.095		
polyr18	177	.104		
polyr19	206	.079		
polyr20	236	.096		
polyr21	340	.105		
polyr22	21	.129		
polyr23	66	.105		
polyr24	136	.119		
polyr25	23	.097		
polyr28	67	.099		
polyr30	23	.114		
k, the policy age			.004	.006
k^2, the quadratic term				−.0000735
Intercept		.641	.641	.641
Year indicator variables		yes	yes	yes
County-level fixed effects		yes	yes	yes
Adjusted R-squared		.972	.972	.972
No. of observations		20770	20770	20770

Note: [1]All variables appear statistically significant at the 0.1 per cent confidence level.

Table 7A.5 *OLS estimation results, model with deferred taxation indicators (equation 7.3)*
Dependent variable: proportion of county land in farming[1]

Explanatory variable	Regression coefficient	Explanatory variable	Regression coefficient	Sum of *polyrk* and *dpolyrk*
polyr1 (1 if k=1, 0 otherwise)	0.043	*dpolyr1* (= *polyrk* if state had deferred tax, 0 otherwise)	−.047	−0.005
polyr2	0.029	*dpolyr2**	−.007	0.022
polyr3	0.030	*dpolyr3*	−.008	0.023
polyr4	0.029	*dpolyr4*	−.028	0.002
polyr5	0.059	*dpolyr5*	−.048	0.011
polyr6	0.041	*dpolyr6*	−.016	0.025
polyr7	0.050	*dpolyr7*	−.020	0.030
polyr8	0.061	*dpolyr8*	−.033	0.028
polyr9	0.075	*dpolyr9*	−.040	0.035
polyr10	0.076	*dpolyr10*	−.044	0.032
polyr11	0.062	*dpolyr11**	−.007	0.055
polyr12	0.075	*dpolyr12*	−.019	0.057
polyr13	0.092	*dpolyr13*	−.050	0.043
polyr14	0.114	*dpolyr14*	−.064	0.050
polyr15	0.074	*dpolyr15**	−.005	0.068
polyr16	0.068	(*dpolyr16* dropped)		
polyr17	0.107	*dpolyr17*	−.031	0.076
polyr18	0.110	*dpolyr18*	−.036	0.074
polyr19	0.081	*dpolyr19**	.0007	0.082
polyr20	0.103	*dpolyr20**	−.018	0.085
polyr21	0.097	(*dpolyr 21–23* dropped)		
polyr22	0.112			
polyr23	0.111			
polyr24	0.116	*dpolyr24**	.006	0.122
polyr25	0.087	(omit *dpolyr25–30*)		
polyr28	0.104			
polyr30	0.101			
Intercept	.641			
Year indicators	yes			
County effects	yes			
Adj. R-squared	.972			
No. of obs.	20770			

Note: [1]All variables except some *dpolyr* indicators appeared statistically significant at the 0.1 per cent confidence level.
*Not significant at the 5 per cent confidence level.

Table 7A.6　Model with more explanatory variables
　　　　　　　Dependent variable: proportion of county land in farming[1]

Explanatory variable (per acre, 1982 dollars)	Model with *polyr* indicators	Model with linear policy effect	Model with quadratic policy effect
[ln(pop. density)	.066	.062	.061
[ln(pop. density)]^2	−.016	−.016	−.016
ln(mkt. val. of farm)	−.025	−.024	−.024
ln(property tax)	−.019	−.018	−.018
ln(value of produce)	−.019	−.019	−.019
polyr1	.021		
polyr2	.023		
polyr3	.023		
polyr4	.016		
polyr5	.038		
polyr6	.031		
polyr7	.032		
polyr8	.030		
polyr9	.059		
polyr10	.053		
polyr11	.052		
polyr12	.055		
polyr13	.063		
polyr14	.082		
polyr15	.068		
polyr16	.067		
polyr17	.085		
polyr18	.086		
polyr19	.081		
polyr20	.093		
polyr21	.109		
polyr22	.140		
polyr23	.130		
polyr24	.109		
polyr25	.107		
polyr28	.141		
polyr30	.133		
k, the policy age		.004	.004
k^2, quadratic term			−.000037*
Intercept	.969	.968	.967
Adjusted R-squared	.974	.974	.972

Note: [1]All models included year indicators and county indicators, and they all had 20 641 observations. All variables appeared significant at the 0.1 per cent confidence level, except for the quadratic term in column three.
*t-statistic = −0.388, not statistically significant at the 5 per cent confidence level.

Table 7A.7 *OLS estimation results, model with interaction terms (equation 7.4)*

Dependent variable: proportion of county land in farming *

Explanatory variable	Regression coefficient	Explanatory variable	Regression coefficient	Sum of coefficients, evaluated at mean of ln(*prop. tax*) = 5.525
ln(*pop. density*)	.070			
[ln(*pop. density*)]²	−.016			
ln(*mkt. val. of farm*)	−.020			
ln(*property tax*)	−.033			
ln(*val. of produce*)	−.019			
polyr1	−.127	polyr1* ln(prop. tax)	.026	0.016
polyr2	−.010*	polyr2* ln(prop. tax)	.006	0.021
polyr3	−.069	polyr3* ln(prop. tax)	.016	0.022
polyr4	−.127	polyr4* ln(prop. tax)	.025	0.013
polyr5	−.106	polyr5* ln(prop. tax)	.025	0.030
polyr6	−.097	polyr6* ln(prop. tax)	.022	0.024
polyr7	−.020*	polyr7* ln(prop. tax)	.008	0.026
polyr8	−.123	polyr8* ln(prop. tax)	.027	0.024
polyr9	−.031	polyr9* ln(prop. tax)	.015	0.051
polyr10	−.133	polyr10* ln(prop. tax)	.031	0.038
polyr11	−.065	polyr11* ln(prop. tax)	.020	0.044
polyr12	−.059	polyr12* ln(prop. tax)	.019	0.049
polyr13	−.068	polyr13* ln(prop. tax)	.022	0.052
polyr14	−.122	polyr14* ln(prop. tax)	.033	0.061
polyr15	−.029*	polyr15* ln(prop. tax)	.015	0.056
polyr16	−.069	polyr16* ln(prop. tax)	.023	0.061
polyr18	.161	polyr18* ln(prop. tax)	−.015	0.077
polyr19	−.229	polyr19* ln(prop. tax)	.053	0.062
polyr20	.028*	polyr20* ln(prop. tax)	.009*	0.077
polyr21	−.121	polyr21* ln(prop. tax)	.037	0.086
polyr22	−.274	polyr22* ln(prop. tax)	.063	0.071
polyr23	−.381	polyr23* ln(prop. tax)	.092	0.126
polyr24	−.269	polyr24* ln(prop. tax)	.062	0.075
polyr25	.043*	polyr25* ln(prop. tax)	.009*	0.093
polyr28	−.365	polyr28* ln(prop. tax)	.087	0.114
polyr30	−.060*	polyr30* ln(prop. tax)	.030*	0.109
Intercept	.969			
Year & county ind's	yes			
County-level effects	yes			
Adjusted R-squared	.975			
No. of obs	20641			

Note: *All variables appear statistically significant at the 0.5 per cent confidence level except those marked with an asterisk, which were not significant, even at the 5.0 per cent confidence level.

8. Incentives, firm location decisions and regional economic performance

William F. Fox and Matthew N. Murray

INTRODUCTION

Many communities seek the siting of large branch plants based on faith that the regional economy will be stimulated by the siting.[1] Communities often make significant tax concessions and provide substantial other incentives to woo plants because of expected jobs and income. Economic analyses of expected effects from plant entry are sometimes performed, either to assist in setting the value of inducements during the recruitment process or to determine the magnitude of impacts after the actual siting decision. These studies are almost always based solely on the effects of the single firm, and possibly its suppliers,[2] with no consideration to potentially offsetting dynamic effects in the region.

Firm sitings are expected to increase economic activity because of the anticipated movement of capital and labour demand from other regions into the area. However, in an analysis of the Nissan siting, Fox (1990) observed there were no signs that either the county or the broader area in which Nissan located showed greater growth after the location than before. One possible explanation for the counter-intuitive finding is that the expectation of faster growth ignores the simultaneity that exists between the siting of a major branch plant and the broader set of siting and contraction/expansion decisions. For example, interdependencies are likely to exist between a major plant siting and overall capital and labour flows of other firms, because the factors affecting expected profits and amenities are altered by the siting decisions of large visible firms. For example, Fox and Murray (1990) describe new start-ups and branch firms making siting decisions by maximizing over the package of expected profitability and amenities available at alternative sites. The siting of a major plant may significantly reduce any excess supply of labour and may bid up wages, causing other firms to locate elsewhere. The chance that other firms see the area as the best location option is reduced to the extent that higher wage rates and less available labour supply reduce an area's relative position among alternative locations. Also, tax concessions granted to a large plant can result in higher tax rates for other new firms, and public service demands imposed by a large plant may crowd service availability for other firms. Substitution for labour demand and capital that would otherwise be in the area means the major location at least partly substitutes for other economic activity. Thus it becomes an empirical question whether the two sources of growth are less than substitutable so that on net the new plant's impact is positive; exactly substitutable so the area can have the same amount of growth with either a new large facility or with other economic expansion; or more than substitutable so the area experiences a greater loss of other firms (and employment) than it receives from the new plant.

An empirical analysis of the extent to which regional economies are spurred by siting of a large employer is provided in this chapter. The next section is a description of the data and methodology. The third section is a discussion of the empirical results on the stimulus to local economies induced by new plants. Section 4 is a description of structural change in local economies that results because of the plants. The final section is a brief conclusion.

DATA AND METHODOLOGY

The goal is to determine the extent to which an area's aggregate economic activity is affected by the location of a large employer. This goal is accomplished by identifying a number of plant siting decisions and examining the effect on aggregate economic activity in the area around each siting. The major criteria in selecting firms for study were that initial announced employment was at least 1000 workers and that the sitings occurred in the 1980s, so that a significant history of data was available both before and after the location. A set of 24 firms making site selection decisions in the 1980s was found in *Site Selection Magazine*, as shown in Table 8.1. Included are seven motor vehicle manufacturing firms, 13 other manufacturing firms, and firms in the financial, transportation, services and retail trade industries. Each of the firms was contacted at the new site to confirm the date of first employment and the initial level of company employment.

The area affected by a large-plant siting could be defined in numerous ways. For our purposes, area is depicted alternatively as the county in which the firm locates and the multi-county region that includes the county of location and all adjacent counties. The latter is defined as the entire metropolitan area when location takes place in a metropolitan area. Two measures of economic activity were used as alternative measures of aggregate economic growth: personal income and employment.

Table 8.1   Selected large-company location decisions, 1983–89

Company	City	State	Opening date	Announced employment
Nissan	Smyrna	TN	1983	3000
Saturn	Spring Hill	TN	1989	6000
Mazda	Flat Rock	MI	1987	3500
Toyota	Georgetown	KY	1989	3000
Fuji-Isuzu	Lafayette	IN	1989	1700
Diamond-Star	Bloomington-Normal	IL	1988	2500–2900
Electronic Data Systems	Fairfax county	VA	1988	3000
American Express	Guilford county	NC	1986	2000
Cincinnati Electronics	Warren county	OH	1985	1000
Fort Howard Paper Co.	Effingham county	GA	1987	1000
Vitro Labs	Rockville	MD	1987	1000
Cannon USA	Newport News	VA	1987	1000
Zayre Corp.	Framingham	MA	1989	2000
3M	Austin	TX	1988	1500
IBM	Southbury	CT	1988	2500
Stouffer's Foods Corp.	Springville	UT	1987	1200
ITT	Fort Wayne	IN	1986	1000
GTE Corp.	Taunton	MA	1987	1000
Mack Trucks	Winnsboro	SC	1987	1200
Iomega Corp.	Salt Lake City	UT	1988	1000
UPS	Dallas	TX	1986	1000
Boeing	Lake Charles	LA	1986	1400
GCA Corp.	Bedford	MA	1986	1000
Grumman Corp.	Salisbury	MD	1984	1000

Source: Conway Data Inc., *Industrial Development and Site Selection Handbook*, Vol. 31, No. 1, February 1986, p. 15 and Vol. 32, No. 1, February 1987, p. 28; William F. Fox and David Mayes, 'Are Economic Development Incentives Too Large?', Proceedings of the Eighty-Sixth Annual Meeting of the National Tax Association, Columbus, Ohio; telephone interviews.

A simple time-series stock adjustment model is posited for regional economic growth. The specification employed here is a 'changes–changes' model that seeks to explain changes in economic performance in response to changes in economic forces affecting the region.[3] The model can be written as:

$$\Delta E = \lambda \beta' \, (\Delta X) + (1 - \lambda) \, \Delta E_{t-1} + \gamma \cdot OPENPLNT + \varepsilon \qquad (8.1)$$

where ΔE is the change in employment (real personal income), λ is the stock adjustment coefficient (with $0 < \lambda < 1$), β are the coefficients for changes in the explanatory variables (ΔX), ΔE_{t-1} is the change in lagged economic activity,

γ the coefficient of a zero–one indicator variable for the year of company opening (*OPENPLNT*) and ε is a normally distributed error term.

The model is specified so that regional growth (ΔE) is determined as a share of state growth (ΔX) through inclusion of separate explanatory variables for changes in state-wide employment (*STATEMP*) and changes in state-wide income (*STATINC*) in the employment and income equations, respectively. The state growth variables account for the range of regional location determinants such as wage rates, taxes and regulatory policy, so variables to account for these influences are not independently included. First differencing of the stock adjustment model implied by equation 8.1 (for example, the changes–changes specification), eliminates local fixed factors (including both county and time-fixed effects) that may influence site attractiveness. The stock adjustment process (ΔE_{t-1}) is modelled by including changes in the lagged dependent variable for employment at the county (*LAGEMPC*) and area (*LAGEMPA*) levels, and for income at the county (*LAGINCC*) and area (*LAGINCA*) levels.

The effects of the large plant sitings on regional economic performance are investigated using an intercept indicator variable (*OPENPLNT*). (A more flexible approach, one that will be pursued in extensions of this work, would allow the impacts to vary depending on, say, the number of new employees.) As new plants typically require several years to gear up to full production, and because local labour markets require some time to adjust, *OPENPLNT* is specified to take on a value of unity in the year of opening as well as the subsequent two years. (Noted below are results for alternative specifications of the indicator variable.) In general, if the new companies enhance regional economic performance, the coefficient of *OPENPLNT* should be positive. If, on the other hand, the new plants displace economic activity, there should be no significant impact associated with the company's entry: the coefficient should be negative if lost activity exceeds that generated by the plant. The indicator variable for plant opening is also included as an interaction term with state growth (*OPEN*STATE*) to allow for changes in the way the region responds to state growth.

There are two issues that affect the choice of estimation technique for the stock adjustment model. First, as a time-series model with a lagged dependent variable, the parameter estimates are subject to bias and inconsistency in the presence of serial correlation. Accordingly, an instrumental variables technique based on the Yule–Walker methodology is used to estimate the model, with the appropriate correction for serial correlation imposed on the estimation. A second issue is the potential for selection bias, since the analysis focuses solely on communities which are hosts to new facilities and does not control for the choice across sites.[4] For two reasons this issue is sidestepped here. First, data limitations preclude examination of why firms locate where they do, since there is no knowledge of the range of sites considered, nor tax (or other) inducements offered by various jurisdictions to attract these facilities. Second, the data on incentive offers represent the most important unobservable in the model. However, major discretionary concessions granted to large new plants are typically dominated by state-level, as opposed to local-level, resources, and have little impact on where a company locates its facility within a state.

EMPIRICAL FINDINGS

The empirical results for time-series/cross-section estimates of the stock adjustment model are presented in Table 8.2 for four alternative specifications of the model. Equations are estimated using pooled data for 1973 through to 1993 for 24 companies, yielding 480 degrees of freedom. The first two equations explain variations in county- and area-wide employment, and the second two explain changes in county- and area-wide personal income. In general the models perform well, with $\bar{R}^2$ values lying between 0.67 and 0.73. The state growth variables, *STATEMP* and *STATINC*, are highly significant and positive, indicating that local areas share in the growth of the state region in which they are located. Coefficients for the lagged changes in the dependent variable are statistically significant only in the income equations where the lag operator λ (which falls within the appropriate zero–one interval) takes on a positive sign. The magnitude of λ suggests that about 17–19 per cent of the adjustment in regional income takes place in the first three years after plant opening. The intercept term, which is included to control for time-trend influences on regional growth, is positive and significant only in the area income equation.

Primary interest lies in the results for the indicator variable on company openings (*OPENPLNT*) and the interaction variable (*OPEN*STATE*). Rather surprisingly, the coefficient of *OPENPLNT* is negative and statistically significant in two instances out of the four equations. The results for the interaction variable *OPEN*STATE* indicate that area and county income grow more rapidly as a share of state income following plant siting. The results for the indicator variable reveal more than complete displacement as large new plants locate, with the real or perceived influences of the plant causing a greater reduction in other economic activity than is created by the plant.[5] A number of reasons can be listed as to why displacement will occur. One is that other large, visible employers may choose not to locate because they want a position of prominence in the community, a position that may be eroded by the major siting. There are also perceptions and realities related to community costs. For example, new business entries to the community may drive up land

Table 8.2   Estimation results: impact of large plants on regional growth

	Employment		Personal income	
Variable	County	Area	County	Area
STATEMP	0.099***	0.262***	–	–
	(.006)	(.018)		
STATINC	–	–	0.078***	0.230***
			(.006)	(.018)
LAGEMPC	0.053	–	–	–
	(.041)			
LAGEMPA	–	0.067	–	–
		(.043)		
LAGINCC	–	–	0.166***	–
			(.044)	
LAGINCA	–	–	–	0.186***
				(.043)
OPENPLNT	–422.0	–4510.6	–132199**	–295020*
	(1646.7)	(4857.4)	(52142)	(159000)
OPEN*STATE	–0.011	0.039	0.058***	0.154**
	(.015)	(.044)	(.016)	(.048)
Intercept	473.3	4412.2	8178.5	164266*
	(1132.3)	(3157.6)	(33292)	(99200)
	.73	.67	.68	.68

   *   Significant at 10%.
  **   Significant at 5%.
***   Significant at 1%.

Note: The Yule-Walker autoregression procedure is used to estimate the model. Coefficient estimates are reported with standard errors in parentheses.

costs and wage rates, while new population may increase residential housing costs. Further, new population may expand the scope of required service delivery, a problem aggravated by the granting of concessions to the new plant. Disentangling the web of potential influences is an important direction for future research.

The finding of neutral or negative impacts arising from plant sitings will surprise many. In an effort to determine the robustness of the results, several alternative specifications of the model were estimated. Alternative specifications confirmed the findings reported in Table 8.2 of complete or more than complete crowding out. The first avenue pursued was the exploration of alternative specifications of the indicator variable *OPENPLNT*. The changes–changes specification was re-estimated constraining the indicator variable to take on a value of unity only in the year of company opening. The results were largely the same, with only one instance of a statistically significant and negative coefficient on *OPENPLNT*. Also examined was an extended changes–changes model wherein the indicator variable was allowed to be unity in all years after plant siting. When significant, the indicator variables took on negative signs and the interaction terms were positive. Finally, a 'levels–levels' specification of the stock adjustment model was estimated, with levels of employment (income) as the dependent variable and explanatory variables expressed in levels form. The indicator variable, which was specified to take on a value of one in the year of opening and all subsequent years, was generally insignificant, while none of the interaction terms were significant.

The changes–changes model was also estimated for the pooled set of six automobile plants included in the sample. The automobile plants may be unique due to their large multiplier impacts (see Fulton and Grimes, 1993) and the extensive supplier networks they create and support (see McAlinden and Smith, 1993). Moreover, some of the most lucrative concession packages have been extended to the automobile sector in anticipation of substantial economic and fiscal rewards. The results, based on specifications identical to those in Table 8.2, show that neither *OPENPLNT* nor its interaction with state growth is statistically significant. In alternative equations that included the intercept and slope variables individually, no instances of statistically significant responses to the new automobile plants emerged.

The stock adjustment model also was estimated separately for each of the 24 individual plants. Despite the limited degrees of freedom, these models had reasonably strong overall explanatory power. The results for the plant opening variables are summarized in Table 8.3. The top half of Table 8.3 corresponds to the same model as summarized in Table 8.2, with both the indicator and its interaction term included in the estimated equation. The results in the bottom half of Table 8.3 include the indicator and interaction variables individually. 'No effect' is the primary finding. For the employment equation, positive responses occur somewhat more frequently than negative responses, while for income the number of positive and negative effects appears to be about the same. Nonetheless, only in a minority of the cases are the dummy variables statistically significant. Moreover, the frequent occurrence of insignificant or negatively signed coefficients provides little support for the view that large company locations consistently provide a boost to regional growth. Together, based on the individual firm regressions, there are 192 opportunities for the dummy variable on plant opening to be significant.[6] The variable *OPENPLNT* is positively associated with regional growth in 25 of the cases, whereas company openings are associated with reduced growth

Table 8.3   *Number of significant coefficients for individual firm equations*

	Dependent variable			
	Employment		Income	
	County	Area	County	Area
Combined				
Intercept	4 positive	1 positive	0 positive	0 positive
	1 negative	0 negative	0 negative	0 negative
Slope	2 positive	0 positive	3 positive	2 positive
	1 negative	1 negative	0 negative	1 negative
Individual				
Intercept	7 positive	5 positive	5 positive	3 positive
	2 negative	1 negative	2 negative	2 negative
Slope	5 positive	3 positive	5 positive	4 positive
	2 negative	1 negative	3 negative	2 negative

Note: Based on the same specification of the empirical model as reported in Table 8.2. Under the 'combined' heading the variables are included jointly, whereas the variables are included individually under the 'individual' heading.

in eight of the cases. Hence while there are some specific instances of positive growth emanating from new company locations, there are far more instances of complete or more-than-complete displacement of existing economic activity.

A final option was pursued to account for the possibility that the sheer size of the county and area-wide economies included in the sample simply mask impacts associated with the new company in question. In general, the larger a company relative to the regional economy, the more pronounced the expected effect on the economy. Accordingly, the empirical analysis was confined solely to those firms whose opening employment exceeded 1 per cent of county employment, a total of 14 firms. The indicator and interaction coefficients have eight opportunities to be statistically significant, four times when both variables are entered together, and four times when entered alone in the equation. The coefficient of *OPENPLNT* was insignificant in all instances, while one of the interaction terms was negative and statistically significant. In contrast, when the analysis is confined to the ten firms whose opening employment accounted for less than 1 per cent of employment, there is weak evidence of more-than-complete displacement, with the coefficient of *OPENPLNT* being negative and statistically significant in two of eight instances. These findings suggest that displacement is more pronounced in cases where the plant is small relative to the regional economy. A possible explanation is that perceptions that cause other economic activity not to occur may be the same regardless of the relative size of the plant, even though the actual impact of the plant in terms of direct employment and income is smaller.

Despite the general consistency of these findings, they must be taken as preliminary in light of the potential for selection bias due to the absence of information on communities considered, but not chosen, for location. In subsequent research, the analysis will be extended to a much larger number of communities, and techniques will be developed to address the selection bias problem. This analysis will first estimate the binary choice of location and then, conditional on location, examine impacts that arise from the amount of income and employment generated by firm entry into the community.

STRUCTURAL CHANGE

This empirical evidence reveals substantial displacement of existing economic activity in the face of new entrants to the regional economy. An important question that remains unanswered is whether large-plant sitings induce significant changes in the structure and composition of the local economy as well. For example, while there may be little or no impact on aggregate income, there may be offsetting impacts in the composition of earnings across sectors or across components of personal income. Similarly, neutral or negative impacts on aggregate employment may be consistent with substantial movements in the distribution of employment in favour of the new industry and at the expense of other sectors. These structural changes in income and employment potentially can have important implications for performance of both regional economies and local governments. For example, regional growth in the automobile sector may have little impact on aggregate employment, but may lead to an increase in the share of employment (income) in one of the most cyclically sensitive economic sectors. This structural change may generate lower troughs on the economy in economic downturns, in turn placing local governments at increased financial risk.

In an effort to understand better the structural implications of large-plant sitings, structural change indices were calculated for each county, area and state included in the database (see Lawrence, 1984). The index of structural change, I, is defined as:

$$I = .5(1/k)\sum_{i=1}^{n}\left|S_{i,t} - S_{i,t+k}\right| *100 \tag{8.2}$$

where $S_{i,t}$ is the share of employment in industry i at the beginning period t, and $S_{i,t+k}$ is the share of employment in the same industry in year $t+k$. Note that the index captures the average annual change in employment structure. In the case of no change in the distribution of employment, the index takes on a value zero, whereas higher values of the index indicate a greater degree of structural change. Consider, for example, a simple case of two industries, with 80 per cent of beginning period employment in the first sector and the remaining 20 per cent of employment in the second sector. If the employment distribution shifted to a 70 per cent–30 per cent split within a five-year window (that is, $k=4$), the structural change index would take on the value of 2.5 per cent. Thus even a modest change in the index represents a rather substantial shift in the structure of regional employment.

The indices of structural change were calculated for employment at the one-digit SIC level for two time periods, as shown in Table 8.4. Consider first the indices for the period extending from the date of company opening to 1993. Note that on average counties hosting a large new company realized an annual structural employment change of nearly 1.1 per cent, substantially higher than the rates of change for the broader area-wide region (0.76) and the state (0.71). Moreover, seven counties had structural change values greater than unity, whereas only two areas and a single state experienced changes in structure of a similar order of magnitude.

To account for the impacts arising through facility construction as well as 'announcement impacts' that may lead incumbent firms and potential new entrants to create employment in other locations in anticipation of the new plant's location, the structural change index was also calculated for two years prior to the date of first employment to 1993. The results are presented in the last three columns of Table 8.4. There are seven instances where the county index exceeds unity and no instances of an area realizing the same degree of change. Again these results are consistent with earlier findings of greater structural adjustments in counties hosting new plants than in the broader area-wide or state region. At the same time, the indices that allow for construction impacts reveal relatively less structural change to 1993 than the measures that rely on the actual date of opening. This suggests that the construction phase and pre-siting announcement impacts have less pronounced influences than those arising from siting itself.

As a final and complementary step, the structural change indices were also calculated for the period 1972 to the date of plant opening, allowing a comparison of structural change both before and after siting. A strength of this comparison is that the analysis provides a pre-siting period of over ten years for each community. At the same time, there are many potential influences on structural change over this period, and the period generally represented one of dramatic structural change in the United States and its regional econo-

Table 8.4   Structural change indices for regional employment

Company name	Index for opening date to 1993			Index for opening date minus 2 to 1993		
	County	Area	State	County	Area	State
Nissan	0.862	0.630	0.710	0.854	0.772	0.800
Saturn	2.358	0.712	0.690	1.221	0.631	0.634
Mazda	0.648	0.533	0.591	0.671	0.665	0.668
Toyota	0.898	0.616	0.513	1.991	0.386	0.502
Fuji-Isuzu	1.177	0.920	0.861	0.589	0.690	0.478
Diamond-Star	0.574	0.635	0.612	0.545	0.579	0.531
Electronic Data Systems	0.878	0.710	0.639	0.853	0.541	0.572
American Express	0.952	0.831	0.631	0.766	0.804	0.664
Cincinnati Electronics	0.792	0.664	0.602	0.853	0.691	0.617
Fort Howard Paper Co.	3.415	0.737	0.676	1.126	0.685	0.675
Vitro Labs	0.802	0.549	0.637	0.587	0.525	0.636
Cannon USA	1.174	0.602	0.568	1.292	0.615	0.582
Zayre Corp.	1.529	1.103	1.077	1.314	0.992	0.953
3M	0.972	0.873	0.593	0.904	0.836	0.690
IBM	0.838	0.966	0.966	0.810	0.892	0.892
Stouffer's Foods Corp.	0.927	0.642	0.645	0.927	0.642	0.645
ITT	0.554	0.477	0.447	0.649	0.539	0.578
GTE Corp.	1.137	0.928	0.953	1.135	0.885	0.875
Iomega Corp.	0.569	0.728	0.735	0.600	0.654	0.633
UPS	0.971	0.962	0.690	0.832	0.867	0.763
Boeing	0.452	0.726	0.552	0.675	0.825	0.596
GCA Corp.	1.261	0.922	0.894	1.218	0.867	0.833
Grumman Corp.	0.897	1.012	0.936	0.653	0.828	1.037
Average	1.071	0.760	0.705	0.916	0.713	0.689

mies. On average the pre-location indices are 0.75 for the counties, 0.71 for the areas and 0.68 for the states. A comparison with Table 8.4 reveals that structural change accelerated for each of these regions following plant siting, with the counties' index up 43.7 per cent, the area's rate up 6.7 per cent and the state's index growing by 3.7 per cent.

The various measures of structural change reveal appreciable transformation in the make-up of county employment following the location of large new plants. The concentration of these structural impacts within the county rather than the broader area of location is not surprising, as the external shock represents a larger share of county-level economic activity.

CONCLUSION

Large incentive packages granted to new firms are typically predicated in anticipation of substantial economic and fiscal gains for the host government. Yet with the exception of impacts specific to the firm in question, little effort has been expended to ascertain the broader impact that new entrants have on regional economies. This chapter has explored the *ex post* implications of large-plant siting decisions on regional economic performance, allowing for job and income displacement in the face of new entrants. In general, while there are some specific instances of positive impacts on regional economies, the evidence points to complete or more-than-complete displacement of other economic activity. These findings, which must be viewed as preliminary, suggest the need for further inquiry into the consequences of firm location. There is also evidence of substantial shifts in the structure of employment following large-plant sitings, especially at the county level.

A likely explanation for displacement is that factors that attracted the large plant are the same as the factors that would have attracted other economic activity. Yet the siting of the large plant changes the actual or perceived attractiveness of these factors for incumbent firms and potential entrants. Thus while a region's economy may be stimulated by the location of a large facility in places where other activity would not have located, the reality is that large plants simply do not appear to locate at such sites.

Together the evidence presented here questions the wisdom of using incentives to attract large new companies to boost regional economic performance. While large new plants may add visibility to the region and may cause restructuring of regional economies, there is little evidence of improved aggregate economic conditions following sitings. The stakes are quite high and further research is clearly warranted in several directions. First, the approach employed here to identify company impacts through indicator variables is only one possible approach. An alternative direction would be to identify the nature and path of adjustment through use of intervention analysis (see Mills, 1990). A second area is the potential for simultaneity between incentive offers and plant siting decisions. If data were available, an extended analysis could explore the choice of plant site across the set of potential options with explicit controls for state and local inducements. This same framework could be used to address the selection bias problem noted above, by first estimating the likelihood of locating and then estimating the conditional impacts of location. A third line of inquiry would be to pursue the underlying causes of displacement, such as perceptions of labour market conditions, escalating input prices or tax burden shifting through provision of incentives. Such research may be of use in efforts to mitigate the actual or perceived negative consequences of large-company sitings on regional economic growth and may improve the targeting of industrial recruitment activities.

NOTES

1. Of course, there are reasons other than actual economic effects as to why plants may be recruited. For example, political leaders may want to recruit firms because their siting in the jurisdiction leads to a perception of success.
2. For example, see Center for Business and Economic Services and Fluor Daniel Siting and Consulting Services (undated) and Center for Business and Economic Research (1992).
3. See Bartik (1991) for a discussion of alternative specifications of the stock adjustment model.
4. One approach to dealing with the selection bias issue is through the application of specialized statistical tools; see Maddala (1983). An alternative is to develop a pseudo-control group, using the quasi-experimental design approach. This latter approach uses multidimensional matching to identify similar communities, one receiving treatment (that is, plant location) and the other not.
5. Largely neutral effects surface under respecifications of the model where the dummy and interaction terms are included individually. In these latter equations, the coefficients of the indicator variables are statistically insignificant, while the interaction terms in the county and area income equations have positive effects.
6. This includes eight equations, four of which include both the slope and intercept dummies and four of which include only the dummy variable and 24 companies. Note that an array of alternative specifications of the model was also estimated, including employment and income growth rate equations. In general, plant openings had either no impact or a negative impact on regional growth.

REFERENCES

Bartik, Timothy J. (1991), 'The effects of property taxes and other local public policies on the intrametropolitan pattern of business location', in Henry W. Herzog and Alan M. Schlottmann (eds), *Industry Location and Public Policy*, Knoxville, TN: The University of Tennessee Press.

Center for Business and Economic Research (1992), *The Economic Significance of Toyota Motor Manufacturing, USA, Inc. in Kentucky*, Lexington: College of Business and Economics, University of Kentucky.

Center for Business and Economic Services and Fluor Daniel Siting and Consulting Services (undated), *Economic Impact Analysis of the Mercedes Benz A. G. MPV Production Facility for the State of Alabama*, Troy, Alabama.

Fox, William F. (1990), 'Japanese investment in Tennessee: the economic effects of Nissan's location in Smyrna', in Ernest J. Vanarella and William C. Green (eds), *The Politics of Industrial Recruitment*, New York: Greenwood Press.

Fox, William F. and Matthew N. Murray (1990), 'Local public policies and interregional business development', *Southern Economic Journal*, **57**, 413–27.

Fulton, George A. and Donald R. Grimes (1993), *The Economic Impact of the Domestic Automotive Industry on the US and its Major Regions*, Ann Arbor: Institute of Labour and Industrial Relations, University of Michigan.

Lawrence, Robert Z. (1984), *Can America Compete?*, Washington, DC: Brookings Institute.

Maddala, G. S. (1983), *Limited-Dependent and Qualitative Variables in Econometrics*, Cambridge: Cambridge University Press.

McAlinden, Sean P. and Brett C. Smith (1993), 'The changing structure of the US automotive parts industry', Office for the Study of Automotive Transportation, University of Michigan Transportation Research Institute, Report VMTRI-93-6.

Mills, Terence L. (1990), *Time Series Techniques for Economists*, Cambridge, MA: Cambridge University Press.

9. Tax increment financing as a tool of redevelopment*

Jeffrey I. Chapman

Local redevelopment activities involve a mixture of politics, demographics, public sector fiscal stress and public financing issues. These activities are often controversial and frequently result in contentious public hearings concerning such problems as the appropriate use of eminent domain, the extensive removal of housing units and subjective definitions of blight. However, methods of redevelopment finance are often overlooked.

This chapter analyses one particular tool of redevelopment finance that has spread throughout the United States – the use of tax increment financing. The first section of the chapter describes the theory and practice of tax increment finance (TIF); the next section raises theoretical and applied policy issues concerning the appropriate use of this technique; the third section examines California as a case study of TIF over a period of nearly 50 years; and the final section draws conclusions based on this analysis.

THE THEORY AND PRACTICE OF TIF

Public redevelopment projects are designed as public sector interventions to mitigate the characteristics of blight. For most states, the legislation authorizing redevelopment explicitly mentions blight elimination. The goals of redevelopment are typically to attract new business, provide better housing and, in general, to stop the growth of urban decay. TIF is a technique that many redevelopment agencies utilize to generate funds for furthering the goals of redevelopment. The controversy that surrounds it comes from the potential use of the technique in unblighted areas or for purposes only distantly related to easing the problems of blight.

TIF is thus a technique that was originally justified to finance the removal of blight but has also become a deliberate policy attempt to use the market

* The author would like to thank Helen Ladd and an anonymous referee for their helpful comments.

process as a tool of economic development.[1] These are not always the same tasks. This differential creates tension between the legal constraints of eliminating blight and the policy concerns revolving around the most efficient mechanisms for stimulating economic development. This chapter will partially examine this tension between the policy concerns and legal constraints that face TIF.

TIF was originally designed to raise matching funds required by national urban renewal grants. After these grants disappeared, the tax increment technique remained viable as a revenue-generating method. TIF is a multi-step process that, in theory, generates enough revenue to enable public financing of urban redevelopment. Its implementation process consists of the following:[2]

1. The relevant public agency (this could be a city, a county or a separate redevelopment agency) delineates a proposed project area and a plan for the redevelopment of that area. In most cases, the project area is blighted and urban. In many cases, the public agency has a series of projects covering different areas within the jurisdiction, with each project generating a revenue stream.

2. The financial feasibility of the redevelopment plan is determined. The estimated public costs of the projects intended to eliminate blight are compared with the estimated increased public revenues that will be generated from the project. The costs of the project typically relate to the service on the debt that the agency issues in order to undertake the project.[3] The increased revenues typically come from TIF.

3. The public agency is able to use TIF after the plan has been adopted. The initial property tax base of the project is 'frozen' on the tax roll. As redevelopment in the project area takes place, the assessed value of the property within the project increases above the frozen base. As this increase occurs, the property taxes collected on the property also increase. Those taxes collected on the original (frozen) base are allocated to the original tax-recipient jurisdictions; for example, school districts, local governments and certain special districts. These overlapping jurisdictions receive the same tax revenues that they realized at the time that the project was approved. However, the increment of taxes collected that is associated with the increased assessed value goes to the public agency that established the district. A political advantage of this approach is that the property owners within the project area pay additional property taxes that are generated only by the increase in the value of their property.

4. The agency converts this long-term tax revenue stream into immediate dollars to be used in redevelopment activities through the issuance of tax-free debt that is backed by this new revenue.[4] The tax increment is

used to pay the principal and interest of the debt that the agency issued to help finance the redevelopment project.

5. When the debt is retired, the project area is returned to the tax base of the jurisdiction.[5] For successful programmes, the new tax base is considerably larger than before the redevelopment activities began. At times, the debt can be refinanced and the length of the project extended.

The underlying theory is that no private economic redevelopment would take place without the stimulation of the public redevelopment activities. Without this stimulation, the assessed value of the blighted area would remain constant, with no change in the tax revenues of the original taxing jurisdictions. What seemingly has occurred is that the redevelopment activities have become self-financing: the increment in land value generates the revenue to pay for the debt that was used to finance the expenditures that helped to cause the increment in land value.

Two additional concerns are important. First, it is likely that the local agency will receive revenues in addition to those generated by TIF. In particular, interest income and intergovernmental grants can play a large role in the agency's budget.[6] These additional funds give the agency the fiscal flexibility to undertake projects that may face some risk in generating a large enough increment to satisfy the demands of the debt service. Second, in order for the bonds to have credibility in the bond market, there must be a demonstrable revenue flow from the increment. Yet this increment may not exist without the development that occurs because of the bond financing. Typically, the local agency jump-starts the project with either grants from another government, loans from the private developers or loans from the community itself (California Debt Advisory Commission, 1995).

TIF was used by over 5400 agencies in 44 states in 1992 (Forgey, 1993, p. 26). Most of the TIF districts were formed on the basis of the original California law. Extremely popular among local officials, these districts have been used to finance a phenomenal variety of projects, ranging from housing construction for very poor people to golf courses. All of the TIF districts follow the same basic structure, with some adaptations for local dissimilarities, principally in the area of tax assessment. In states with TIF, nearly all cities with populations over 50 000 use TIF and most of the time they are successful in covering their costs.[7] Finally, in most cases, TIF money is only part of a complicated 'package' of financing, especially where housing is concerned. Because the use of TIF continues to grow, several policy and outcome issues need to be addressed.

ISSUES FOR CONCERN

Questions concerning the use of TIF and the development activities that it finances are often intertwined. In particular, for TIF to be successful, it must generate an increment large enough to cover its debt service. For this coverage to exist, TIF may be utilized to stimulate redevelopment in areas that are already growing. Alternatively, TIF-financed redevelopment may be used to generate economic incentives for new development in order to alleviate municipal fiscal stress, not because of any blight in the area. The following policy and output questions are not independent. Answers to any one question influence the answers to the others.

Policy Issues of TIF

1. Is TIF really self-financing?

In the short run, with a fixed supply of land in the project area, if redevelopment acts as an exogenous influence to increase demand for that site, then land value will increase. This increase is an increase in the economic rent to the owner of the land. Part of the increased rent is taxed to provide the increment to support the improvements. This tax is analogous to the benefit charge approach to property tax incidence, since the redevelopment benefits are accruing to the property owner.[8]

TIF often appears to be a perpetual motion machine. Areas are declared blighted, debt is issued, improvements are made, property values increase, the increment appears and the debt is financed. But in the long run, it is likely that there will be diminishing marginal returns to redevelopment. Diminishing returns will lead to a decline in the projected increment, which will force a lower amount of debt to be issued. Ultimately, the increment will not be large enough to sustain a perpetual motion process.

In addition, the normal business cycle will affect the increment. Even with new redevelopment, there may be years in which the increment is not as large as anticipated, and the bonds could teeter towards default. If the increment from a specific project area becomes smaller than anticipated, the agency could reduce its expenditures in other project areas or utilize intergovernmental grants or interest income in order to sustain its credit rating by maintaining the debt service schedule.

2. How is blight defined?

Tax increment financing was originally designed and justified as a policy technique to mitigate blight. If blight did not exist, this financing technique was not to be used. However, blight was often not clearly defined. In practice, redevelopment agencies often depend upon the interpretation of economic and social data rather than on absolute numbers in identifying areas as blighted. At times, TIF projects reflect this subjectivity. If TIF is used for economic development, the entire question of blight may be irrelevant, since the goal is to stimulate development on unblighted land (even if the implementing jurisdiction declares the land blighted). In this case, the choice of the project is based on the maximization of the increment, not the necessity of redevelopment activities.

3. Is TIF used as a tool of redevelopment finance or a tool to relieve fiscal stress?

In practice, it is feasible for the goal of projects financed by TIF to be the relief of fiscal stress rather than the mitigation of blight. However, when used in this manner the TIF technique may not be consistent with its political and legal foundations.[9]

Fiscal stress is defined in specific contexts and may vary by the political will of the jurisdiction to raise taxes or cut services. However, it is also evident that some jurisdictions are more fiscally stressed than others. While 'unstressed' jurisdictions may consistently run budget surpluses, others are continually dipping into contingency accounts, borrowing from separate funds, instituting an array of new fees and charges, dramatically reducing services or allowing public infrastructure to deteriorate. If these jurisdictions raise taxes, they are likely to face increasing job loss and ultimately declining revenues (Inman, this volume).

Fiscal stress comes from many sources. In some jurisdictions, it comes from an exogenously imposed tax or expenditure limit. In others, it comes from a sudden exodus of a large employer or the impact of a new retail mall opening in an adjacent city. Some jurisdictions may have a population that requires a multitude of services. In others, stress may come from the deterioration of the property tax base. If this deterioration is related to urban blight, then successful redevelopment will increase the base and may ease some of the fiscal stress.[10] Therefore, by facilitating redevelopment, TIF may be alleviating fiscal stress.

To the extent that TIF facilitates redevelopment, it is also alleviating fiscal stress. However, this relief is indirect. The property tax increment does not go directly into the general fund of the jurisdiction that contains the blight, but rather is earmarked for debt service. Blight may be reduced, but there are no direct tax revenues that can be used for general purposes. However, if the redevelopment that is encouraged by the use of TIF generates non-property tax revenues, these may be claimed by the jurisdiction. For example, if commercial development is fostered, any new sales tax revenue flowing to the jurisdiction can be claimed for general use. In addition, if new infrastructure for the blighted area is financed through the tax increment, the funds that the jurisdiction might have used for that purpose can be used for other purposes.

Generally, if a project area is blighted, then TIF is being used for the reduction of blight and is only indirectly used as a general public financing tool. However, if TIF is used to address non-blight problems, it is being used as a tool to reduce indirectly the jurisdiction's fiscal constraints.

This latter use is observable in at least two instances. The first occurs if TIF is used for economic development (not redevelopment) purposes. If unblighted vacant land is declared blighted by the redevelopment agency and a development project is instituted, then there is some justification for believing that TIF is being used to address directly local fiscal distress. This use of TIF is especially apparent when large retail development is enticed into undeveloped areas through the use of TIF. The second instance can be observed when projects are designed to attract a particular new business into the community and away from another community. Part of the offer package may be a particular site that the new business desires, which might not be in a blighted area. If the potential new business can dictate its future location to a redevelopment area, it is likely that the jurisdiction is more concerned about fiscal stress than blight removal.

4. What are the interjurisdictional consequences of TIF?

In addition to the issuing agency, the jurisdictions that overlap the project area are also concerned about the size and allocation of the increment because of the hurdles of either increased costs or foregone revenues.[11] They may believe that the project has caused an additional financial burden because of an increase in the need for services or the loss of the incremental property tax revenues that they would have received if the project had not been implemented. For example, if a fire district has to provide additional fire protection because of the project, or if in the early stages of the project the value of adjacent property falls, the overlapping jurisdictions often argue that they deserve some of the tax increment. Again, if the project is extraordinarily successful and generates a tax increment larger than necessary to support the debt and associated expenses, an additional argument for sharing at least some portion of the increment exists. Finally, the overlapping jurisdictions may believe that the redevelopment would have occurred regardless of the agency's activities. These jurisdictions could then argue that they should receive part of the increment. All the governments that received any of the property tax that originated in the project area have an incentive to claim a share of the tax increment. This interjurisdictional sharing of the increment is often politically contentious, since in the short run the sharing is a zero-sum game.

The problem of tax increment sharing may also include a vertical dimension. This dimension occurs when different levels of government have commitments to maintain service levels for the overlapping jurisdictions. In particular, this commitment is true for school districts that have state-set expenditure floors. If a school district does not receive an expected increase in revenues, the state might be forced to increase its aid to the district. In addition, if the national government allocates any aid on the basis of low local funding levels, it too may discover pressure to increase aid to these jurisdictions.

Three basic outcomes can emerge from this controversial process: the agency that is in charge of the redevelopment can ignore the other relevant jurisdictions; it can negotiate with them; or a higher level of government can mandate the sharing rules. To complicate matters, the first two options also involve the courts which are invoked by aggrieved parties. Moreover, much of the discussion concerning the sharing revolves around arcane legal and financing constrictions and is impenetrable by the general public.

Outcome Issues of TIF

1. How much economic development would have occurred if TIF were not used for a specific project?
This is the most important question for TIF. If economic redevelopment would have occurred regardless of the redevelopment activities, then the increment would have also occurred and would be automatically included in the tax base of the overlapping jurisdictions. In this case, earmarking the increment to the implementing jurisdiction provides that agency with unjustified revenue. In addition, the private developers in the project area are unnecessarily subsidized through this procedure, since many of the costs that they would have been willing to absorb are assumed by the public through the TIF procedure.

Unfortunately, it is impossible to know what level of development would have occurred in the absence of TIF. This level of development depends on at least three conditions. The first is the amount of blight initially within the project area; the second is the state of the local economy; and the third is the package of other economic incentives that may be offered. It is very difficult, if not impossible, to disentangle the effects of these conditions.

If a project contains a large amount of blight, small and independently owned parcels, and poor capital infrastructure, it is not likely to attract many private investors. The worse the blight, the greater is the need for some public intervention. In this case, the majority of any increment generated presumably reflects the results of the TIF-financed project.

If the local economy is in the midst of a recession, private investment is likely to be limited throughout the community. Assuming blight exists, the odds of the private investment locating in the project area are small. In this case, TIF-financed redevelopment is necessary in order to generate any economic growth activity, but even so the project is likely to generate only a small increment. However, if the local economy is robust, then redevelopment is possible without extensive government intervention, even in the blighted area. TIF-financed redevelopment may not be as necessary, although if it occurs the increment is likely to be large.

Finally, jurisdictions can offer the private sector other incentives either to augment or substitute for TIF redevelopment. For example, instead of indirectly subsidizing developers by providing infrastructure, the jurisdiction can directly subsidize them through tax abatement policies (Fox and Murray, this volume). In this case, the abatement cost of the redevelopment will be on the particular jurisdiction that gave the tax subsidy – not on the other overlapping jurisdictions that act as free-riding beneficiaries as they observe their tax base increasing.[12]

There have been several site-specific case studies in Illinois (Davis, 1989; Ritter and Oldfield, 1990), Wisconsin (Huddleston, 1984) and Minnesota (Stinson, 1992), which indicate that TIF projects do stimulate economic development. A secondary benefit occurs because the focus on debt repayment schedules as part of the redevelopment plan forces the agency to establish an economic rationale for the debt in order to meet the demands of the public debt market. Unfortunately, there has been almost no empirical work beyond the individual case study to examine the success of TIF at generating redevelopment activity.[13] It is thus impossible to generalize as to the net benefits of TIF. It is likely that the focus on debt repayment schedules as part of the redevelopment plan forces the agency to develop a plan that makes economic sense in order to meet the demands of the public debt market.

2. What are the distributional outcomes of TIF?

In addition to the distributional consequences generated by the sharing of the increment, at least two other distributional concerns are important.

TIF was originally designed to generate a match for urban renewal funds from the federal government. To some degree, especially in the mid 1950s, these federal funds were to be used to improve housing conditions. One of the failures of these early programmes was the loss of housing units not replaced after the urban renewal (Rothenberg, 1967). The same concerns arise in connection with TIF redevelopment. TIF redevelopment must generate a revenue stream that is sufficient to provide a large enough tax increment to service the debt. In many cases, new housing will not by itself generate this large a stream. In addition, new housing will maintain or increase the population of the district, and thus generate additional service costs. If low cost housing is not replaced during the TIF redevelopment, the displaced inhabitants are bearing a burden that is regressive.

A second set of distributional concerns arises from the unanticipated budgetary consequences for the jurisdiction that undertakes the redevelopment.[14] Since at least one goal of TIF is to ensure that the tax increment is large enough to cover the debt, not much attention may be given to any additional costs generated by the project. For example, as redevelopment increases, some local service costs may increase (for example, police protection) while others may decrease (for example, welfare). If the net costs increase, service quality will deteriorate or taxes and fees will be forced up.

A BRIEF CASE STUDY: CALIFORNIA

California passed redevelopment legislation in 1945 and was the first state to allow TIF, beginning in 1952. The stimulus for TIF occurred when voters in several jurisdictions failed to approve the necessary one-third match for federal urban renewal grants and loans. Local officials viewed TIF as a substitute method to generate revenues to provide the match. Since 1945 the redevelopment laws have been tightened several times, in each case to ensure that redevelopment was actually occurring. The most recent major changes occurred in 1993.

Redevelopment in California is implemented by a unit of local government called a redevelopment agency. The existence of these agencies is inherent in the powers of all cities and counties and can be established, following the proper protocol, at the will of the relevant legislative body. They have the power to exercise eminent domain, to issue debt, to impose land use and development controls, and to engage in TIF. More than 95 per cent of the agencies are governed by city councils or boards of supervisors (California State Senate Committee on Local Government, 1989). Redevelopment finance occurs disproportionately in the larger jurisdictions. While only 42 per cent of cities with less than 10 000 population have instituted redevelopment projects, 47 out of 48 cities of more than 100 000 population have active projects.[15] The 686 current projects range from the very small (less than 50 acres) to the very large – there are 15 projects between 6001 and 25 000 acres. Redevelopment agencies claim that redevelopment activities generated over 27 million square feet of new or rehabilitated construction and created slightly more than 26 000 jobs during 1992–93.[16]

Table 9.1 indicates that until very recently the story of TIF redevelopment has been one of continuous and accelerating growth. In 1950 (before the legalization of TIF) there were two active redevelopment project areas in the state. By 1990, there were 658 project areas. The growth of the increment has been equally dramatic. In 1984–85, the tax increment was $0.4 billion and total redevelopment revenues were $0.9 billion. In 1992-93, the increment

Table 9.1   Project areas in California

Ending date	Number of areas
1950	2
1960	13
1970	76
1980	299
1990	658
1993	686

Source: California State Controller's Office (1995).

had more than tripled to $1.5 billion and total redevelopment revenues were $2.2 billion. The total assets of redevelopment agencies in this later year were $23.9 billion (California State Controller's Report, 1995). In this same year, the total assessed value of the tax increment was about 7.9 per cent of the total assessed property value for all counties. However, this percentage ranged from zero to slightly over 17 per cent, indicating that TIF was very important for some counties.[17]

TIF and Fiscal Stress in California

California faces many sources of fiscal stress. Two of the most important are demographic changes and self-imposed tax and expenditure limits. Both affect the use of redevelopment financed by the tax increment.

Between 1977–78 and 1994–95, California's population grew by nearly 44 per cent (about 10 million people). This growth put increasing pressure on both operating and capital expenditures for all levels of government. In addition, Proposition 13 was passed in 1978. This constitutional amendment reduced aggregate property tax revenues by about 60 per cent by lowering the property tax rate to a maximum of 1 per cent and reducing the property tax base. The growth rate of the property tax base was capped at 2 per cent until the property was sold, and new construction was added to the base at its market value. Because TIF is dependent on rising property tax revenues, the reduction in the property tax rate forced the new construction component to play a larger role in generating the increment. Some predicted that because of Proposition 13, only a few projects could generate sufficient increments and TIF would disappear (Merrill Lynch, 1979).

As Table 9.1 shows, this outcome did not happen. City councils (and some County Boards of Supervisors) quickly shifted into their concurrent roles as members of the boards of redevelopment agencies. They recognized that TIF could become a major tool for public improvements and that this tool was under their control. By carefully defining the project area and working with private developers who were anxious to expand, TIF could be made to work to relieve some of the stress. In particular, redevelopment agencies often set two goals.[18]

The first was to ensure that redevelopment would not only generate large property tax increments, but that it would also generate additional sales tax revenues.[19] The agency would use the increment to service the debt, and the jurisdiction in which the project was located would gain the sales taxes. Redevelopment was used for economic competition among jurisdictions. Automobile dealerships and 'big-box' retailers, such as Wal-Mart, were especially revered.

The second goal was to ensure that at least some new capital infrastructure would be financed by TIF redevelopment projects. Because of Proposition 13, local general obligation bonds were impossible to issue between 1978 and 1986.[20] The full faith and credit pledge required for these bonds could not be met because local governments did not have the ability to increase the property tax. Although some fascinating debt instruments were developed to raise money (Horler, 1987), the ease of issuing bonds backed by the tax increment made this method increasingly attractive, and tax increment debt rose from $2.9 billion in 1984-85 to $7.3 billion in 1992-93.

TIF might contribute to fiscal stress in the future. For 1995–96, approximately 40 per cent of a sample of redevelopment project areas showed decreases in the size of the tax increment (although the increment was still positive). Several of these decreases were over 40 per cent (California Redevelopment Association, 1995). Although no redevelopment debt has yet to go into default, these recent declines raise concern about the ability of the redevelopment agency to continue to fully fund the debt service.

TIF and Blight

Sometimes lost in the rush to use TIF was the underlying concept that this technique was intended to be used to eliminate blight. Until 1993, the redevelopment laws in California did not explicitly define blight, but rather described its characteristics (California State Senate Committee on Housing and Land Use, 1995). This language was such that almost any parcel of land could be termed blighted. Redevelopment agencies established projects that attempted to redevelop golf courses, included non-contiguous areas in the same project or included large non-blighted sections. Farmland was especially prized for its potential. Perhaps the most unusual example was the city of Hemet. The city council, acting as the redevelopment agency, declared the entire city blighted, although 60 per cent of the land was vacant or in agricultural use.[21] Many projects were designed to maximize the potential tax increment or sales tax receipts rather than eliminate blight.[22] Litigation was frequent, and the legislature passed reform bills narrowing the scope of redevelopment activities in 1976, 1984 and 1993.[23]

The existence of substandard housing is often a major cause of blight, and the need for the elimination of slum housing has been a common justification for the adoption of redevelopment projects. However, low and moderate cost housing generates less of a tax increment than commercial revitalization, and there was little financial impetus for agencies to replace the blighted housing with more attractive, but still affordable, units. Legislation in 1976 and 1983 mandated that 20 per cent of the property tax increment be used to support low and moderate income housing, and that at least 30 per cent of all new or rehabilitated housing units that the agency developed must be affordable by persons of very low income. The 1993 legislation strengthened these provisions.

Interjurisdictional Concerns

In the early history of the procedure, the tax increment went back to the redevelopment agency and was used as a source for bond servicing. But as TIF became increasingly more important and as fiscal stress increased, the disposition of the increment became more controversial.

The redevelopment agency typically argued that no redevelopment would have occurred if it had not initiated the project. Thus with no redevelopment, there would be no increment. The overlapping jurisdictions argued that some redevelopment would have occurred in any case and that under Proposition 13, which allowed a 2 per cent yearly property value increase for assessment purposes, at least 2 per cent should be shared. The 1983 legislative reform mandated negotiation among the affected parties on a case-by-case basis in a fiscal review process and mandated annual increases of 2 per cent in the 'frozen' base of the taxing jurisdictions. The distribution of the increment above the debt service reflected the bargaining power of the individuals involved in the fiscal review process, as well as the ability of any of the participants to institute litigation to stop the project. Redevelopment agencies began passing through more of the increment to reduce the probability of a law suit being filed.

A second interjurisdictional concern involved the state, the overlapping school district and the redevelopment agency. As part of the solution to the initial problems caused by Proposition 13, the state took over primary responsibility for the financing of K-12 education, thereby significantly reducing the school districts' dependence on the local property tax.[24] School districts were unconcerned about their share of the increment, because they were aware that the state would replace any lost revenues. But over time, the state went through a series of budget crises and ultimately shifted more of the education burden to the local property tax, with the state backfilling only when necessary. By 1994–95, out of each property tax dollar collected, the schools received 51 cents. As a result, the method of sharing the increment became more important to the state since the dollar cost of school finance could become very large. The estimates of the state backfill depend upon the assumptions made about how much redevelopment would have occurred in the absence of redevelopment activity. They vary widely, and in 1993-94 the estimates ranged from a high of \$500–800 million to a low of zero, with a median estimate of about \$82 million.[25]

Another technique that the state used to extricate itself from its ongoing fiscal crises was to take some of the property tax revenues away from cities, counties, special districts and redevelopment agencies, and place them in a special fund earmarked for education. In 1992–93, redevelopment agencies lost \$205 million in this property tax shift. The redevelopment agencies were expected to absorb this reduction by reducing administrative costs.

Because of the increasing complexity of negotiations and the magnitude of the state backfill and property tax shifts, the redevelopment lobbyists cooperated with the legislature to encourage the development of a formula that would determine the exact sharing of the redevelopment increment to the overlapping jurisdictions, including schools. Among other provisions, a set of 1993 redevelopment reforms replaced the negotiated sharing arrangements with a series of complex formulae that mandated specific amounts of the tax increment to be passed through to counties, special districts and school districts. This gave somewhat more certainty to the process, but at the cost of decreased flexibility.

Redevelopment Reform Once Again

Other major changes were also included in the 1993 reforms. Merely listing the mandated changes accurately indicates the myriad of problems that have been associated with TIF development and indicates areas for other states to investigate.[26] The important changes were as follows:

1. The definition of blight was tightened.
2. Agencies were forced to adopt public implementation plans that linked their planned expenditures to the elimination of blight in the project area.
3. Statutory time limits were adopted. Old plans were given up to 30 years to incur new debt and up to 40 years to carry out other activities. New plans were given only 30 years.
4. Statutory pass-through agreements with overlapping jurisdictions

(including schools) were mandated, replacing the fiscal review negotiations.

5. The authority to provide financial assistance to automobile dealerships and large volume retailers proposing to locate on previously undeveloped land was eliminated.

6. Agencies were given more flexibility in how to achieve the inclusionary housing percentage requirements, but the penalties for failing to use the 20 per cent set-aside monies were increased.

In the year before the law was finally adopted, and perhaps in anticipation of its more stringent requirements, redevelopment agencies placed about 100 square miles of land under redevelopment – about three times the land placed under redevelopment in the year before (Legislative Analyst's Office, 1994).

CONCLUSIONS

The principal question in evaluating TIF redevelopment projects revolves around how much redevelopment would have occurred in the absence of the project. When studied *ex post* on a case-by-case basis, some projects seem to stimulate significant redevelopment while others do not. However, the limited empirical work results in few conclusions that can be generalized. Because of this *ex ante* ambiguity of the success of any particular project, it is important for all of the participants to be continually aware of what might go wrong as they use TIF to attempt to generate economic growth.

In particular, redevelopment might go wrong in two ways. The first relates to the underlying motivation of the local agency that is implementing TIF. There may be strong incentives for this agency to define blight loosely in order to establish a project in an area that will ensure a large increment and thus a large potential for agency activity. If TIF is established in order to solve fiscal stress problems rather than problems of blight, the result is circumvention of the legal constraints under which TIF was established. Redevelopment has become development, and to the extent that the TIF process shifts resources from needy areas to areas that can generate a large increment, regardless of need, this use of the tool is inconsistent with its original policy justification.

The second area with potential for distortion of the purpose of TIF implementation relates to the interjurisdictional sharing of the tax increment revenue. Because some of this increment might have occurred because of inflation or exogenous growth, other jurisdictions probably have a legitimate claim for a share. The opportunity cost of their not getting this share is a reduction in their capacity to deliver services. When the vertical dimension is then added to this mix, as has occurred when the state became involved with property tax distribution and education, the distribution of the increment presents a nearly intractable problem.

To prevent these problems, legislation must be enacted to ensure that TIF is used appropriately. The California case study indicates that this legislation must be continually examined for appropriateness. In California, blight is now defined in a series of complex statutes, penalties for not replacing housing are significant, and interjurisdictional fiscal flows are set by formula. But even in this case, redevelopment agencies are still searching for exceptions.[27]

TIF can be a desirable tool if it is correctly monitored. The project can generate a revenue stream that can be turned into a self-financing instrument. But it only works correctly if it is carefully planned, monitored and implemented under the light of public scrutiny.

NOTES

1. TIF was later expanded to finance the construction of affordable housing for low and moderate income residents, in itself a controversial activity (California State Senate Committee, 1996).
2. This discussion will follow the California redevelopment process (California Debt Advisory Commission, 1995). Other states typically follow this same process.
3. This debt can be issued by the local agency without a vote of the populace.
4. This debt is not automatically tax-exempt. However, careful structuring of the issue and definition of purpose enables the issuing agency to make the debt exempt.
5. In reality, this almost never happens.
6. For example, in California, interest income and grants made up nearly 17 per cent of redevelopment agency revenues in 1992–93 (California State Controller, 1995; Beatty *et al.*, 1994).
7. According to Forgey (1994), only 10 per cent of the districts have revenues that fall short of covering project costs by more than 5 per cent.
8. Positive externalities also occur in the case of successful redevelopment. Their existence can be used to explain partially why additional sources of revenue are used in these redevelopment projects.
9. For example, in California, the Community Redevelopment Act specifically only authorizes the establishment of redevelopment agencies to address the effects of blight.
10. It might also be that some redevelopment is designed to chase low income service demanders out of the area and therefore ease fiscal stress from the demand side.
11. California State Senate Committee on Local Government (1989). Remember that the overlapping jurisdictions have no control over the size of the project or the amount of debt that is issued. The debt service determines the necessary increment.
12. Other popular incentives include streamlining building permits, waiving some regulations and allowing the formation of development agreements.
13. For exceptions, see Anderson (1990), or Man and Rosentraub (1993).
14. These are separate and in addition to the interjurisdictional consequences.
15. Since most urbanized land in California is in the incorporated cities, TIF is used less often by counties – 24 out of the 58 counties have their own redevelopment agency. Sacramento and San Francisco have joint city–county agencies.
16. The 'new and rehabilitated construction' and 'job creation' numbers are self-reported by the agencies.

17. In 1984–85, about 4.4 per cent of total county-assessed value was in TIF projects, with the county range of 0 to 6.7 per cent.
18. One additional effect also occurred. In real, per capita, terms, the total revenue received by all units of government in California increased between 1977–78 and 1991–92. A good part of the stress was associated with the earmarking of this revenue for specific programmes (ranging from education to spending on anti-smoking ads), rather than the aggregate level of revenues. TIF continued this trend because the increment was earmarked for debt service, and the sales taxes ultimately generated went back to the jurisdiction.
19. Sales tax revenues are subvened by the state to the local jurisdiction by point of sale.
20. A constitutional amendment passed in 1986 that allowed property tax rate increases for GO financing upon a two-thirds vote.
21. Multiple lawsuits forced Hemet to repeal the redevelopment project. Hemet has a population of about 50 000.
22. As the California State Senate Committee notes, the 're' in redevelopment became less important. The average size of a redevelopment project increased by 80 per cent in the five years following Proposition 13 (California State Senate Committee on Housing and Land Use, 1995).
23. The 1993 legislation was the first to define blight in statute. Generally, the project area must be urbanized, with conditions that cause serious physical and economic burdens that can't be ameliorated without economic development (California Redevelopment Association, 1994). The new definition eliminated lack of public infrastructure as a justification for TIF and social blight is ignored.
24. Schools still received about 20 per cent of their revenues through the property tax. The state was also under a court order to reconstitute the public school financing mechanisms, and thus it used this opportunity to attempt to solve both Proposition 13 and school financing problems at the same time (Fischel, 1994).
25. This range was derived as follows. For the worst case, assume that no redevelopment activity was necessary and therefore assessed value would increase by $1.5 billion, of which about $750 million would go to schools. If schools received no money through negotiation, the state would have to give them the $750 million under its current education funding laws. For the best case, assume that there would have been no increment without the redevelopment activity. In this case, the schools would have lost no money through negotiation and the state would not have had to provide any additional backfill (Gumucio, 1995).
26. Although these are California changes, many of the case studies indicate that similar types of problem appear whenever TIF is used.
27. Declaring that a disaster has occurred appears to be becoming more popular (Legislative Analyst's Office, 1994).

REFERENCES

Anderson, John E. (1990), 'Tax increment financing: municipal adoption and growth', *National Tax Journal*, **XLIII** (2), 155–63.

Beatty, David F., Joseph E. Coomes, Jr, T. Brent Hawkins, Edward J. Quinn, Jr and Iris P. Yang (1994), *Redevelopment in California*, 2nd edn, Pt Arena, CA: Solano Press.

California Debt Advisory Commission (1995), *Recommended Practices for California Redevelopment Agencies*, Sacramento: California Debt Advisory Commission.

California Redevelopment Association (1994), *Legal Clinic on AB 1290*, Sacramento: California Redevelopment Association.

California Redevelopment Association (1995), 'Redevelopment tax increment decreases between 1992–93 and 1995–96', unpublished survey, 11/1/95, Sacramento, California Redevelopment Association.

California State Controller's Report (1995), *Annual Report 1992–93: Financial Transactions Concerning Community Redevelopment Agencies of California*, Sacramento: State Controller's Office.

California State Senate Committee on Housing and Land Use (1995), 'Redevelopment and blight', background paper, Sacramento, California State Senate, 16 November.

California State Senate Committee on Housing and Land Use (1996), 'End or means? Redevelopment agencies housing programs', briefing paper, Sacramento, California State Senate, 13 November.

California State Senate Committee on Local Government (1989), 'Redeveloping California: finding the legislative agenda for the 1990s', background paper, Sacramento, California State Senate, 7 December.

Davis, Don (1989), 'Tax increment financing', *Public Budgeting and Finance*, 9 (1), 63–73.

Fischel, William A. (1994), 'How *Serrano* caused proposition 13', working paper No. 94–23, Dartmouth College, Hanover, NH, Department of Economics, September.

Forgey, Fred Allen (1994), 'Tax increment financing: equity, effectiveness, and efficiency', in *Municipal Yearbook, 1993*, Chicago: International City Managers Association, pp. 25–33.

Gumucio, Dante (1995), unpublished testimony, California State Senate Select Committee on Redevelopment. Introductory hearing: The impact of redevelopment on communities, property owners, and state and local revenues, 25 October.

Horler, Virginia L. (1987), *Guide to Public Debt Financing in California*, San Francisco: Packard Press.

Huddleston, Jack B. (1982), 'Local financial dimensions of tax increment financing: a cost–revenue analysis', *Public Budgeting and Finanacing*, 2 (1), 40–49.

Huddleston, Jack B. (1984), 'Tax increment financing as a state development policy', *Growth and Change*, 15 (2), 11–17.

Legislative Analyst's Office (1994), 'Redevelopment after reform: a preliminary look', Sacramento, Legislative Analyst's Office, 29 December.

Man, Joyce Y. and Mark S. Rosentraub (1993), 'Tax increment financing and its effect on property values', 93-U10 (October): Center for Urban Policy and the Environment, School of Public and Environmental Affairs: Indianapolis: Indiana University.

Merrill Lynch Pierce Fenner and Smith, Inc. (1979), *California's Tax Allocation Bonds: Victims of Proposition 13*. Los Angeles: Merrill Lynch Municipal Bond Research.

Ritter, Kevin and Kenneth Oldfield (1990), 'Testing the effects of tax increment financing in Springfield, Illinois: the assessor's role in determining policy outcomes', *Property Tax Journal*, 9 (2), 141–7.

Rothenberg, Jerome (1967), *Economic Evaluation of Urban Renewal*, Washington, DC: Brookings Institute.

Stinson, Thomas F. (1992), 'Subsidizing local economic development through tax increment financing', *Policy Studies Journal*, 20 (2), 241–6.

PART III

Fiscal and Distributional Impacts

10. Fiscal impacts of business development in the Chicago suburbs*

William H. Oakland and William A. Testa

Many suburban communities experienced rapid business development and employment growth during the past two decades. Planners and development officials encouraged business growth not only because of increased employment opportunities for their constituents, but also because they may have believed it would result in fiscal benefits paid for by non-resident business owners.[1]

These beliefs have recently been challenged, however, by some urban planners and other analysts of the suburban growth process who maintain that business development brings along high costs in associated public services and infrastructure, and that intergovernmental aid to pay for these costs is too low (see White, 1975; DuPage County, 1991; Gómez-Ibáñez, 1993; Ladd, 1994). Critics of urban land use expansion further contend that job suburbanization isolates the urban poor from gainful employment, contributes to overdevelopment of land and spoilage of agricultural land at the urban fringe, and raises overall metropolitan-area public service costs by requiring new infrastructure that duplicates what already exists in the urban core. This chapter assesses the local fiscal impact of business development by first reviewing previous studies and then investigating the statistical relationship between business development and residential property tax rates for 115 Chicago suburbs during the 1980s.

WHAT DO PREVIOUS STUDIES TELL US?

Previous studies have assessed the fiscal impact of business development using two different methodologies. One approach generalizes from the outcomes of many different case studies that tabulate the fiscal costs and benefits of individual business developments. The other examines the statistical rela-

* Tulane University and the Federal Reserve Bank of Chicago, respectively. The authors acknowledge financial support from the Metropolitan Planning Council of Chicago.

tionship between general business growth and community fiscal well-being. So far, both approaches have produced ambiguous or contradictory findings; studies can be found suggesting that business development brings a net fiscal benefit and others that it does not.

Fiscal Impact Studies

So many local officials have become concerned about the fiscal impact of land development that an entire methodology has been developed to address the question in specific circumstances. This methodology, known as fiscal impact analysis, compares the public service costs of land development in a particular use with the public revenues that the development is expected to generate.[2]

Although most recent fiscal impact studies share this general methodology, these studies vary widely in sophistication (see Burchell and Listokin, 1993; Gómez-Ibáñez, 1993; Oakland and Testa, 1995). Nonetheless, the findings of fiscal impact studies over the past four decades indicate a dichotomy between business and residential development with respect to fiscal impact. Generally speaking, and with important exceptions, commercial and industrial development (hereafter referred to as 'business development') appears to more than pay its way fiscally. For example, the Saturn plant is expected to produce local revenues that exceed associated public service costs by a factor of three (Fox and Neel (1987) and Bartik *et al.* (1987) cited in Bartik (1991)). In contrast to most business development, most types of residential development, especially single-family detached housing, are found to be losing propositions. Elementary and secondary education is commonly implicated as the major factor producing the adverse fiscal outcome.[3]

The divergence between the fiscal impact of residential development and that of business development may disappear if households tend to follow job opportunities, and vice versa. The fiscal benefits of new job growth might thereby be eroded by subsequent population growth. This may prompt some communities to admit only the most lucrative types of business development and/or act to exclude subsequent in-migration of population. The presence of linkages between jobs and population has been observed in studies that focus on the aggregate city versus suburban location of jobs and people (for a recent review, see McDonald (1989) and Thurston and Yezer (1994)). Evidence that jobs follow people behaviour has also been provided by Luce (1994) in his study of the Philadelphia suburbs. Such interactions between employment and population have typically been ignored in fiscal impact analysis.

Some analysts have questioned the validity of simple fiscal impact analysis because it does not sufficiently allow for the added costs of public infrastructure. As evidence, they point to some recent case studies where infrastructure cost is explicitly considered and which indicate that business development fails to cover its public service costs (see, for example, Gómez-Ibáñez (1993)). This may explain why some communities that experienced rapid employment growth in the 1980s also experienced rising property tax rates.[4]

Statistical Studies of Fiscal Impact

Unlike fiscal impact analysis, which is based upon presumed relationships, statistical studies of the actual consequences of business expansion have been much less definitive concerning the presence of fiscal benefits. Some studies examine the correlation between business development and changes in local property tax rates. From the standpoint of community residents, falling property tax rates are a fiscal benefit because lower property tax rates allow a greater proportion of personal income to be devoted to consumption (assuming that public service consumption does not decline).[5] However, evidence that residential property tax rates are rising can be more difficult to interpret. Rising property tax rates imply either: (1) that community residents have taken advantage of their enhanced ability to tax non-resident business property owners in order to increase public services; or, to the contrary; (2) that business development has imposed higher costs on the community, which must now raise tax rates.

Danielson and Wolpert (1991) examined 365 contiguous municipalities of northern New Jersey that gained 400 000 new jobs and 150 000 new residents during the 1980s. They assessed whether the growth in jobs and population affected several indices of fiscal and non-fiscal benefits. In general, the authors concluded that employment growth benefited local communities, while population growth was largely detrimental. With specific regard to fiscal benefits, community employment growth significantly lowered property tax rates while raising local government revenues per capita.[6]

Studying the educational spending decisions of communities in the Boston metropolitan area, Ladd (1975) found that a greater proportion of commercial and industrial property signals to local voters that they face a lower 'tax price' for education.[7] That is, for every additional dollar that voters decide to spend, they behave as if part of the additional costs will be borne by out-of-community people associated with the business property.[8] In effect, business property is perceived as reducing the taxpayer's price of public services, providing a benefit over-and-above the direct tax payments made by the business community.[9] Similar conclusions were reached by Fischel (1975) and more recently by Danielson and Wolpert (1991) for northern New Jersey communities. In the latter study, the tax price effects were found to increase per pupil school spending significantly. Fischel found evidence of higher educational spending and lower property tax rates in association with business development.

Statistical studies do not always support the hypothesis that community pursuit of commercial and industrial property is advantageous. Margolis (1956, 1957) examined both the real effective property tax rate of municipalities in the San Francisco Bay area in 1953–54 and their total property value per resident. Margolis classified cities according to their intensity of commercial/industrial property land use, and then compared the distribution of property value and real tax rate by type of city. He found that 'dormitory' cities (that is, those choosing to specialize in residential property) tended to display lower property tax rates than did 'balanced' cities (those with substantial proportions of both non-residential and residential property).[10]

RESEARCH QUESTION

We direct our analysis to the following question: has business development been associated with reductions in tax burdens in the Chicago suburbs? To address this question it is not sufficient to show a negative simple correlation between business growth and tax burden. As is widely known: 'correlation does not imply causation'. A negative simple correlation could just as well be a signal that high taxes deter growth, instead of the other way around. Insight into the linkages between taxes and development can only be provided by more sophisticated modelling and statistical techniques. Economic modelling can help us to identify the many factors and mechanisms which come into play in determining tax burdens and business development. In turn, simultaneous multiple regression analysis can help us sort out the separate effects of the many influences upon a community's tax burden.

In the next section we develop a model of community fiscal behaviour which takes into account feedbacks from the fiscal outcomes, such as tax rates, to economic development, residential public services and other important community characteristics such as housing prices. In addition, the model recognizes the interdependence between business growth and population growth within a particular community as well as among communities. The latter enables us to identify potential spillover benefits and costs among the suburban communities.

THEORETICAL FRAMEWORK

To understand better the relationship of business activity to tax burdens, several key relationships must be considered: (1) the government's budget constraint; (2) the government's expenditure decisions; (3) locational choices of households; (4) locational choices of firms; and (5) the determinants of housing values.

Budget identity

Property tax rates and the business property tax base are determined within a budget identity which links government expenditures to revenues. Local government property tax revenues are the product of the tax rate and the tax base. An increase in tax base, holding expenditure constant, requires a reduction in tax rate. This is true whether the increase in the tax base is the result of greater population (increased residential units), greater employment (increased business property) or housing value appreciation (increased value per residential unit). To understand changes in tax rate, and hence tax burden, one must understand each of these underlying terms in the budget identity: population, employment, housing appreciation and public expenditures.

Expenditure Levels

A community's expenditure for public services will reflect the need for services by its population (residential services) and by its business community (business services). Residential services will reflect population size, the income of the average resident and the perceived cost ('tax price') of public services. Tax price is often approximated by the share of residential property in the tax base.[11] Business services will be tied to employment within the community.[12]

Population

A community's population will reflect the demand for residential sites within the community and the supply of such sites by local government authorities. On the demand side, important factors include the price of housing, proximity to employment opportunities, and community amenities such as low crime rate, environmental quality and the quality of public education. On the supply side, the most important factor may be the income of existing residents. Large lot zoning may be applied by wealthy communities in order to promote exclusivity, low density and to avoid subsidizing the public services of new residents. It should be noted that this sector determines not only community population but the price of housing as well.

Employment

Like population, a community's employment will be the product of demand
and supply forces. On the demand side, businesses will prefer communities
with good access to markets and labour supplies and low property tax rates.[13]
On the supply side, high existing tax rates increase the potential fiscal benefit
from new development. Conversely, affluent communities will find the environmental disamenities created by business activity to more than offset the
fiscal benefits. The actual employment within a community will reflect the
relative importance of the supply and demand factors. Some communities
will eschew business development altogether, and others may allow only
'clean' industry. For such communities there is no price to equilibrate supply
and demand forces.

THE EMPIRICAL MODEL

The relationships defined above can be expressed as a set of five interdependent
relationships which explain the following community variables: (1) the property tax rate; (2) public expenditure; (3) housing prices; (4) population; and (5)
employment. The interrelationships between these variables are as follows:

Property tax rate: Housing prices, employment, population, expenditure
Public expenditure: employment, population[14]
Housing prices: population, employment, public expenditure, property
                       tax rate
Population: employment, **nearby employment**, housing price, pub-
                       lic expenditure, property tax rate[15]
Employment: population, **nearby population**, **nearby employment**,
                       property tax rate.[16]

The italicized terms represent the dependent variables in question. The terms
to the right of the colon are those other dependent variables which influence
the outcome for that dependent variable. The relationships are seen to be
highly interrelated, suggesting the potential for misleading interpretation of
the data. Also, the emphasized terms indicate interrelationships among communities. These exist primarily through population and employment interdependencies. Because of a lack of data it was necessary to combine
relationships (1) and (2); fortunately this aggregation does not mask tax price
effects. The remaining four relationships were estimated using multiple regression techniques. The precise form of each of the relationships, including
a list of other intervening variables, is provided in the Appendix.

THE DATA

The model is applied to a sample of suburban communities drawn from the six-county Chicago metropolitan area.[17] The unit of observation was the municipality. We defined sample communities by municipal boundaries rather than, say, school districts, because significant control over land use is vested with municipal governments. Our sample included incorporated municipalities with populations of more than 10 000 in Cook County and the six counties that border it. We excluded the city of Chicago because of its size and economic maturity. The 115 suburbs we included account for just over two-thirds of the suburban population. The period of observation was roughly 1980–90.[18] During the period under study, population in the overall suburban area grew by 9.2 per cent, with growth most rapid in the farthest-outlying suburbs. The continued decentralization of metropolitan employment also meant rapid employment growth over the same period – a blistering 37 per cent increase.

Measures of Tax Burden

In most of the municipalities numerous local taxing jurisdictions overlap. Therefore we found it necessary to estimate an aggregate property tax rate for each municipality, reflecting the combined burden of all the levies imposed within the municipality's boundaries.[19] We consider two measures of tax burden: (1) the average effective tax rate on owner-occupied housing (*rate*), which is computed as the ratio of aggregate residential property tax payments to aggregate market value of housing; and (2) the average effective tax rate in terms of income (*burden*), which is measured as the ratio of aggregate residential tax payments to aggregate household income in the community. *Rate* is of interest because it reflects the degree to which residential property is taxed, and is thus relevant to decisions to build or improve residential property.[20] *Burden*, on the other hand, measures tax burdens in terms of the fraction of the household's budget absorbed by residential property taxes.

SIMPLE CORRELATION ANALYSIS

Let us begin by examining the simple correlation between business development and tax burden. While such an analysis may tell us little about causal relationships, it is the easiest to understand by the layman. It is also the measure most likely to be publicized in the media and in political campaigns. As our measure of business development, we use the change in business assessed valuation from 1981 to 1991 as a fraction of the total property tax base in 1991 (*grbus*). This measure reflects the maximum potential reduction in tax burden afforded by the growth in taxable business property. The results, displayed in Table 10.1, indicate a very weak ($R^2 = 0.07$) marginal negative relationship with *rate* and a strong negative relationship with *burden*. Whether business development is associated with a reduction in tax burden therefore depends on which measure of burden one adopts. It appears that those communities with the most rapid business development during the 1980s experienced a reduction in the share of their income which they had to devote to property taxes.[21] Even so, because of the bi-directional and complex nature of the relationship between tax burden and business development, simple correlation analysis is inadequate for the task at hand.

Table 10.1   Simple correlation of growth in tax burden and growth in business tax base

	Parameter estimate	Standard error	*t*-statistic	Prob.>*t*	Adj.R^2
GRRATE					0.0712
INTERCEPT	13.86	1.58	8.75	0.0001	
GRBUS	−1.22	20.39	−3.12	0.0023	
GRBURDEN					0.4940
INTERCEPT	21.03	2.05	10.23	0.0001	
GRBUS	−5.50	0.05	−10.59	0.0001	

MULTIPLE REGRESSION ANALYSIS

Each of the major relationships identified above was tested within a simultaneous equations framework. Essentially, this involved the identification of exogenous variables to supplement the list of endogenous variables in each of the relationships. These exogenous variables will also serve as instruments for dependent variables when the latter are themselves used as explanatory variables. Space will not permit an exhaustive discussion of the logic for each chosen instrument, but a complete list is contained in the Appendix. Suffice it to say that it includes the usual income and wealth variables, locational and environmental characteristics of communities, and variables that reflect important institutional factors or adjustment processes. As an example of the latter, the initial tax burden was employed in order to capture constraints imposed by state tax rate caps as well as to reflect political pressure for fiscal relief.

We will discuss each important relationship in turn.

Tax Burden

The major issue of interest here is how business and population growth impact own-community tax burdens. Of secondary interest is whether business development is associated with significant tax price impacts. The results are shown in Table 10.2 for our two measures of tax burden. With respect to the effective tax rate on housing (*rate*), the coefficient for employment growth has a negative sign and is significant at the 95 per cent level of confidence. Since the coefficient can be interpreted as a partial elasticity, it implies that a 1 per cent growth in employment produces a 12 per cent decrease in effective tax rate. The coefficient of population growth, though positive, is significantly different from zero at only the 80 per cent level, below the threshold usually adopted in empirical work. However, we can feel reasonably comfortable in concluding that population growth is not associated with measurable *decreases* in effective property tax rate. Finally, the coefficient on tax price is positive and significant at the 99 per cent level. Given that the coefficient applies to the level, rather than the change, in tax price, this implies that those communities which began the period with a relatively high tax price experienced greater increases in tax burdens, as measured by effective tax rate. For such communities, as the demand for residential public services grows with income, business contributes a smaller share of the accompanying tax increase, thus raising residential tax burdens.[22] Thus business development provides dynamic as well as static tax relief.

Table 10.2   Two-stage least squares estimates of the growth in tax burden*

	Parameter estimate	*t*-statistic	Prob.>*t*	Adj.R^2
GRRATE				0.46
GREMPLOY	−0.12	−2.02	0.046	
GRPOPULA	0.17	1.35	0.179	
TAX PRICE	0.99	3.32	0.001	
GRBURDEN				0.80
GREMPLOY	0.09	1.16	0.250	
GRPOPULA	0.26	1.78	0.077	
TAX PRICE	0.51	1.67	0.100	

Note: *   Not all explanatory variables shown

When burden is measured in terms of income share, the results are less conclusive. The elasticity for population continues to be positive and is now significant at the 90 per cent level of confidence. The coefficient on tax price remains positive, although its significance falls to marginal levels. A major change, however, is that the coefficient on employment growth changes sign. Though it fails the usual tests for significance, the result would appear to rule out favourable employment growth impacts with respect to this measure of tax burden.[23]

Employment and Population Growth

Key issues here involve the relationship between employment growth and population growth. Of particular interest is whether employment growth in a community gives rise to population growth in that community and/or nearby communities. Also of interest are the effects of property tax rates upon employment growth. Finally, although tangential to the issue of fiscal interactions, we have the question of whether population growth spawns employment growth or vice versa – an issue of perennial interest in the planning and urban economic literature. Our findings are shown in Table 10.3.

First consider the population–employment growth relationship. A 1 per cent increase in a community's employment gives rise to a 0.12 per cent increase in that community's population. Moreover, a 1 per cent increase in employment in *neighbouring communities* is associated with a 0.40 per cent

Table 10.3   Two-stage least squares estimates of the growth in employment and growth of population*

	Parameter estimate	*t*-statistic	Prob.>*t*	Adj.R^2
GRPOPULA				0.64
GREMPLOY	0.12	2.50	0.014	
GREMPLOY	0.40	3.73	0.003	
NEARBY				
GRTRATE	−0.01	−0.08	0.940	
GREMPLOY				0.44
GRPOPULA	0.18	0.36	0.718	
GRPOPULA	−0.11	−0.18	0.854	
NEARBY				
GRTRATE	−1.00	−1.58	0.118	

Note: *Not all explanatory variables shown

increase in a community's population.[24] Both of these relationships are statistically significant. Access to jobs located outside the community is more important than to those located within the community. Since own-population growth results in higher tax burdens, the basis for a fiscal externality is seen to exist. It is interesting to note that no statistically significant connection exists in the employment growth relationship. Neither own-population growth nor neighbouring population growth is seen to have an impact on local employment growth.[25] Thus it appears that people follow jobs rather than the other way around. With respect to how property taxes affect business development, both the level and change in statutory property tax rates were negatively associated with employment growth, although the relationships were of marginal statistical significance. This is weak evidence that higher property tax rates are associated with slower economic development. Given that some communities with high property tax rates may be more receptive to business development, the existence of even a marginal negative relationship may be interpreted as confirmation of business's aversion to high property tax rates.

Housing Price Growth

The last relationship investigated is the implication of employment growth and property tax rates for housing appreciation (Table 10.4). Employment growth can influence housing prices through its positive impact on own population growth and its negative effect on the quality of life within the community. Given these opposite effects, it is not surprising that no relationship emerged from our sample.[26] On a more definite note, a high initial property tax rate and rapidly growing property tax rate were associated with sub-par rates of real housing price appreciation. This suggests the presence of

Table 10.4   *Two-stage least squares estimates of the growth in real housing prices**

	Parameter estimate	*t*-statistic	Prob.>*t*	Adj.R^2
GRHPRICE				0.612
GREMPLOY 1981	−0.006	−0.05	0.963	
TXRATE	−7.37	−4.55	0.001	
GRTRATE	−0.822	−2.94	0.004	

Note: *   Not all explanatory variables shown

tax capitalization, although the point elasticity of –0.82 seems unreasonably large in that context. Increasing property tax rates may also be serving as a proxy for fiscal and economic stress within the community.

DISCUSSION AND CONCLUSIONS

The popularly held position that business development provides fiscal benefits to host communities is supported by the experience of the Chicago suburbs during the 1980s. Tax burdens, particularly when measured relative to income, increased relatively more slowly in those communities with rapid employment growth during the period. By itself, such an association is not proof of the proposition because low tax growth can also be expected to give rise to greater business development. Further complicating the picture is the expectation that, as the business share of the property tax base increases, expenditures for both business and household government services will increase. These in turn will put upward pressure on property tax rates. Thus the relationship between property tax rates and business development may be quite complex. However, when examined within the context of a general equilibrium model which allows for all of these nuances, the data continue to suggest that increased business development will lead to property tax relief. The data are also consistent with the hypothesis that population growth increases a community's tax burden. These two findings, together with evidence that business development in one community leads to population increases in other communities, point to a negative fiscal externality in the development process. This linkage between communities keeps open the possibility that, as a whole, local governments suffer fiscal losses from suburban job growth. The present model is inadequate for assessing this possibility. Perhaps the parameters developed here could be embedded into a computational model which takes into account actual geographic patterns. Alternatively, a more aggregative framework might afford important insights into the issue. Whatever approach is taken, it is clear that host communities have fiscal incentives to engage in competition for job growth. This does not auger well for the central city.

NOTES

1. Fiscal benefit is defined from the perspective of a typical household in the home community and implies an enhanced ability of such a household to consume more publicly provided goods and/or private goods and services. A fiscal benefit can arise from an increase in the community's taxable resources or, on the expenditure side, from a reduced need for public services. For example, a new business development typically adds to a

community's tax base – property or other. As the community levies taxes on this addition to the tax base, new revenues will be generated. If these revenues exceed the public service demands that accompany the new development, then the community household will be able to: (1) lower its own tax rate, thereby enabling increased consumption of private sector goods; (2) consume more residential services as financed from the added tax base; or (3) both. Note also that the accrual of fiscal benefit does not necessarily imply greater overall levels of general welfare for community residents. Business development may cause congestion and environmental degradation that lower the quality of life for residents.

2. An extensive handbook details how to measure the fiscal impact associated with any particular property development; see Burchell and Listokin (1993).
3. On average, and with much variation, education accounts for 40 per cent of local government spending in the United States (Advisory Commission on Intergovernmental Relations, 1993).
4. In addition, fiscal impact studies may be turning up more negative findings because revenue assistance from state and federal government has become less responsive to community growth. See Gómez-Ibáñez (1993) and Ladd (1994).
5. Falling residential property tax rates are not necessarily a signal of fiscal benefit. Non-property taxes borne by community residents may increase as a result of the business expansion. Moreover, the new business property tax payments may be shifted to residents through lower wages or land prices. Since the property tax is the overwhelming source of revenue for the communities in our study, non-property tax payments are not an issue here. As for shifting of business property taxes, the increased business activity is more likely to increase local wages and land prices.
6. Unlike reduced property tax rates, increased revenues may or may not signal taxpayer benefit. The expanded business community will likely require added public services.
7. Commercial and industrial property is defined by most local governments as that land and building used (and assessed for tax purposes) in profit-making enterprises. Hence it is closely aligned with what we refer to in our empirical work as 'business development'. Of course, some job-creating businesses are not subject to the local property tax – for example, government operations and private colleges – and hence are not included in measurements of commercial and industrial property.
8. Unlike the assumption of some statistical studies and most fiscal impact studies, Ladd's study suggests that local residents comprehend that part of local taxes imposed on businesses is shifted forward to local consumers or backward to local wage earners or landowners. Ladd found that in their selection of property tax rates, communities act as if 39–45 per cent of the property taxes paid by industrial property are borne by that property rather than by local residents.
9. In the lexicon of the economist, the taxpayer enjoys 'substitution benefits' from being able to purchase public services at lower prices.
10. The evidence for this conclusion is not totally persuasive. The study excluded the type of community – so-called industrial enclaves – that contains the largest proportion of commercial and industrial property. It is arguable whether such an exclusion is justified and has the effect of biasing the results. In any case, as discussed earlier, higher property tax rates do not necessarily indicate fiscal losses to community residents.
11. The implicit assumption is that voters perceive that business property tax payments are passed on to non-residents.
12. This is meant to capture needs of businesses *per se* and services provided to their employees in connection with travel to and from work.
13. While property taxes are not a big ticket item, as, for example, labour costs, there may be little the firm can do to influence significantly labour costs. Rather, only modest savings in wages can be made through strategic location choice, and these savings may be similar in magnitude to tax variations among communities.
14. Note that population and employment influence both the demand for public services and the tax price faced by voters.
15. Tax price may be a better proxy of fiscal conditions than outlays and tax rates.

16. In principle, business public services should also be included; however, they are not measurable.
17. This area is not identical to the present Metropolitan Statistical Area as defined by the US Department of Commerce; rather, it is the former SMSA area that continues to be used by local government-related planning agencies.
18. We say 'roughly' because some data were available only for the Census years 1979 and 1989, or for the fiscal years 1981 and 1991.
19. We did this by overlaying maps of each type of jurisdiction upon that of the municipality in question. The fraction of a municipality's tax base that was subject to the property tax levy of an overlapping jurisdiction of a particular type (for example, school district) was assumed to equal the fraction of municipal land area accounted for by that particular jurisdiction. A detailed description of the methodology and the data themselves will appear in a forthcoming working paper, 'Does business development raise taxes? An empirical analysis of Chicago's suburbs', Federal Reserve Bank of Chicago, working paper, 1995.
20. This measure differs from the statutory rate of tax because, by convention, the assessed value of housing for tax purposes is but a fraction of its market value. Moreover, this ratio may vary from community to community.
21. This probably understates the implied elasticity because of the use of the terminal value of business assessed property in computing the growth of business.
22. The change in tax price was not included in the regression because these effects would be subsumed by the growth of business and population variables. Thus the coefficients on the latter include tax price change effects on expenditures.
23. To be consistent with our finding for effective tax rates on housing, it must mean that the ratio of housing value to income rises with employment growth; but this is just the opposite of what one would expect on quality-of-environment grounds.
24. Neighbouring employment is defined as employment in communities located within five miles of the community in question.
25. We also tested for a relationship between own employment growth and neighbouring employment growth but found no relationship.
26. However, we did find that those communities most developed at the beginning of the period enjoyed less price appreciation over the period. This offers some support for the position that business activity creates negative disamenities.

REFERENCES

Bartik, Timothy (1991), 'The effects of property taxes and other local public fiscal policies on the intrametropolitan pattern of business location', in *Industry Location and Public Policy*, Henry W. Herzog, Jr and Alan Schlottmann (eds), Knoxville: The University of Tennessee Press.

Bartik, Timothy, Charles Becker, Steve Lake and John Bush (1987), 'Saturn and state economic development', *Forum for Applied Research and Public Policy*, **2**, 29–40.

Burchell, Robert W. and David Listokin (1993), *The Development Impact Assessment Handbook and Model*, Cambridge, MA: Urban Land Institute.

Carlino, Gerald and Edwin Mills (1985), 'Do public policies affect county growth?', *Business Review*, Federal Reserve Bank of Philadelphia, July/August, 3–16.

Danielson, Michael N. and Julian Wolpert (1991), 'Distributing the benefits of regional economic development', *Urban Studies*, **28** (3), 393–413.

Danielson, Michael N. and Julian Wolpert (1992), 'Rapid metropolitan growth and community disparities', *Growth and Change*, Fall, 494–515.

DuPage County Development Department Planning Division (1991), *Impacts of Development on DuPage County Property Taxes*, prepared for the DuPage County Regional Planning Commission, 9 October.

Fischel, W. (1975), 'Fiscal and environmental considerations in the location of firms in suburban communities', in E.S. Mills and Wallace E. Oates (eds), *Fiscal Zoning and Land Use Controls*, Lexington, MA: Lexington Books.

Fox, William F. and C. Warren Neel (1987), 'Saturn: the Tennessee lessons', *Forum for Applied Research and Policy*, **2**, 7–16.

Gómez-Ibáñez, José A. (1993), 'Does development pay its own way?', in Alan A. Altschuler (ed.), *Regulation for Revenue: The Political Economy of Land Use Exactions*, Washington, DC: Brookings Institute.

Ladd, Helen F. (1975), 'Local education expenditures, fiscal capacity, and the composition of the property tax base', *National Tax Journal*, **28** (2), 145–58.

Ladd, Helen F. (1992), 'Population growth, density, and the costs of providing public services', *Urban Studies*, **29** (2), 273–95.

Ladd, Helen F. (1993), 'Effects of population growth on local spending and taxes', *Research in Urban Economics*, **9**, 181–223.

Ladd, Helen F. (1994), 'Fiscal impacts of local population growth, a conceptual and empirical analysis', *Regional Science and Urban Economics*, **24** (6), 661–86.

Luce, Thomas F. (1994), 'Local taxes, public services, and the intrametropolitan location of firms and households', *Public Finance Quarterly*, **22** (2), 139–67.

Margolis, Julius (1957), 'Municipal fiscal structure in a metropolitan region', *Journal of Political Economy*, **64**, 226–36.

Margolis, Julius (1956), 'The variation of property tax rates within a metropolitan region', *National Tax Journal*, **9**, 326–30.

McDonald, John F. (1989), 'Econometric studies of urban population density: a survey', *Journal of Urban Economics*, **26** (3), 361–85.

Oakland, William H. and William A. Testa (1995), 'Does business development raise taxes?: an empirical appraisal', *Economic Perspectives*, Federal Reserve Bank of Chicago, March/April, 22–32.

Thurston, Lawrence and Anthony M.J. Yezer (1994), 'Causality in the suburbanization of population and employment', *Journal of Urban Economics*, **35** (1), 105–18.

US Advisory Commission on Intergovernmental Relations (1993), *Significant Features of Fiscal Federalism*, 2, September, M-185-II, p. 85.

US Department of Commerce, Bureau of the Census, *Census of Population, 1990*, (1993), Washington DC: US6PC.

White, Michelle J. (1975), 'Firm location in a zoned metropolitan area', in Edwin Mills and Wallace Oates (eds), *Fiscal Zoning and Land Use Controls*, Lexington, MA: Lexington Books.

APPENDIX

10A1   Complete specification of estimating equations

Endogenous variables are in bold.

Dependent variable: *Grburden or Grrate* (*Gr* = percentage increase)
Gremployment, grpopopulation, grhouseprice, Grincome, Taxprice 1981, Property tax rate 1981, Average home price 1981, Assessment ratio (Grburden only), Percentage of renters 1980, Cook County dummy variable.

Dependent variable: *Grpopulation*
Grrate, Gremployment, Grhouseprice, Gremployment nearby, Property tax rate 1981, Average home price, 1981, Population density 1980, Change in land area 1980–90, Percentage of renters 1980, Per pupil education spending (average of 1981, 1991).

Dependent variable: *Gremployment*
Grpopulation, Grrate, Gremployment nearby, Grpopulation nearby, Property tax rate 1981, Per capita income 1980, Manufacturing employment density 1980, Average home price 1980, Access to highways, Dissipation index 1980, Cook County dummy.

Dependent variable: *Grhousingprice*
Grpopulation, Gremployment, grrate, Employment–population ratio 1980, Population density 1980, Distance to Loop, Access to highways, Grincpercap, Average home price 1980.

10A2   Descriptive statistics

Data definitions follow table.

Variable	#Observ	Mean	Standard deviation
ANNEX	115	0.8219	1.578
ASSRAT0	115	20.59	5.484
CHASS	115	−2.307	12.82
GRBURDE	115	10.82	27.35
GRBUS	115	23.03	42.77
GRRATE	115	0.1154	0.1557
CHRENT	116	−2.675	15.87
GRTRATE	116	14.02	12.32
COOK	116	0.6637	0.4744
DISDEXB	115	5.671	4.366
DIST	116	23.89	11.28
EMPPOP0	115	0.3668	0.2589
GREMP	115	26.94	42.87
GREMPNB	115	13.81	11.57
GRHPRIC	115	5.58	31.18
GRINC	116	14.80	13.44
GRN_POP	115	6.739	11.05
GRPOP	116	7.079	15.83
HIGHWAY	116	1.215	1.002
HPRICE0	115	7335	3716

INC0	116	4079	1237
MANDENS	115	464.4	674.7
POPDEN0	115	4349	2204
RATE81	115	1.605	0.3396
RENTAL0	116	28.20	13.71
STR81	116	0.0800	0.0139
TAXPRIC0	115	0.2271	0.0543
TORATE81	115	0.0334	0.0103
WOPEXPB	115	9035	2674

Variable	Definition
ANNEX	Change in land area, 1980–90
ASSRAT0	Average assessment ratio, 1981
CHASS	Change in average assessment ratio, 1981-91
GRBURDE	Growth rate of property tax as a fraction of income, 1981–91
GRBUS	Growth in assessed value of business property, 1981–91
GRRATE	Growth rate of effective property tax rate, 1981–91
CHRENT	Change in the percentage of households which rent, 1980–90
GRTRATE	Growth rate of the statutory property tax rate, 1981–91
COOK	Cook county dummy variable
DISDEXB	Average dissipation index, 1981, 1991
DIST	Distance to central business district
EMPPOP0	Ratio of employment to population, 1980
GREMP	Growth rate of employment, 1980–90
GREMPNB	Growth rate of nearby employment, 1980–90
GRHPRIC	Growth rate of average house price, 1980–90
GRINC	Growth rate of income per capita, 1980–90
GRN_POP	Growth rate of nearby population, 1980–90
GRPOP	Growth rate of population, 1980–90
HIGHWAY	Access to interstate highway
HPRICE0	Average house price, 1980
INC0	Income per capita, 1980
MANDENS	Manufacturing density, 1980
POPDEN0	Population density, 1980
RATE81	Effective tax rate, 1981
RENTAL0	Percentage of households renting, 1980
STR81	Statutory tax rate, 1981
TAXPRIC0	Residential share of property tax base, 1981
TORATE81	Average property tax to income ratio, 1981
WOPEXPB	Average per pupil educational operating expenditure, 1981, 1991.

11. Who pays development fees?*

John Yinger

INTRODUCTION

The tax revolt and the high costs of rapid residential development have induced many jurisdictions to implement development fees, also called impact fees or exactions, as a way to finance new infrastructure. Special assessments are also used for this purpose in a few states, such as Minnesota.[1] Using some well-known tools of urban public finance, this chapter asks who ultimately pays these fees and special assessments.

This question, which involves what economists call the incidence of alternative infrastructure financing mechanisms, has been explored in many papers.[2] Most of this literature employs supply and demand curves and intuitive arguments. Although the technical details are not presented here, this chapter builds on a more formal treatment of the topic which confirms some points, adds precision to others and reveals some new conclusions that the literature has missed.[3] The formal analysis on which this chapter builds does not consider all the institutional details presented in some previous work, but includes, I believe, the most central features of the topic.[4]

PROPERTY TAXES, INFRASTRUCTURE AND THE VALUE OF HOUSING

The key relationship on which this analysis builds is the relationship between house values on the one hand and property taxes, fees and infrastructure on the other. As many economists have pointed out, and many empirical studies confirmed, people will pay more for houses that face lower effective property tax rates or receive better infrastructure or other public services, all else

* The author is grateful for comments from the participants in the 1995 TRED conference at the Lincoln Institute of Land Policy, Cambridge, Massachusetts, 29–30 September 1995. Comments by Jeff Chapman, Bob Einsweiler, Carol Heim (my formal discussant) and Bob Inman were especially helpful. The author is Professor of Economics and Public Administration at the Maxwell School, Syracuse University.

equal.[5] To put it another way, property tax rates and public service levels are 'capitalized' into property values. Development fees have no direct impact on house values, because they are paid by the developer not the homeowner, but house values may be affected by the infrastructure that these fees purchase.

The relationship between house values and property taxes, infrastructure and other public services can be expressed in a simple equation. Let V stand for the price of a house; let $TB(C)$ measure the total annual benefits from living in a house as a function of the level of infrastructure, C (and other things);[6] let i indicate the appropriate discount rate; and let t be the effective property tax rate. Now the value of a house is the present value of the stream of benefits from owning it, net of property taxes, which equal tV per year. In symbols:[7]

$$V = \frac{TB(C)}{i} - \frac{tV}{i} \tag{11.1}$$

or, solving for V:

$$V = \frac{TB(C)}{i+t} \tag{11.2}$$

This so-called capitalization equation shows how C and t affect the value of a house.

The value of a house can also be expressed in another simple way. Let H stand for the quantity of housing in a house (measured, perhaps, by quality-adjusted square feet of living space), and let P stand for the amount a household is willing to pay for housing per unit H. This price term, P, is often called the household's 'bid'. Thus a household is willing to pay PH per year to rent a house that contains H units of housing or to pay a purchase price equal to the present value of its stream of benefits, PH/i; that is:

$$V = \frac{PH}{i} \tag{11.3}$$

Equating these two expressions for V, (11.2) and (11.3), we obtain the following expression for household housing bids:

$$\frac{PH}{i} = \frac{TB(C)}{i+t} \text{ or } P = \frac{TB(C)i}{H(i+t)} \tag{11.4}$$

Now suppose the level of infrastructure is increased by some amount, dC. Then, holding H constant,[8] simple differentiation reveals that:

$$\frac{dP}{dC} = \frac{(\partial TB/\partial C)i}{H(i+t)} = \frac{Bi}{H(i+t)}P \tag{11.5}$$

where B is the marginal benefit per year from the infrastructure improvement.

The striking thing about this result is that the change in a household's annual bid per unit of H does not equal its annual benefit per unit of H, namely B/H, but instead equals this annual benefit multiplied by $i/(i+t)$. Thus the change in bid is less than the added benefit from the infrastructure. This result reflects the fact that any increase in house value due to an infrastructure improvement is subject to property taxes. The household does not get to 'keep' the full value of the benefit because some of it is taxed away.

The property taxes in question are not the property taxes required to pay for the infrastructure, but instead are the property taxes levied to cover other public services. The infrastructure itself must be paid for by a development fee, a special assessment or a property tax increase. Each of these cases will be considered in turn.

PAYING FOR INFRASTRUCTURE: DEVELOPMENT FEES, SPECIAL ASSESSMENTS AND PROPERTY TAX INCREASES

Development fees are paid for by a developer. Because the market for new houses appears to be reasonably competitive, developers can be expected to earn the same profit wherever they build. To use economists' terms, developers earn zero economic profits; that is, profits in one jurisdiction cannot exceed profits elsewhere. Thus if one jurisdiction imposes a development fee, either housing prices or land prices must adjust to maintain developers' profits in that jurisdiction.

Suppose the development fee per house, F, is set to cover the cost of the new infrastructure, such as water and sewer lines and streets, associated with development. Suppose further that increments to infrastructure are optimal in the sense that the present value of their benefits equals their costs. In other words, suppose infrastructure improvements meet a benefit–cost test, which can be written as follows:

$$\frac{BdC}{i} = F \tag{11.6}$$

Now it is straightforward to show that the increase in the price of housing that accompanies new infrastructure will not be sufficient to compensate fully a developer for the associated development fee. Full compensation requires that the present value of the housing price increase be equal to the fee. In symbols:

$$\frac{dPH}{i} = F \tag{11.7}$$

Equation (11.5) reveals that (11.6) and (11.7) cannot both hold. In fact:

$$\frac{dPH}{i} = BdC\left(\frac{i}{i+t}\right) < BdC(i) \tag{11.8}$$

Thus the actual price change always falls short of the price change needed to compensate fully developers.

The intuition of this result is straightforward. The added infrastructure raises the price of housing, but this price increase is subject to the property tax so it does not equal the full value to consumers of the infrastructure alone. Since the development fee is set equal to this full value, the housing price increase is not sufficient to compensate developers for the development fee. Thus new residents bear some of the burden of the fee in the form of higher housing prices associated with the infrastructure, but household mobility prevents complete shifting of the fee into higher housing prices.

It follows that the price of land must drop to preserve zero profits. In other words, equation (11.8) shows that changes in housing prices alone will not be sufficient to maintain zero economic profits for developers who must pay development fees, and landowners in jurisdictions with such fees will bear some of the burden of those fees in the form of lower prices for their land.

The literature recognizes that landowners may bear some of the burden of development fees in extreme cases. However, most previous studies ignore the capitalization of infrastructure benefits into house values, and no previous study recognizes the impact of property tax capitalization on the incidence of development fees.[9] This impact leads to the new finding that landowners usually bear some of the burden of these fees.

In principle, the burden on landowners might be eliminated with tax increment financing. This burden arises because the house value increment associated with infrastructure is subject to the property tax, and the resulting property tax revenue is not connected to the infrastructure project. Tax increment financing creates the required connection. In particular, if the property tax on the house value increment associated with the infrastructure is devoted to pay for the infrastructure (or to back infrastructure bonds), thereby offsetting some of the development fee, the mismatch between project benefits and project costs might disappear, so that the burden of the fee would fall entirely on the buyers of new homes, even if they are fully mobile.

In fact, however, tax increment financing cannot, in general, eliminate the burden on landowners because the infrastructure-induced increase in the price of housing will result in a decrease in the quantity of housing consumed. Because of this quantity decrease, the property tax collected on the house value increment associated with infrastructure inevitably falls short of the amount needed to eliminate all burden on landowners. Moreover, a housing price elasticity above one in absolute value (which is larger than most estimates) would actually increase the burden on landowners, because it implies that an infrastructure-induced housing price increase is more than offset by the resulting housing quantity decrease.

Tax increment financing also faces a formidable practical problem, namely that it requires an assessor to isolate the impact of infrastructure on the price of housing. If infrastructure varies across jurisdictions, a researcher might be able to estimate this impact with a sample of houses from many jurisdictions. In contrast, an assessor must work with data for a single jurisdiction, which cannot provide the required estimate. The usual method for estimating a tax increment is to subtract property values before a project is undertaken from values after it is in place. This method is flawed in any application because it does not control for factors other than the project that might influence property values, but it is particularly absurd in this case. An assessor can observe house values after the infrastructure is in place but can only observe land values, not house values, before the infrastructure is built. The difference between these two values obviously overstates the required value increment by a large amount.

Because tax increment financing is not practical, even with a housing price elasticity near zero, the increase in house values due to an infrastructure improvement raises the property tax base in a jurisdiction and increases the revenue that could be raised at the old rate, t. To keep the jurisdiction's budget balanced, t must drop.[10] This drop in t raises the price of new houses and therefore further compensates developers for the fee they must pay. In principle, this additional price boost might be high enough so that land prices will not have to drop to maintain zero profits. In fact, however, unless the value of a new house is many times greater than the average house value in the jurisdiction, the extra price boost from the property tax cut will not be sufficient to compensate developers fully for the exaction they must pay, and land prices will still fall with a development fee. Because the property tax break is spread out over all houses in the jurisdiction, not just over new houses, the impact on the price of new houses is likely to be small.

The magnitude of the final burden imposed on landowners can be quite high.[11] With an interest rate of 5 per cent, an effective property tax rate of 1 per cent, new houses selling for twice the value of existing houses, and new houses equal to 5 per cent of the total stock, the total burden on landowners is only 13 per cent of the burden on new residents. Raising the property tax rate to 3 per cent, setting the value of new houses equal to the value of existing houses, and increasing the share of new houses to 50 per cent raises the total burden on landowners to 59 per cent of the burden on new residents. In this latter case, therefore, landowners pay 37 cents out of every dollar spent for new infrastructure and new residents pay the rest.

This analysis also implies that existing residents get a capital gain from the fee.[12] Because infrastructure boosts the price of new houses and expands the tax base, the jurisdiction-wide cut in property taxes that is needed to keep revenue constant raises the value of existing houses. Development fees not only insulate existing residents from the costs of infrastructure for new development, but also give them a capital gain.

These results are illustrated in the first panel of Figure 11.1. Let P' be the price of housing that would exist without the infrastructure financed by the development fee. When one unit of infrastructure is built (so $dC = 1$), equation (11.5) indicates that the price households are willing to pay jumps to $P' + dP = P' + Bi/[H(i + t)]$. According to (11.7) the price developers need to maintain zero economic profits is $P' + iF/H$. Thus the household bid, indicated by P_B, is less than what developers need to receive, called P_S, and land prices must fall.[13]

The final price buyers are willing to pay will actually be somewhat higher than $P' + Bi/[H(i + t)]$ because, as explained above, the tax base expansion allows a decrease in the property tax rate for other purposes. The resulting increase in household bids is indicated by the upward arrow in Figure 11.1. This small upward shift in P_B lowers the extent to which land prices must decline. The final required decline in land prices depends on the shaded region in the diagram.

A development fee does not affect a household's bid for housing because the fee is paid by the developer, not the household. In other words, imposing a development fee does not alter the amount households are willing to pay for housing, although household bids do increase to reflect the infrastructure that the fee finances. In contrast, a special assessment is a one-time property tax payment. Although special assessments are usually based on frontage or on some other lot or housing characteristic, it will prove convenient (and roughly accurate) to consider special assessments that are levied on house value.[14]

Thus with special assessments, an additional term, namely aV, must be subtracted from equation (11.1). This term is not divided by i because the special assessment is paid just once, not every year. Following the same steps as before, equation (11.4) now becomes:

$$P = \frac{TB(C)i}{H(i+t+ia)} \tag{11.9}$$

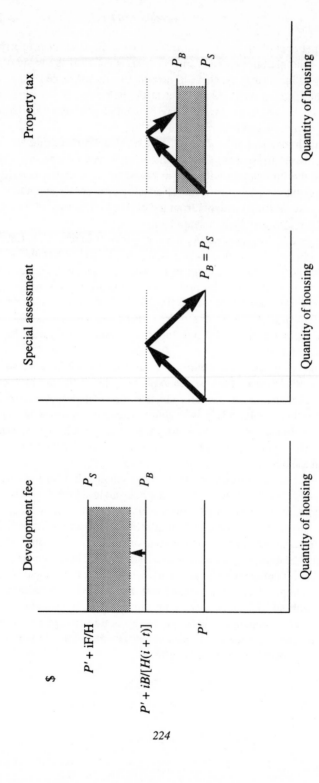

Figure 11.1   The incidence of options for financing infrastructure

We want to know what happens to P when the rate of special assessment increases. Simple differentiation reveals that:

$$\frac{dP}{da} = -P\left(\frac{i}{i+t+ai}\right) \qquad (11.10)$$

If the initial special assessment rate is zero, then equation (11.10) indicates that the change in household bids with respect to a change in a equals the initial bid multiplied by $[i/(i+t)]$.

The benefit–cost condition is simply that the present value of the benefits from the infrastructure increase (dC) equals the revenue raised by the change in the rate of special assessment (da), or:

$$\frac{B}{i}dC = daV \qquad (11.11)$$

Solving (11.11) for da, substituting the result into (11.10) (under the assumption that the initial a is zero) and remembering that $V = PH/i$, we find that the decrease in P induced by the increased special assessment exactly equals the increase in P induced by the added infrastructure.[15]

In short, with a special assessment, the increased housing price associated with better infrastructure and the decreased housing price associated with the special assessment both affect property tax liability, so the asymmetry present in the case of development fees does not appear. Thus the two price impacts exactly offset each other and net housing bids do not change. As a result, land rents do not need to fall to ensure equilibrium for developers, and landowners do not pay any of the special assessment. In fact, the burden of the special assessment falls entirely on new residents, who are, of course, the ones who receive the entire benefit from the new infrastructure.[16]

This case is illustrated in the second panel of Figure 11.1. The infrastructure increase boosts the price of housing to $P' + iB/[H(i+t)]$, but the special assessment pushes the price back down to P'. With no change in housing price, there is no reason for a change in land prices, either.

Finally, property tax financing spreads the cost of infrastructure over all property owners, not just new residents. Even if the amount of infrastructure is set so that its benefits to new residents equal the cost per household of the property tax increase needed to pay for the infrastructure, which is the benefit–cost condition, a large share of the tax increase will be paid by existing residents. Hence the infrastructure benefits will raise the price of new housing much more than the property tax increase will lower this price. It follows that landowners will be able to raise the price of undeveloped land and that existing homeowners in the jurisdiction will experience a capital loss on the value of their houses.

As shown in the third panel of Figure 11.1, property tax finance results in an increase in the price households are willing to pay for housing. This net price increase will be larger, the smaller the number of new residents relative to the number of existing residents, and the smaller the value of new houses relative to the value of existing houses.[17] If both these ratios are very small, most of the property tax increase will be paid by existing residents and the increase in the price of housing will be only slightly less than the increase caused by the infrastructure benefits alone. The resulting gap between the price buyers are willing to pay and the price sellers need to receive, illustrated by the shaded area, leads to an increase in the price of land.

QUALIFICATIONS AND EXTENSIONS

This analysis assumes that households are mobile across jurisdictions, that the housing construction industry is competitive, and that infrastructure investments meet a benefit–cost test. This section briefly considers the consequences of relaxing these assumptions.

The assumption of mobile households implies that there is only one possible price for housing in each jurisdiction, namely the price that will attract households away from other jurisdictions. In more formal terms, the housing demand curve facing firms in a single jurisdiction is horizontal. If the demand curve is downward-sloping, which many authors assume, new residents may bear a higher share of the burden of development fees than the share derived above. Moreover, in traditional analysis of this topic, which does not consider the capitalization of infrastructure benefits, none of the burden falls on new households unless the demand curve slopes downward.

However, the literature does not provide a satisfactory explanation for the causes of a downward-sloping housing demand function in a single jurisdiction. Several articles claim that demand will slope downward in a jurisdiction that has uncommon or non-reproducible characteristics,[18] but these articles do not explain why the value of non-reproducible characteristics is not simply capitalized into the price of housing – with no impact on the slope of the demand curve. Thus a formal analysis of imperfectly mobile households has yet to appear. This analysis may or may not lead to downward-sloping demand curves and a higher burden of development fees on new residents.

The housing construction industry appears to be reasonably competitive. It is dominated by small firms, entry and exit are relatively easy, and estimated supply curves are infinitely elastic (see Stover, 1986). Nevertheless, some evidence suggests that there may be modest economies of scale in construction and that large firms are increasing their market share in some metropolitan areas (Stover, 1986). Without perfect competition, construction firms will earn profits, but also might lose some of those profits if development fees are imposed, and therefore pick up some of the burden that would otherwise fall on landowners. They also might be able to pass this burden on to immobile households.[19] The literature does not contain any formal analysis of these possibilities.

Finally, the burden of development fees changes if infrastructure investment does not meet the benefit–cost condition. If marginal benefits exceed marginal costs, for example, then the price of housing will rise more than the above analysis indicates. In this case, landowners would be able to charge more for their land and the losses imposed on landowners by development fees might disappear or even turn into capital gains. Similarly, if marginal benefits fall short of marginal costs, landowners suffer additional capital losses.

This issue is particularly important when development fees are used to finance something other than infrastructure for new housing.[20] In this case, the benefits to new residents almost inevitably fall far short of the fees, and landowners will experience a large drop in the value of their land. Moreover, the revenue that flows into the city treasury after infrastructure for new housing is built leads to capital gains for existing owners, regardless of whether this revenue is used to boost other public services or to cut property taxes.

To some degree, this type of outcome is now discouraged, if not outlawed, by the 'rational nexus' test, which requires development fees to be related to the infrastructure needs of new development (see Stegman, 1986). Strict adherence to this test implies that development fees, as such, cannot be used to shift on to existing landowners the burden of infrastructure that is designed to serve current – not new – residents.

However, the rational nexus test does not cover agreements negotiated between individual developers and local governments.[21] In return for expedited processing of the necessary permits, zoning changes or other considerations, developers may be willing to provide payments to the local government or to build infrastructure not covered by development fees. If developers anticipate that such agreements will be required in a particular community, they may be able to shift some of their resulting costs on to landowners in the form of lower bids for land there.

CHOOSING A FINANCING MECHANISM

The analysis in this chapter reveals how different parties rank the various financing mechanisms for new infrastructure. In particular, because all three financing mechanisms are designed to provide the same infrastructure, comparing the above results reveals which party ultimately pays for any given infrastructure improvement under each of the financing mechanisms. In making this comparison, we will restrict our attention to infrastructure additions that meet a benefit–cost condition.

The above results imply that special assessments are the most neutral policy: the burden falls entirely on the people who receive all the benefit from the infrastructure, namely the new residents. By comparison, development fees shift some of the burden of paying for that infrastructure on to the owners of undeveloped land and confer a capital gain on existing homeowners. Property tax financing does the opposite: it places some of the burden on existing homeowners and gives a capital gain to the owners of undeveloped land.

These results provide guidance to a community that is trying to select a financing mechanism for new development.[22] Two lessons are particularly striking. First, a community should not expect new residents to pay for infrastructure improvements that mainly benefit existing residents. Because such improvements fail a benefit–cost test, the burden of financing them will fall largely on existing landowners, not on new residents, regardless of the financing mechanism selected.

Second, development fees are not a particularly good mechanism for shifting the burden of new infrastructure on to new residents. In fact, development fees appear to impose a significant burden on existing landowners, and to confer a small capital gain on existing residents, even when the benefit–cost test is met. Communities interested in matching benefits and costs should select special assessments, not development fees.

A related lesson applies if a community wants to place some of the burden of new infrastructure for existing residents on to the owners of undeveloped land. Although their ability to do this through development fees is limited, they may, as pointed out earlier, be able to do it through negotiated agreements. A developer who is already holding land that has appreciated in value since he purchased it (for reasons unconnected with infrastructure) may expect to receive such high profits from development that he is willing to share some of these profits with the community in order to facilitate or speed up the development.

EMPIRICAL EVIDENCE

This analysis implies that, controlling for the characteristics of housing and for other determinants of housing price, the price of new housing should increase with the anticipated quality of public infrastructure, decrease with special assessments and property taxes, and be unaffected by development fees. It also implies that, all else being equal (including the quality of the infrastructure), the price of undeveloped land should fall as one moves from a jurisdiction that finances infrastructure with property taxes to one that uses special assessments to one that uses development fees. In addition, the larger the development fee, again all else being equal, the lower the price of undeveloped land.[23]

Unfortunately, the impact of the infrastructure financing mechanism on housing and land prices has proven difficult to measure. Data sets with all the required control variables are not yet available. Moreover, the impacts of development fees in any community depend on the nature of the alternative financing system that the fees replaced. As several articles point out, if a community that has financed infrastructure with a property tax shifts to development fees, the price of both new and existing housing should go up and the price of undeveloped land should fall (see, for example, Singell and Lillydahl, 1988). The trouble is that expectations about the alternative financing system are difficult to observe.

In contrast, the impact of property taxes on house values has been extensively studied (see Yinger *et al.*, 1988). Although there is some disagreement about whether a $1 increase in the present value of property taxes results in a full $1 decrease in house values, as the theory presented here predicts, the vast majority of studies find a statistically significant negative impact of property taxes on house values. These results support the framework in this chapter but do not directly shed light on incidence because new infrastructure is rarely financed with property taxes.

Two well-known studies examine the impact of development fees in Loveland, Colorado and Dunedin, Florida.[24] The study of Loveland finds that the price of a new house increased by about $3800 at the time the fee increase was implemented. This increase was far greater than the actual fee increase of $1182. The authors conclude that these results, 'imply that the buyers of new homes in Loveland, rather than land owners or developers, bear the burden of the impact fees' (Singell and Lillydahl, 1990, p. 89). If, indeed, house values increase $3800 for a fee increase of only $1182, then the fees are being 'overshifted' on to new homeowners, with developers or landowners receiving a bonus and existing homeowners receiving capital gains due to the expanded property tax base.

The paper also contains several puzzling results, however, that call this interpretation into question. First, the price of existing housing also increased, by $7000, when development fees were implemented. It makes some sense to argue that the price of existing housing would rise when the threat of higher property taxes for new infrastructure disappeared, but the magnitude of this impact on existing housing prices seems far too great. Moreover, it is not clear why this property-tax effect would lead to a larger impact on existing than on new housing, which also benefits from the shift away from property taxes. Finally, this study has relatively few control variables, and therefore cannot rule out explanations of these results that have nothing to do with development fees. For example, housing price increases that are larger for existing than for new houses could be explained by external events, such as the opening of a new factory combined with a shift towards smaller (and hence lower valued) new houses at about the time that the development fees were implemented.

Another study looks at the impact of development fees in Dunedin, which imposed development fees of $1150 in 1974.[25] This study finds that the price of new housing in Dunedin increased almost three. times as much as the fee. Unfortunately, however, the methodology of the study has limitations. In particular, the data set contains few control variables and the estimating technique is subject to severe conceptual and econometric problems. For example, the authors do not discuss expectations about infrastructure finance before development fees were implemented. Moreover, land value is included as a 'control' variable, even though it is influenced by the same forces that influence housing price.

In sum, empirical studies of the impact of development fees on housing prices face formidable obstacles, such as the need for information on expectations about infrastructure benefits and about the fall-back financing mechanism are difficult. In addition, the impact of development fees on the path of housing prices over time must be isolated from other time-related events that affect property values, and studies based on variation in development fees across properties must carefully control for determinants of property value with which the fees might be correlated. No study has yet overcome all these obstacles.

CONCLUSIONS

Development fees are often seen as a way to shift the burden of new public infrastructure on to the new residents that require it. As it turns out, this view is only partially correct. The buyers of new houses will indeed bear some of the burden of these fees as the benefits of associated infrastructure are capitalized into the prices of this housing. Even with mobile households, competitive housing markets and infrastructure investments that meet a benefit–cost test, however, one-quarter or more of the burden of these fees could fall on the owners of undeveloped land.

The analysis in this chapter also reveals that fees or negotiated charges on developers for infrastructure that does not benefit new residents will only increase the burden landowners bear. In addition, development fees generally confer a small capital gain on existing homeowners and, to the extent that housing construction is competitive, do not place any burden on developers.

Special assessments appear to provide a better way to ensure that the costs of new infrastructure fall on the beneficiaries. Under the same assumptions listed above, the burden of special assessments falls entirely on the people who benefit, namely the people who buy new housing. Thus with well-functioning markets and sensible decisions about infrastructure investment, special assessments avoid the problems of unfair burdens on landowners and unfair gains to existing homeowners.[26]

Finally, empirical research concerning the impact of development fees on housing and land prices faces severe obstacles and so far has not yielded clear-cut results. Although a few studies suggest that the implementation of development fees to pay for new infrastructure raises housing prices, these studies raise more questions than they answer. Given the growing popularity of development fees, more empirical work is clearly needed.

NOTES

1. Recent developments concerning development fees and special assessments are reviewed in Altshuler and Gómez-Ibáñez (1993).
2. See, for example, Huffman *et al.* (1988), Altshuler and Gómez-Ibáñez (1993) and the references therein.
3. The formal analysis can be found in Yinger (1995).
4. For example, this chapter does not explore the impact of fees on the timing of develop-ment. For an analysis of this issue, see Downing and McCaleb (1987) and Nelson *et al.* (1992).
5. For reviews of this literature see Ross and Yinger (1995) and Yinger *et al.* (1988).
6. *TB* may be a function of other locational variables too, such as school quality and access to employment. These other variables are not relevant for our analysis and are ignored.
7. Recall that the present value of a long-lived and constant stream of annual benefits, B, equals B/r, where r is the appropriate discount rate.
8. In practice, changes in P may lead to changes in H. This possibility has no impact on the results presented here. See Yinger (1995).
9. Levine (1994) recognizes that the impact of infrastructure changes on house values is tempered by property tax capitalization (with an equation equivalent to (11.2) above), but he does not recognize the implications of this result for development fee incidence.
10. The answer would be the same as the one given here if the extra revenue were used to purchase better public services, which also would raise the value of all houses in the jurisdiction.
11. For details of these calculations, see Yinger (1995).
12. Huffman *et al.* (1988) say that development fees lead to a higher property tax base due to higher housing prices. However, the cause of higher housing prices in their analysis is a

shift to higher quality houses, not the capitalization of infrastructure benefits. At another point, Huffman *et al.* say that: 'If housing prices in a community rise because of impact fees, the price of existing homes that are close substitutes for new homes will also rise. That results in a windfall profit to owners of existing homes' (p. 52). This effect cannot arise in my analysis because the higher price for new houses simply reflects infrastructure benefits, which do not apply to existing houses. Benefits to new houses flow only through increases in the property tax base.

13. Although not indicated in Figure 11.1, a drop in land prices pulls down the price developers are willing to accept – and, indeed, pulls it down until it equals P_B.

14. Special assessments often are linked to frontage because the cost of infrastructure, such as water or sewer pipes, often varies with frontage. This linkage could be incorporated into the following analysis, including the benefit–cost condition, with little or no impact on the principal results.

15. In more formal terms, these steps prove that if the benefit–cost condition is met, $(\partial P/\partial C)dC+(\partial P/\partial a)da = 0$.

16. This result may seem at first to contradict the well-known theorem that switching a tax from the supply side (developers) to the demand side (households) does not change its incidence. In this case, however, the switch from development fees to special assessments also changes the form of the tax from one that is fixed to one that depends on housing consumption; this change in form explains the change in incidence.

17. For a precise formula, see Yinger (1995).

18. See, for example, Altshuler and Gómez-Ibáñez (1993), Delaney and Smith (1989a), Downing and McCaleb (1987), Huffman, *et al.* (1988), and Stegman (1986).

19. Several authors also argue that timing issues and uncertainty about the final fee may affect the sharing of the burden between developers and landowners. See, for example, Downing and McCaleb (1987), Huffman *et al.* (1988) and Stegman (1986).

20. Another complication not considered here is that the marginal cost may vary by house. This complication is typically ignored with development fees, but special assessments often account for it, at least in part, by basing payments on frontage instead of value. This practice undoubtedly leads to deviations between actual special assessments and the benefit–cost condition in the text, but these deviations are beyond the scope of this chapter.

21. I am grateful to Bob Einsweiler for pointing this out to me.

22. These results also lead to predictions about the actual behaviour of communities. See Yinger (1995).

23. Predictions could also be developed for the quantity of housing, H, which moves in the opposite direction from P. Empirical work usually holds H constant by including housing characteristics in the analysis, but Singell and Lillydahl (1990), discussed below, find that lot size decreased (and price increased) after development fees increased.

24. These studies are, respectively, Singell and Lillydahl (1990) and Delaney and Smith (1989a, b). More details on these studies are in Yinger (1995), who also examines Nelson *et al.* (1992), which looks at the impact of development fees on the price of developable land in Loveland, Colorado and in Sarasota County, Florida. For an alternative review of the empirical literature, see Altshuler and Gómez-Ibáñez (1993).

25. Delaney and Smith (1989a, b). The discussion in the text focuses on the first of these studies. The second study uses a similar methodology to compare the prices of existing houses in Dunedin and in another city and to compare the prices of new and existing houses in Dunedin.

26. Carol Heim pointed out to me that a burden on landowners could be considered fair on vertical equity grounds if landowners are rich compared with new owners.

REFERENCES

Altshuler, Alan A. and José A. Gómez-Ibáñez, with Arnold M. Howitt (1993), *Regulation for Revenue: The Political Economy of Land Use Exactions*, Cambridge, MA: The Lincoln Institute of Land Policy.

Delaney, Charles J. and Marc T. Smith (1989a), 'Impact fees and the price of new housing: an empirical study', *AREUEA Journal*, **17** (1), 41–54.

Delaney, Charles J. and Marc T. Smith (1989b), 'Pricing implications of development exactions on existing housing stock', *Growth and Change*, Fall, 1–12.

Downing, Paul P. and Thomas S. McCaleb (1987), 'The economics of development exactions', in J.E. Frank and R.M. Rhodes (eds), *Development Exactions*, Washington, DC: Planners Press, pp. 42–69.

Huffman, Forrest E., Arthur C. Nelson, Marc T. Smith and Michael A. Stegman (1988), 'Who bears the burden of development impact fees?', *Journal of the American Planning Association*, Winter, 49–55.

Levine, Jonathan C. (1994), 'Equity in infrastructure finance', *Land Economics*, **70** May, 210–22.

Nelson, Arthur C., Jane H. Lillydahl, James E. Frank and James C. Nicholas (1992), 'Price effects of road and other impact fees on urban land', *Transportation Research Record*, **1305**, 36–41.

Ross, Stephen and John Yinger (1995), 'Sorting and voting: a review of the literature on urban public finance', in P. Cheshire and E.S. Mills (eds), *Handbook of Regional and Urban Economics, Volume 3, Applied Urban Economics*, draft chapter, North-Holland.

Singell, Larry D. and Jane H. Lillydahl (1990), 'Housing impact fees', *Land Economics*, **66** (February), 82–92.

Stegman, Michael A. (1986), 'Development fees for infrastructure', *Urban Land*, May, 2–5.

Stover, Mark Edward (1986), 'The price elasticity of the supply of single-family detached urban housing', *Journal of Urban Economics*, **20**, November, 331–40.

Wheaton, William C. (1993), 'Land capitalization, Tiebout mobility, and the role of zoning regulations', *Journal of Urban Economics*, 34, November, 102–17.

Yinger, John (1995), 'The incidence of development fees and special assessments', Center for Policy Research Occasional Paper No. 171, The Maxwell School, Syracuse, NY: Syracuse University, November.

Yinger, John, Howard S. Bloom, Axel Boersch-Supan and Helen F. Ladd (1988), *Property Taxes and House Values: The Theory and Estimation of Intrajurisdictional Property Tax Capitalization*, New York: Academic Press.

12. Regional tax base sharing: the Twin Cities experience

Thomas Luce*

INTRODUCTION

The Minnesota Fiscal Disparities Act of 1971 created the only metropolitan-wide tax base sharing system in the United States. More than 20 years later, it is still the only system of its kind. However, tight fiscal conditions at both the federal and state level in the 1990s have focused attention again on tax base sharing. At the state level, tight budgets in the early 1990s led to lower than average growth or real declines in state aids to local governments and school districts in many states. Because of budget concerns, federal aid to states is also likely to decline by significant amounts during the next decade, placing further stress on state–local fiscal systems. Current trends clearly imply that the federal declines will be concentrated in redistributive programmes, increasing the need for state and local approaches to general equity concerns. At the same time, American metropolitan areas continue to decentralize in ways that may be both inequitable and inefficient.[1]

In such an environment, tax base sharing at either the regional or state level is a likely candidate for discussion. This chapter reviews the pros and cons of tax base sharing, assesses recent experience in the Twin Cities with the Fiscal Disparities Programme, examines the motivations and implications of some recently proposed changes to the programme, and looks at some of the implications for establishing similar programmes in other metropolitan areas.

* The author wishes to acknowledge support by grants from The Pew Charitable Trusts and the Center for Urban and Regional Affairs, University of Minnesota that helped support the work reported in this chapter. The opinions expressed in this report are those of the author and do not necessarily reflect the views of those organisations. The author also wishes to acknowledge the excellent research assistance received from Humphrey Institute graduate assistant Anne Heitlinger.

RATIONALES FOR REGIONAL TAX BASE SHARING

For the purposes of this work, tax base sharing is defined as a system that combines some portion of local tax bases into a regional or state-wide pool, taxes that pool at a uniform rate, and distributes the resulting revenues based on some criteria other than contributions to the pool. Distribution criteria may involve measures of local tax capacity, tax effort, service needs, land use decisions or other indicators. The central point is that the criteria do not simply return funds to the collection location (as with piggy-back arrangements), finance a specific service (as with multi-jurisdictional special districts), or finance a range of public services at a wider geographic scale (as with county or state taxes).

Regional tax base sharing proposals generally have both efficiency and equity rationales. Efficiency objectives deal directly with land use issues, while equity questions touch only indirectly on land use. Two types of land use are usually at issue in both dimensions: commercial–industrial and high-end residential.

Efficiency Rationales for Business Tax Base Sharing

The central issue in the efficiency debate regarding business tax base sharing is whether inter-local competition for business in a fragmented system of local government generates rational land use patterns in metropolitan areas. Inter-local competition for business activity may be inefficient on two grounds. First, from a regional or national point of view, there is likely to be a clear zero-sum aspect to the game. Business activity lured to one locality with local incentives of some sort is unlikely to represent net new activity for the region or the nation since, in the absence of the incentive, it would have located somewhere else. In this light, unless the resources that are expended in the competition are necessary to ensure that firms end up in their least-cost locations, the competition leads to inefficient location decisions. Second, the competition will not account for inter-local cost or benefit spillovers, such as congestion or pollution, that differ from place to place since localities will ignore the costs or benefits of development that accrue outside their boundaries.

Commercial–industrial tax base sharing could reduce the efficiency costs of zero- or negative-sum inter-local competition in two ways: (1) by reducing incentives for inter-local competition for commercial–industrial activities; and (2) by affecting location decisions of firms indirectly through its effects on tax rate differentials (see Reschovsky (1980) and Bell (1994)). In the first instance, since business tax base sharing means that a locality can keep only a portion of the tax generated by new commercial–industrial development, the costs (fiscal and other) that a locality will be willing to absorb for a given development will be lower than in the absence of the tax base sharing. Since costs or benefits might vary from place to place (due to differences in availability of unused infrastructure or relatively immobile unemployed labour, for instance), a reduction in the overall fiscal incentive to compete for business development might push development towards lower cost or higher benefit areas, increasing overall regional net benefits.

In the second instance, since tax base sharing should reduce inter-local tax rate disparities, it should also reduce the extent to which local fiscal considerations distort private market location incentives for firms, making the tax system more neutral. Recent evidence implies that, controlling for public service levels, tax disparities do have significant and potentially large effects on the intrametropolitan location decisions of firms (see Bartik, 1991).

The other argument for the inefficiency of inter-local competition – that it will ignore benefit or cost spillovers – implies that the incentive structure of a tax base sharing system is important. Since pooling tax base in and of itself provides no incentives to account for inter-local spillovers, the criteria used to distribute revenues from the pool and the type of tax base pooled are of central concern. If, for instance, revenues are distributed simply based on fiscal capacities, there is no reason to think that inefficiencies resulting from spillovers are being addressed directly. Similarly, tax base associated with spillover-generating activities is the more logical target for pooling. Again, the pooling itself will not necessarily reduce spillovers, but the reduced competition might make the spillover-generating activity more amenable to other types of control.

Efficiency Rationales for Residential Tax Base Sharing

Efficiency rationales for residential tax base sharing are much less clear-cut. The primary argument is that residential base sharing would reduce the incentives for excessive exclusionary zoning or other local land-use regulations that increase housing costs. Dubbed the 'regulatory commons' problem by William Fischel, the argument is essentially that localities do not face adequate constraints on their ability to regulate local housing and land markets (Fischel, 1994). This is a result of the fact that the costs of such regulations are borne largely by non-residents (usually in the form of restricted choice in the housing market), while the benefits are borne locally (usually in the form of higher home values). Local fiscal and housing market incentives generally push localities to exclude new low and (often) middle income housing in favour of high-end development. Since many (if not all) localities in a region face the same incentives, the regional result can be an under-supply of low or moderate priced housing. If targeted for tax base associated with expensive housing, the pooling mechanism in a regional tax base sharing system can reduce the incentives for localities to limit new development to the high end of the market. Similarly, the distribution mechanism might be tailored to reward low and moderate priced housing programmes.

Conclusions from the Tiebout model of intrametropolitan location decisions provide fairly strong counterpoints to these arguments, however. The most relevant is that efficient provision of local public services in a regional system requires relatively homogeneous local populations. In this context, region-wide programmes promoting more diverse local housing stocks may have significant efficiency costs. Overall, most analysts would regard the efficiency rationales for residential tax base sharing as significantly less cogent than those for business tax base sharing.

Equity Rationales for Tax Base Sharing

The primary equity rationale for either form of tax base sharing is that fragmented local government systems generate uneven spatial distributions of tax base across jurisdictions within a metropolitan area. This inequality generates horizontal inequities in the price that residents of different jurisdictions face for local services. The issue is most pronounced in the case of the components of local tax base that are not directly associated with demand for particular local services, such as, for example, the business tax base and local schools.[2] In such cases, greater than average commercial–industrial tax base is not directly associated with greater than average demand for the service. This means that residents who do consume the service receive it at a lower tax price than equivalent residents of other places with less business property contributing to the tax base. If this difference is not fully offset by negative externalities associated with the business activity, then horizontal inequities exist.

Another possible rationale involves sharing the costs associated with regional problems such as poverty and blight that tend to concentrate in central cities. While some of these costs are borne locally, many of the benefits are likely to be regional in nature. Similarly, tax base sharing has been touted as a means to spread the benefits from local tax windfalls resulting from arbitrary local advantages, such as closeness to natural amenities.[3]

There is also an important argument against pursuing equity goals at the local or regional level of government. The conventional wisdom is that income redistribution is a task best left to higher levels of government. If pursued at the local level, high income residents can escape to localities that do not pursue redistributive goals. The implication in the context of regional tax base sharing is that the 'region' must be defined broadly enough to minimize location effects of this sort. This suggests that the minimum scope for a tax base sharing programme would be the metropolitan area (encompassing an entire labour and/or housing market).

THE TWIN CITIES FISCAL DISPARITIES PROGRAMME

The Fiscal Disparities Programme was implemented in the Twin Cities in 1975 based on legislation passed in 1971. Under the programme, each taxing jurisdiction in the seven-county area that constituted the metropolitan area in 1971 contributes 40 per cent of the growth in the value of its commercial–industrial tax capacity since 1971 into a regional pool. 'Tax capacity' in Minnesota is defined as the tax forthcoming from the local tax base at rates that are set by state law. For commercial–industrial property the rates are 3 per cent of the first $100 000 of market value and 4.6 per cent of the remaining value. Localities determine their actual tax revenues by taxing their tax capacity at more or less than 100 per cent.[4] Taxing jurisdictions in the programme include municipalities, counties, school districts and special districts, and number roughly 300. However, contributions to, and distributions from, the pool are computed at the municipality level (195 in 1995). Municipalities receive a distribution of tax base from the pool based on population and total market value of property per capita relative to the rest of the region.[5] A municipality with average market value per capita receives a portion of the pool equal to its share of regional population. If its market value per capita is lower than average, it receives more than its population share. Other coterminous or overlapping taxing districts then tax at their own rates that part of the jurisdiction's distribution from the pool that is within their boundaries.

Overall, Fiscal Disparities cleverly balances regional goals with local autonomy. It is designed so that it both narrows property tax rate disparities by taxing part of the local tax base at a uniform rate and maintains local control over local property tax rates. A jurisdiction taxes its distribution from the pool at the local tax rate. However, owners of business property pay a rate that is a weighted average of their home jurisdiction's tax rate and a region-wide rate applied to the pooled base. The region-wide rate is determined by computing the revenue needed to cover tax payments (at local rates) to all jurisdictions and dividing by the value of the area-wide pool. This means that, as the share of total business tax capacity in the pool increases towards 40 per cent, the share of business property value that is taxed at the regional average rate will increase and effective inter-local property tax disparities will narrow.

Several implications of the contribution and distribution systems are worth noting in the context of the various rationales for tax base sharing. First, the programme is limited to 40 per cent of new tax capacity from only a portion of the total property tax base. The 40 per cent share preserves some incentive for localities to accept cost-generating business activities. However, 40 per cent (or any other percentage) is an essentially arbitrary cut-off and it is not clear what percentage would provide the 'correct' reduction in the incentive for localities to compete for tax base. The cut-off also means that, at a maximum, only 40 per cent of commercial–industrial tax capacity can be shared. In 1995, commercial–industrial property represented 37 per cent of the regional total property tax capacity, limiting the pool to a maximum of just 15 per cent of total property tax capacity in that year.

Distributions from the pool are based solely on market value per capita. This means that variation across municipalities in the capacity to raise revenues via fees, charges or other non-tax instruments is not considered. Potentially important contributors to local revenue-raising capacity (as the phrase is normally used) are therefore ignored. Distributions are also independent of expenditure needs. This means that the programme does not explicitly redistribute resources to places with characteristics such as high poverty, high density, greater than average proportions of the young or old, ageing infrastructure or other characteristics usually associated with fiscal stress or need. Combined, these two features of the system mean that it is very likely that some jurisdictions that would normally be considered good candidates for net subsidies under tax base sharing (such as central cities) will instead be net contributors. This feature of the system has been noted by most analysts and is important for any analysis of the actual equalizing effects of the programme.

The growth of Fiscal Disparities over its first 20 years is shown in Table 12.1, which displays the size (absolute and per capita) of the shared pool and the pool's changing shares of commercial–industrial and total tax capacities. (Note that, since 'tax capacity' in Minnesota is the tax that would be forthcoming from the local tax base at state-determined rates, tax capacity is generally of the same order of magnitude as tax revenue rather than tax base as that term is normally defined.) All four measures show steady growth from the beginning of the programme to the early 1990s. By 1992, the pool represented nearly $300 million, or $125 per capita, in tax capacity. The size of the pool was roughly constant from 1991 to 1993 and declined significantly in subsequent years. A relatively mild recession in late 1990 and early 1991 halted the growth in the pool, while the subsequent declines were the combined result of decreases in the state-set rate structure for business property taxes and declining commercial–industrial property values in some areas.[6] By 1995 the absolute size of the pool had declined by roughly 17 per cent ($50 million) from its peak in 1992 and by slightly more (18 per cent) in per capita terms. However, increases in the tax rate on the pool offset much of the

Table 12.1   Growth of the Fiscal Disparities Programme, 1975–95

Year	Pooled tax capacity		% of business tax base	% of total tax base
	$ millions	*$ per capita*	*In shared pool*	*In shared pool*
1975*	19	9	6	2
1980*	46	21	11	3
1985*	179	80	22	8
1989	250	107	26	10
1990	265	114	26	12
1991	290	125	28	12
1992	292	124	29	14
1993	289	121	29	13
1994	277	118	30	13
1995	241	103	26	11

*   Extrapolated using Baker *et al.* (1991) with Minnesota House of Representatives Research Department data for 1989 as the base.

Sources: Baker *et al.* (1991), Minnesota House of Representatives Research Department and Minnesota Department of Revenue.

decline. The tax rate on the pool increased from roughly 100 per cent of tax capacity in 1990 to 135 per cent in 1995. As a result, revenues from the pool (not shown in Table 12.1) increased from about $114 per capita in 1990 to a high of $157 per capita in 1994. Rate increases failed to offset capacity declines only in the final year, when revenues fell to $139 per capita. Despite some recent erosion in the size of the pooled tax base, the Fiscal Disparities pool still generates significant revenues.

The capacity trends are reflected in the data for the pool's share of commercial–industrial and total tax capacity. The percentages increased to peaks of 30 per cent and 14 per cent respectively and then fell to 26 per cent and 11 per cent in 1995. Thus roughly one-quarter of the taxes paid on business property is equalized across the region, but the extent to which Fiscal Disparities narrows tax rate disparities has declined in recent years.

Efficiency Implications of Fiscal Disparities

Two aspects of the Fiscal Disparities Programme are important in the context of the efficiency implications of the programme: the inclusion of 40 per cent of new commercial–industrial property value and the programme's effects on tax rate disparities. As noted above, the 40 per cent rule significantly reduces the fiscal pay-off to localities associated with new business development while preserving some incentive for localities to accept cost-generating activities. It is impossible to evaluate whether 40 per cent is the proper cut-off on efficiency grounds. However, it is clear that in spite of Fiscal Disparities, many localities in the metropolitan area still compete very hard for business tax base. A good indicator of this is the extensive use of tax increment financing (TIF) across the region. TIF is a financing tool that captures the increased tax revenues generated by new economic development to pay for public subsidies associated with the development. In Minnesota, TIF has been an important part of the inter-local competition for economic activity. By 1991, for instance, 46 of the 61 municipalities in the region's two central counties had a total of 343 tax increment finance districts that captured roughly 8.5 per cent of total tax capacity in the counties.[7] This is a proportion that rivals the Fiscal Disparities pool in magnitude, indicating that competition for commercial–industrial tax base is still heated.[8]

The effect of Fiscal Disparities on actual tax rates has always been relatively modest. Calculations for 1989 and 1995 show that the program's effect on average tax rates (as opposed to tax base) measured at the county level was less than 10 per cent in 1989 and less than 5 per cent in 1995.[9] However, tax rate effects in some individual jurisdictions are also significantly greater than the county-level averages, implying proportionately greater potential impacts in specific places. St Paul, for example, would have had to increase property tax rates by about 9 per cent in 1995 in order to maintain revenues if Fiscal Disparities had been eliminated. Most recent work on the effects of tax rate disparities on intrametropolitan location decisions implies that even relatively modest disparities of this magnitude can have significant long-run impacts on local economic activity (see Bartik, 1991).

In sum, it is difficult to evaluate the efficiency effects of Fiscal Disparities in exact terms. The programme is structured in a way that should reduce inter-local tax disparities and competition for business tax base. However, the effects on actual tax rates are modest and the competition for business tax base is still quite spirited in the region, suggesting that there is room for improvement in the programme in these dimensions.

Overall Equalizing Effects of Fiscal Disparities

A shared tax base of the magnitude of Fiscal Disparities clearly has the potential to offset a significant amount of tax base inequality across jurisdictions. However, Fiscal Disparities is designed in a way that does not guarantee that it will reduce inequality in *total* tax base per capita. Nor is it guaranteed that the programme will redistribute tax base to places with high expenditure needs (however measured) relative to their tax bases.

Table 12.2 shows two measures of the overall equalizing effect of Fiscal Disparities on property tax base for the period from 1987 to 1995. Shown are Gini coefficients of total tax capacity per capita and the ratio of tax capacities per capita at the 95th and 5th percentiles, all measured at the jurisdiction level before and after contributions and distributions from the Fiscal Disparities pool. The before and after measures are meant to compare what the distribution of tax base would have been in the absence of the programme with the actual distribution with the programme. However, strictly speaking we cannot know what the distribution of tax base around the region would have been in the absence of the programme because relative tax rates and incentives for localities to pursue business development would have been different for a period of 20 years without the programme. In spite of this problem, net distributions are still the best measure available to see the way that the separate rules governing contributions to, and distributions from, the pool interact to determine the total tax base actually available to localities for raising revenues.

Table 12.2   Equalizing effects of Fiscal Disparities, 1987–95

	Gini coefficients*		Tax capacity per capita: ratio of 95th percentile to 5th percentile	
	Before Fiscal Disparities	After Fiscal Disparities	Before Fiscal Disparities	After Fiscal Disparities
1987	0.19	0.16	4.3	3.1
1988	0.20	0.16	4.7	3.2
1989	0.19	0.16	4.3	3.2
1990	0.23	0.18	6.1	3.8
1991	0.23	0.17	5.7	3.7
1992	0.22	0.16	5.8	3.4
1993	0.22	0.17	4.9	3.2
1994	0.21	0.16	4.8	3.4
1995	0.21	0.17	4.8	3.6

* Computed for total tax capacity per capita at the jurisdiction level.

Sources: Computed from data from Minnesota House of Representatives Research Department and Minnesota Department of Revenue.

The Gini coefficients are relatively stable over the period, with increasing inequality indicated early in the period (both before and after Fiscal Disparities) and improvements later in the period.[10] The reductions in the Gini coefficients due to Fiscal Disparities are relatively small in absolute terms (0.03 to 0.06), but they imply that the programme reduces the measured inequality in total tax base per capita by roughly 20 per cent. Although the percentage is declining in the later years, this is still a non-trivial effect given that the programme shares only 10–15 per cent of total tax base.

The 95th to 5th percentile ratios are intended to show effects of the programme in the tails of the tax capacity distributions. The patterns are much the same as for the Gini coefficients, with two differences.[11] First, Fiscal Disparities removes a greater proportion of the measured inequality in the tails of the distribution than in the middle, with reductions in the ratios in a range from 25–40 per cent.[12] Second, the ratio implies that after-Fiscal Disparities inequality was worsening late in the period, with a sustained three-year, 10–15 per cent increase in the after-Fiscal Disparities ratio. The implication is that tax base growth in very low capacity places has been disproportionately in commercial–industrial property, compared with very high capacity places. Examination of the jurisdiction-level data shows that contributions did grow more rapidly in very low capacity places than at the high end, while changes in distributions were roughly proportionate in the two kinds of place.

Overall, the data suggest that Fiscal Disparities reduces property tax base inequality in the region to a significant extent. However, the data also suggest that commercial–industrial growth patterns in recent years have reduced the extent to which Fiscal Disparities equalizes total tax base, especially for the places at the extreme low end of the distribution.

Effects of Fiscal Disparities by Type of Jurisdiction

Just as Fiscal Disparities is not designed necessarily to benefit places with low total tax capacities, it also contains no explicit provisions that redistribute tax base according to local needs or stages of development. Table 12.3 explores the effects of Fiscal Disparities on different types of place by showing Fiscal Disparities and tax base data broken down by type of jurisdiction. The region is broken down into categories developed by the Twin Cities Metropolitan Council to classify communities in the metropolitan area by a combination of type of economy, location and stage of development. The classifications used for this analysis include the two central cities, fully developed inner suburbs, developing outer suburbs, free-standing growth areas (small urban centres in the outer part of the region) and rural areas (many of which include significant commercial–industrial and residential development).[13]

Table 12.3 *Tax base and Fiscal Disparities data for metropolitan council policy areas, 1990–95*

	Ratios of Fiscal Disparity distributions to Fiscal Disparity contributions			Net Fiscal Disparity Distribution: Tax Base Per Capita		1989 Median Income	1990 Median Owner-Occupied Housing Value
	1990	1995	1990–95	1990	1995		
Central cities (2)							
Minneapolis	0.69	1.22	0.85	–$43	$20	$25 324	$71 200
St. Paul	2.27	2.51	2.33	75	79	26 498	70 200
Developed suburbs (23)	0.75	0.70	0.73	–43	–39	37 796	90 428
Developing suburbs (55)	0.91	0.82	0.87	–9	–21	44 924	101 479
Free-standing growth areas (11)	1.27	0.90	1.15	41	–11	38 777	89 407
Rural (96)	3.80	2.26	3.14	102	51	45 574	99 227
Metropolitan area	1.00	1.00	1.00	0	0	37 837	90 806

Sources: Minnesota House of Representatives Research Department, Minnesota Department of Revenue and *1990 Census of Population and Housing.*

The data for the two central cities highlight the extent to which Fiscal Disparities fails to account for many traditional indicators of need. By most measures, Minneapolis and St Paul are similar kinds of place. They are of similar size and show nearly identical median incomes and housing values. In some dimensions (such as strength of the central business district) Minneapolis shows the healthier signs, while in others (such as murder or poverty rates) it looks worse. However, the two places are treated very differently by Fiscal Disparities. During much of the 1980s and up until 1994, Minneapolis was a net contributor, showing net contributions as high as $45 per capita, or distributions that were less than 70 per cent of its contributions. Extensive redevelopment in the Minneapolis central business district was largely responsible for this. St Paul, on the other hand, was consistently one of the largest net recipients in the system, receiving roughly $75 per capita in additional tax capacity per year from the system, or distributions that were more than 200 per cent of contributions.

Data for other parts of the region also show revealing contrasts. Compared with developed inner suburbs, developing outer suburbs in the region showed greater incomes in 1990 (by nearly 20 per cent) and housing values (by more than 10 per cent). Yet in the same year, the inner suburbs contributed $43 per capita more tax base to the Fiscal Disparities pool than they received, while the outer suburbs contributed just $9 more per capita than they received. This was true despite the fact that many of the inner suburbs were beginning to show signs of social and economic stress during the 1980s much like those in the central cities (Orfield, 1997). Similarly, rural areas showed median incomes and housing values 18 per cent and 11 per cent greater, respectively, than outlying urban centres. Yet rural areas were net recipients of $102 per capita in tax base compared with just $41 for the urban centres. Clearly, growth in commercial–industrial tax base since 1971 is an imperfect indicator of overall fiscal needs.

Changes in the indicators between 1990 and 1995 show a very clear pattern. With the exceptions of St Paul and outer suburbs, net distribution rates moved closer to zero. This implies that the overall distribution of commercial–industrial property in the region became more homogeneous over the period. Consistent with the data in Table 12.2, the magnitude of tax base redistribution accomplished by the system clearly declined.[14]

Another method available for evaluating how well Fiscal Disparities reflects local needs is comparison of the net distributions from Fiscal Disparities to more formal calculations of local fiscal capacities and needs that are available for a subset of communities in the region. Regression-based calculations of expenditure needs and comprehensive estimates of revenue-raising capacities are available for the late 1980s for all cities larger than 2500 in Minnesota, including 88 of the 195 jurisdictions covered by Fiscal Disparities.[15]

Revenue-raising capacity measures how revenues from a standardized tax rate on local bases would vary from place to place as a result of differences in local tax bases. Expenditure needs capture how the costs of providing a standardized level of services vary from place to place as a result of local conditions beyond the control of local officials. The difference between the two measures – the need–capacity gap – is a measure of a city's overall fiscal condition, or of its relative need for outside help in order to finance a typical level of public services. Normally one thinks of state aids as the mechanism to fill this kind of gap, but net distributions from Fiscal Disparities also have the potential to meet this need.

The correlation between 1989 net distributions from Fiscal Disparities for those 88 places and estimates of the 1989 need–capacity gaps is strong and positive ($r = +0.58$). Places in more tenuous fiscal condition (places with larger gaps between needs and capacities) do indeed tend to be net recipients from Fiscal Disparities. The data further show that, on average, a dollar increase in the gap between needs and capacities was associated with a $0.64 increase in the net distribution per capita from Fiscal Disparities, which implies that Fiscal Disparities alleviated a sizeable portion of fiscal stress in the region.[16] However, the correspondence between net distributions and fiscal stress was far from perfect. The central cities again provide a good example. Minneapolis and St Paul both showed need–capacity gaps among the greatest across the 88 places, with gaps of $261 and $260 per capita, respectively. However, in that same year, Minneapolis was a net contributor to Fiscal Disparities, contributing roughly $25 per capita more tax base to the pool than it received back, which, in effect, worsened its gap by about 10 per cent. In contrast, St Paul received a net distribution from Fiscal Disparities of $59, in effect closing about 23 per cent of its gap.

Decomposing the need–capacity gap into its two components (expenditure needs and revenue capacities) shows that the source of the problem is that needs are not accounted for by Fiscal Disparities. The correlation between revenue-raising capacities and net distributions from Fiscal Disparities in 1989 was strong and of the expected sign ($r = -0.78$). Places with lower revenue-raising capacities received larger net distributions from Fiscal Disparities on average. This reflects the fact that Fiscal Disparities distributions are determined by total market value, which is the primary determinant of the base for the dominant local tax in Minnesota, the property tax. However, the correlation of net distributions with expenditure needs was weak and of the wrong sign ($r = -0.17$). Places with greater than average needs tend to receive lower than average net distributions from Fiscal Disparities. Net distributions from Fiscal Disparities thus track capacities fairly well but needs rather poorly.

In sum, the sub-regional and jurisdiction-level data show that Fiscal Disparities net distributions correlate fairly well with fiscal stress overall, but that there is also an element of arbitrariness to the net distributions when they are viewed case by case in the context of more general equity measures. This at least partly explains why proposals to reform or expand the system have come forward in recent years.

Proposed Reforms of Fiscal Disparities

There have been several proposals in recent sessions of the Minnesota legislature to reform Fiscal Disparities in ways intended to increase the redistributive power of the system. Most prominent among these were bills sponsored by Minneapolis Representative Myron Orfield to extend Fiscal Disparities to part of the owner-occupied residential tax base. Two variations are examined here: one that would pool all of owner-occupied residential tax base above $150 000 in assessed value; the other that would pool all value above $200 000.[17] Both of these values represent relatively highly valued homes in the Twin Cities housing market, where the median value of a single family house was roughly $90 000 in 1990. In the proposals, the pooled tax base would be added to the Fiscal Disparities pool and distributed in the same manner as the current business tax base pool.

Table 12.4 shows 1995 statistics corresponding to those in Table 12.2 for the two proposals. Adding all residential value above $200 000 to the current Fiscal Disparities pool would increase the size of the pool by about $44 million (or by 18 per cent). This represents roughly 5 per cent of owner-occupied residential tax capacity in the region. The addition would decrease the Gini coefficient to 0.15 (from an after-Fiscal Disparities value of 0.17). The effects on the tails of the distribution would be more substantial, decreasing the ratio of the 95th percentile tax base per capita and the 5th percentile to 3.0 (from 3.6 for Fiscal Disparities alone). Implementing this proposal

Table 12.4   Equalizing effects of residential tax base proposals, 1995

| | | Gini coefficient | | Ratio of 95th to 5th Percentile | |
| | | | | | |
Programme	Pooled value	Added to Fiscal Disparities	Implemented alone	Added to Fiscal Disparities	Implemented alone
> $200 000	$44M	0.15	0.20	3.0	3.9
> $150 000	$88M	0.14	0.18	2.6	3.4

Sources: Computed from Minnesota House of Representatives Research Department data.

alone, however, would result in less redistribution than the current Fiscal Disparities programme – generating a Gini of 0.20 and a ratio of 3.9.

The effects of implementing the second proposal – adding all residential value above $150 000 – are stronger but similar. Adding it to the existing programme would increase the pool by $88 million, and decrease the Gini to 0.14 and the 95th to 5th percentile ratio to 2.6. Implementing the programme alone would reduce the Gini coefficient by less than the existing programme. However, this proposal affects the extremes of the distribution more dramatically than either the >$200 000 plan or the current programme. The >$150 000 plan actually reduces the 95th to 5th percentile ratio by more than the current programme despite the fact that the pool would be only about one-third the size of the existing pool.

These patterns are reflected in the comparisons of the need–capacity estimates with the net distributions from the residential tax base pooling proposals. The simple correlations between the two sets of net distributions and the need/capacity data look much like those for the existing programme – net distributions correlate strongly with revenue capacity ($r = -0.44$ for the >$200 000 programme and -0.46 for the >$150 000 programme), weakly and in the 'wrong' direction with needs ($r = -0.08$ and -0.10, respectively) and moderately with the need–capacity gap ($r = 0.34$ and 0.33, respectively). However, the data also imply that the larger of the residential programmes (the >$150 000 proposal) would be significantly more efficient at filling need–capacity gaps than the smaller programme. A dollar increase in need–capacity gap per capita would be associated with an increase of $0.59 per capita in the net distribution from the >$150 000 programme – a magnitude consistent with the much larger existing programme. The equivalent figure from the >$200 000 programme is only $0.39. This suggests that the >$150 000 programme would narrow need–capacity gaps to the same extent that the current pool does, with roughly one-third the amount of pooled tax base ($88 million compared with $250 million), while the smaller programme (the >$200 000 programme) would narrow gaps by about 60 per cent as much as the current programme, with a pool one-sixth the size of the current pool. Further, if either of the programmes were implemented as a supplement to the current programme, a need–capacity gap increase of one dollar would, on average, be met with a roughly equal increase in the net distribution from Fiscal Disparities.[18]

Thus the existing distribution of business and high-end residential tax bases in the Twin Cities implies that the overall ability of Fiscal Disparities to relieve fiscal stress in the region's localities would be enhanced by the addition of some residential tax base to the programme. Although net distributions from the residential alternatives do not track expenditure needs alone any better than the existing programme, the residential programmes are more efficient at filling the need–capacity gap than the existing business tax base programme.

A final advantage of residential base sharing proposals is worth noting. Because the residential tax base distribution is more skewed than the commercial–industrial base in the Twin Cities, net winners tend to outnumber net losers by a greater margin for residential programmes than for one limited to business tax base. For instance, in 1995, jurisdictions that were net receivers from Fiscal Disparities included roughly two-thirds of the region's population. The corresponding percentages for the >$150 000 and >$200 000 proposals (implemented independently) are 78 per cent and 81 per cent respectively. These differences are even greater for earlier years, when Minneapolis was a net contributor to Fiscal Disparities but would have been a net recipient from a residential programme. Numbers like these help to explain why a variation of one of the residential programmes described here actually passed the Minnesota legislature in 1995 (although it was subsequently vetoed by the Governor who had a strong base of support in the high income suburbs that would be net contributors under the new programme.).

IMPLEMENTING TAX BASE SHARING IN OTHER METROPOLITAN AREAS

The primary weakness of the Twin Cities model for tax base sharing is that the basic structure of the programme does not *guarantee* outcomes that correspond to commonly accepted notions of equity. Contributions are based solely on growth in business tax base and distributions are based entirely on total market value of property. The system makes no explicit allowances for public service needs or the possibility that business tax base growth might occur disproportionately in places with low tax capacities in other dimensions. In practice, Fiscal Disparities does, in fact, redistribute tax base on average towards low capacity places and communities showing high gaps between needs and capacities. However, this is the result of the specific distributions of business growth and market values in the Twin Cities since 1971. It is worth examining whether this result carries over into other metropolitan areas. The literature includes simulations of the outcomes of the Fiscal Disparities model in two other areas (the state of Maryland and the Milwaukee metropolitan area), and new simulations were performed for this research with Chicago area data. Simulations from all three metropolitan areas generate results much like those for the Twin Cities.[19] In all three places, the Fiscal Disparities model would redistribute tax base from high capacity places to low capacity places on average.

The Maryland simulation shows that a programme that based contributions on business tax base growth from 1985 to 1990 and distributions on 1990 total market value would generate a pattern of net distributions per capita with a relatively strong negative correlation with total tax base per capita ($r = -0.45$).[20] The only major city in the Maryland simulation – Baltimore – would be the largest net recipient of tax base (as a percentage of pre-programme tax base) by far, which also suggests that the net distributions would track fiscal stress reasonably well.[21]

The Milwaukee simulation yields similar results. Net distributions from a programme modelled on Fiscal Disparities instituted in the late 1970s (with contributions based on business tax base growth from 1973 to 1978) would have been correlated very strongly with total tax base per capita ($r = -0.70$) (Fischer, 1982, Table 3). The plan would also have resulted in the greatest net distribution (as a percentage of pre-programme tax base) going to Milwaukee, the only major city in the simulation.

Simulations of both business and residential property tax base sharing proposals for the Chicago metropolitan area were also carried out for this research. Net distributions per capita from a programme that pooled 40 per cent of business tax base would correlate very strongly with total tax bases per capita ($r = -0.73$). Sharing residential tax base above \$150 000 or \$250 000 would result in even stronger associations ($r = -0.95$) for both proposals. The Chicago area simulation differs from Maryland and Milwaukee in that Chicago is not a major receiver in either the business or residential runs. In both instances, Chicago's relatively large total tax base per capita limits its net distributions per capita to positive, but relatively modest, levels, putting it about 60th among more than 250 jurisdictions.

The Fiscal Disparities model also generates anomalous results in all of the simulations similar to those evident in the Twin Cities data, regardless of whether equity is expressed in terms of tax base redistribution or assistance to places likely to be enduring fiscal stress. For instance, the Maryland and Milwaukee simulations compare the Fiscal Disparities model with other methods of distribution, and find that overall equity goals are more consistently met when distribution formulae explicitly account for variations in expenditure needs. Thus although the Twin Cities model does in fact redistribute tax base in the 'right' direction in all of the cases, it is clear that specific redistributive goals are best met by explicitly building them into distribution formulae.

CONCLUSIONS

Regional tax base sharing has the potential to enhance the efficiency and equity of metropolitan economies and public sectors. It is difficult to evaluate the efficiency implications of tax base sharing as implemented in the Twin Cities under the Fiscal Disparities Programme. However, the programme is structured in a way that reduces the incentives for inter-local competition for tax base and narrows tax rate disparities in the region (although this effect is rather modest). Equity outcomes are more clear-cut. Despite the fact that the programme's design ignores many general equity concerns, its net effect is a significant equalization of total local tax base. This effect has diminished slightly in recent years, especially at the lowest end of the tax base distribution, and exceptions to the pattern exist, but the overall association is relatively strong. Evaluating equity outcomes using a more general measure of local fiscal needs (the need–capacity gap) also shows fairly strong correlation between net distributions from Fiscal Disparities and local needs. Again, notable exceptions are evident – Minneapolis is the clearest example – but, on average, net distributions from Fiscal Disparities operate to relieve local fiscal stress in the region.

Proposals to extend Fiscal Disparities to residential tax base would enhance all of these relationships. Simulations show that the redistribution per dollar of shared tax base is greater for the residential tax base sharing programmes than in the existing programme. For instance, a proposal that would create a residential pool from residential assessments in excess of $150 000 would generate a tax base pool just one-third the size of the current business tax base pool but would narrow tax base disparities at the extremes of the distribution to a greater extent, on average, than the current programme and relieve local fiscal stress to roughly the same extent. This type of reform has shown itself to be relatively viable politically – one variation actually passed the Minnesota legislature in 1995 only to be vetoed by the Governor. However, such reforms still generate anomalies like those in the current programme: relatively low capacity/high need places that are net contributors to the pooled tax base and relatively high capacity/low need places that are net receivers. Simulations from the Twin Cities and elsewhere show that explicit consideration of these factors in distribution formulae is necessary to ensure that such inconsistencies do not occur.

NOTES

1. See Gold (1995) for a review of the fiscal conditions of state governments in the early 1990s and Downs (1994) on decentralization patterns in metropolitan areas.

2. Businesses are likely to care about the quality of school systems. However, most businesses draw from regional (or national) labour markets, implying that it is the overall quality of regional schools, rather than nearby schools, that concerns them.

3. Implicit in both of these arguments is the notion that mobility barriers of one sort or another prevent the capitalization process from compensating residents for local problems (by lowering housing costs) or from offsetting local windfalls (by raising housing costs). In this context, the first issue (concentrated poverty) seems likely to be more acute, given the mobility constraints on low income inner city residents in US metropolitan areas.

4. The tax does not apply to all business property, so effective rates are lower than the nominal rates imply. Note that the contribution to the pool includes increases in the value of properties that were on the roles in 1971. Inflationary growth is clipped at 40 per cent along with growth due to new development. Tax capacities are calculated with a one year lag, for example, 1994 tax base data determined the contribution for 1995.

5. Prior to 1991, jurisdictions were guaranteed a minimum distribution by the 'factor of two' rule that substituted two as the ratio of local market value per capita to regional value per capita if the actual ratio exceeded two. The rule was removed in 1991. This is the most significant change in the programme since the descriptions found in the early literature on the programme, including Lyall (1975), Vogt (1979), Reschovsky (1980) and Fischer (1982).

6. See Metropolitan Council (1995). During 1993 and 1994, the region saw a rash of court cases that led to significant reductions in commercial–industrial property assessments, especially for office buildings in the central cities and commercial property in inner suburbs.

7. Data are from unpublished reports of the Research Department of the Minnesota House of Representatives.

8. The structure of property tax rates in Minnesota contributes significantly to this phenomenon. Property tax rates are much higher on commercial–industrial property than on most residential property. Commercial–industrial property is taxed at 3 per cent for the first $100 000 of value and at 4.6 per cent above that. Owner-occupied residential property, on the other hand, is taxed at just 1 per cent on the first $72 000 of value and at 2 per cent above that. The implication is that 'capturing' 40 per cent of new business tax base would reduce incentives for tax base competition by more in most other states (where business and residential property are taxed at the same or similar rates).

9. See Baker *et al.* (1991) and Baker and Hinze (1995). Part of the reason for this finding is that the analysis (correctly) controls for changes in state school aids that would result directly from the elimination of Fiscal Disparities. State school aid programmes in the state have significant equalizing components. This effect may be declining since most state aid programmes have been in decline in the early 1990s (see Luce (1995)).

10. The increase in the Gini coefficients in 1990 is at least partially an artefact. In that year, the state-set rate structure for owner-occupied residential property was changed in a way that reduced tax capacities (revenues forthcoming from the state-set rates) across the board. The reductions were proportionately greater in low capacity places, increasing the Gini coefficient. However, the capacity reductions were replaced dollar for dollar with state aid. Low capacity places were thus reimbursed for the disproportionate decrease in capacities. Subsequent distributions of state aid have not necessarily moved with the value of the lost tax base, however, meaning that inequality probably has increased to some extent in the long run as a result of the 1990 changes.

11. Alternative measures, such as the ratio of tax capacity in the top 10 per cent of places to capacity in the bottom 10 per cent, generate similar patterns but with some anomalies generated by one or two outliers at both extremes of the distribution. The 95th to 5th percentile ratio avoids these problems while still picking up effects in the tails of the distribution.

12. Computing the ratio of the 75th and the 25th percentiles bears this out as well.

13. Metropolitan Council definitions of policy areas: central cities: Minneapolis and St Paul. Developed suburbs: places that were more than 85 per cent developed at the end of 1984. Developing suburbs: the rest of the portion of the region in the path of urban growth (within the 'metropolitan urban service boundary', or MUSA) and that part of the region

where regional services, such as waste water collection and treatment, are provided by the Metropolitan Council. Free-standing growth areas: urban centres outside the MUSA. Rural: areas outside the MUSA and free-standing growth areas – largely in agricultural use, but including some commercial, industrial and residential development. See Metropolitan Council (1988).

14. This can be seen in the jurisdiction-level data as well. Between 1990 and 1995, the standard deviation of net distributions from the system declined each year, from 116 in 1990 to 101 in 1995.

15. See Ladd *et al.* (1991). Modified capacity estimates using the 'income with exporting approach' are used for this work. The published estimates are modified to remove net distributions from Fiscal Disparities. This is accomplished by applying the formula for revenue-raising capacity on p. 64 of Ladd *et al.*

16. This comes from a simple regression of the need–capacity gaps (modified to exclude net distributions from Fiscal Disparities) on net distributions from Fiscal Disparities. The estimated regression equation was Net Fiscal Disparities Distribution = –71.15 + 0.640 (need–capacity gap). The *t*-statistic on the need–capacity gap coefficient was 6.54 (d.f. = 86), which is significant at the 99 per cent confidence level.

17. Only the portion above $150 000 (or $200 000) for each individual property would be pooled. For a house assessed at $250 000, for instance, the first $150 000 ($200 000) would be taxed by the locality as usual, while the remaining $100 000 ($50 000) would go into the regional pool.

18. The estimated regressions supporting these findings were: net distribution from the >$200 000 programme = –79.33 + 0.393 (need–capacity gap); net distribution from the >$150 000 programme = –118.86 + 0.586 (need–capacity gap); net distribution from the combination of the existing programme and the >$200 000 programme = –150.49 + 1.033 (need–capacity gap); and net distribution from the combination of the existing programme and the >$150 000 programme = –190.01 + 1.227 (need–capacity gap). The *t*-statistics for the slope coefficients were 3.27, 3.33, 6.40 and 5.81, respectively – all significant at the 99 per cent confidence level.

19. See Bell (1994) for the Maryland simulation and Fischer (1982) for Milwaukee. Data for the Chicago area simulations are from county assessor records and the 1990 Census of Housing and Population.

20. This was computed from Tables 6A1 and 6A2 of Bell (1994). The correlation is significant at the 95 per cent level of confidence.

21. Bell is less positive in his assessment of the redistributive effects of the Fiscal Disparities model in Maryland. However, he bases much of his assessment on estimates of net increases in tax revenues as a result of the programme that seriously understate the revenue changes in places with higher than average tax rates. This is due to a misinterpretation of the way that localities tax net distributions from Fiscal Disparities in the Twin Cities case. Bell assumes that local revenues from tax base received through fiscal disparities are determined by applying the regional average rate to the net distribution, when in fact it is the local tax rate that determines a locality's revenues. This means that Bell seriously understates the revenue increases that would result for places with higher than average tax rates, a group that includes Baltimore and several other of the low capacity places in the Maryland sample.

REFERENCES

Baker, Karen and Steve Hinze (1995), *Minnesota Fiscal Disparities Programme*, St Paul: Minnesota House of Representatives Research Department.

Baker, Karen, Steve Hinze and Nina Manzi (1991), *Minnesota Fiscal Disparities Programme: A Presentation to the Fiscal Disparities Task Force of the House Tax Committee*, St Paul: Minnesota House of Representatives Research Department.

Bartik, Timothy J. (1991), *Who Benefits from State and Local Economic Development Policies?*, Kalamazoo: W. E. Upjohn Institute for Employment Research.

Bell, Michael (1994), 'Tax base sharing revisited: issues and options', in John E. Anderson (ed.), *Fiscal Equalization for State and Local Government Finance*, West Port: Praeger.

Downs, Anthony (1994), *New Visions for Metropolitan America*, Washington, DC: The Brookings Institution and Cambridge: Lincoln Institute of Land Policy.

Fischel, William A. (1976), 'An evaluation of proposals for metropolitan sharing of commercial and industrial property tax base', *Journal of Urban Economics*, **3**, 253–63.

Fischel, William A. (1994), review of Alan A. Altshuler and José A. Gómez-Ibáñez with Arnold Howitt, 'Regulation for revenue: the political economy of land use exactions', *Journal of Policy Analysis and Management*, **13** (4), 792–6.

Fischer, Peter S. (1982), 'Regional tax base sharing: an analysis and simulation of alternative approaches', *Land Economics*, **58**, 497–515.

Fox, William F. (1981), 'An evaluation of metropolitan area tax base sharing: a comment', *National Tax Journal*, **34**, 275–9.

Gold, Steven D. (ed.) (1995), *The Fiscal Crisis of the States*, Washington, DC: Georgetown University Press.

Ladd, Helen L., Andrew Reschovsky and John Yinger (1991), *Measuring the Fiscal Condition of Cities in Minnesota: Final Report to the Minnesota Legislative Commission on Planning and Fiscal Policy*.

Luce, Thomas F. Jr (1995), 'Minnesota: innovation in an era of constraint', in Steven D. Gold (ed.), *The Fiscal Crisis of the States*, Washington, DC: Georgetown University Press.

Lyall, Katherine C. (1975), 'Tax base sharing: a fiscal aid towards more rational land use planning', *Journal of the American Institute of Planners*, **41**, 90–100.

Metropolitan Council (1988), *Metropolitan Development and Investment Framework: Metropolitan Development Guide*, St Paul: Twin Cities Metropolitan Council.

Metropolitan Council (1995), *Tax base Sharing in the Twin Cities Metropolitan Area: Taxes Payable in 1995*, St Paul: Twin Cities Metropolitan Council.

Orfield, Myron (1997), *Metropolitics*, Washington, DC: Brookings Institute.

Reschovsky, Andrew (1980), 'An evaluation of metropolitan area tax base sharing', *National Tax Journal*, **33**, 55–66.

Vogt, Walter (1979), 'Tax base sharing: implications for San Diego County', *Journal of the American Planning Association*, **45**, 134–41.

Index